The Ins and Outs of Selective
Secondary Schools

The Ins and Outs of Selective Secondary Schools

A Debate

Geoff Barton
Graham Brady
Nicole Chapman
John Coldron
Nic Dakin
Nigel Genders
Gabriel Heller Sahlgren
Peter Hitchens
Chris Keates
Neal Lawson
Charlotte Marten
Alice Phillips
Eddie Playfair
Stephen Pollard
Sally Power
Jonathan Romain
Neil Roskilly
Gillan Scott
Alan Smithers
Emer Smyth
Henry Stewart
Peter Tait
Margaret Tulloch
Geoff Whitty
Joanna Williams

With Forewords by David Davis *and* Fiona Millar

Anastasia de Waal (ed.)

CIVITAS

First Published March 2015

© Civitas 2015
55 Tufton Street
London SW1P 3QL

email: books@civitas.org.uk

ISBN 978-1-906837-71-6

Independence: Civitas: Institute for the Study of Civil Society is a registered educational charity (No. 1085494) and a company limited by guarantee (No. 04023541). Civitas is financed from a variety of private sources to avoid over-reliance on any single or small group of donors.

Designed and typeset by
lukejefford.com

Printed in Great Britain by
Berforts Group Ltd
Stevenage, SGI 2BH

Contents

Authors   vii
Acknowledgements   xiv
Foreword *David Davis*   xv
Foreword *Fiona Millar*   xviii

Introduction *Anastasia de Waal*   1

Selective, Comprehensive and Diversified Secondary
Schooling in England: A Brief History
Sally Power and *Geoff Whitty*   9

The Twenty-First Century Case for Selection
Graham Brady   29

The Case for Comprehensive Schools
Henry Stewart   55

Free to Pursue an Academic Education
Joanna Williams   80

Education for New Times
Neal Lawson   98

How We Got Into This Mess
Stephen Pollard   108

Will Selection at 11 Ever End?
Margaret Tulloch   128

The Case for Grammar Schools
Charlotte Marten   140

(Un)natural Selection
Peter Tait   152

Why Is Selection by Wealth Better
Than Selection by Ability?
Peter Hitchens   167

Assessing the Damage:
The Fracturing of Our Comprehensive System
Nic Dakin   183

The Dilemma of Selection in Schools
Alan Smithers   194

Selection by Stealth
Chris Keates   206

Church of England Schools for the Common Good
Nigel Genders   221

Divisive Faith Schools Urgently Need Reform
Jonathan Romain   233

In Defence of Faith Schools and Religious Selection
Gillan Scott   245

Banding: Selecting for a Comprehensive Intake
John Coldron   261

Selection and the Independent Sector
Neil Roskilly   275

Using the Comprehensive Ideal to Drive Education
Standards and Equality
Geoff Barton   290

School Selection by Gender: Why It Works
Alice Phillips and *Nicole Chapman*   306

What Does the Research Tell Us About Single-Sex
Education?
Emer Smyth   320

Selection by Choice
Gabriel Heller Sahlgren   329

Unlimited Potential
Eddie Playfair   345

Endnotes   363

Authors

Geoff Barton began teaching English at Garforth Comprehensive School, Leeds, in 1985, and has been Head of English and Deputy Head in various schools subsequently. In 2002, he was appointed Head Teacher of King Edward VI School, Bury St Edmunds, a 13-18 upper school of 1,440 students. Barton has written and edited more than 100 books on grammar and literature, and is a monthly columnist for the *Times Educational Supplement*.

Graham Brady has been the Member of Parliament for Altrincham and Sale West since 1997. He served as a shadow minister for employment, schools and Europe, resigning from the last of these positions in 2007 so that he would be free to speak out in support of selective education. Brady is currently Chairman of the 1922 Committee, which represents all back-bench Conservative MPs:

Nicole Chapman is Joint President of the Association of State Girls' Schools and has been Head Teacher of Chelmsford County High School for eight years. A Fellow of the Royal Society of Arts, she has taught in and led both mixed and girls' schools (in the London Boroughs of Barking, Havering and Bromley, as well as Kent), in comprehensive and selective settings.

John Coldron was Assistant Dean and before that the founding director of the Centre for Education and Inclusion Research, Sheffield Hallam University, a teacher educator and a primary school teacher. He directed two large projects in 2001 and 2008 mapping admissions in England, the results of which were used in the development of the admissions codes, and has published widely on admissions to schools.

Nic Dakin worked for over 30 years as a teacher, both in the UK and abroad. Before being elected as Scunthorpe's Member of Parliament in 2010 he was Principal of John Leggott College, a 2,200 student open access sixth-form college. Since his election, he has continued to contribute to the debate on the future direction of education, serving on the Education Select Committee and chairing the All-Party Parliamentary Group on Skills and Employment.

David Davis worked as corporate trouble-shooter and strategist for Tate and Lyle PLC for approximately fifteen years, becoming a main board director in 1987. Since 1987 he has been a Member of Parliament, representing a constituency in Yorkshire. In 1990, he was invited to join the Government and served in the Cabinet Office and the Foreign and Commonwealth Office. Thereafter, he served as Conservative Party Chairman, then shadow Deputy Prime Minister, and then shadow Home Secretary.

Nigel Genders has lead responsibility for the development of the Church of England's strategies and policies for education – in schools, colleges and universities, and in parishes, deaneries and dioceses -

to promote the highest quality of educational practice and to promote and support the Church's voluntary work among children and young people.

Gabriel Heller Sahlgren is research director at the Centre for the Study of Market Reform of Education (CMRE), affiliated research fellow at the Research Institute of Industrial Economics in Stockholm, Sweden, and a PhD student at the London School of Economics. He has authored numerous publications on issues relating to applied microeconomics, including the book *Incentivising Excellence: School Choice and Education Quality* (CMRE and IEA, 2013).

Peter Hitchens is a columnist for the *Mail on Sunday*, and the author of a series of books on Britain's cultural, moral and religious revolution. He was privately educated in various boarding schools until the age of 15, after which he attended a College of Further Education.

Chris Keates was appointed as NASUWT Deputy General Secretary in 2001. She has been General Secretary since 2004, overseeing the NASUWT becoming the largest teachers' union operating across the UK, representing teachers and school leaders in all sectors.

Neal Lawson is Chair of the good-society pressure group Compass, and author of *All Consuming*. He serves on the boards of UK Feminista and We Own It, is a contributing editor of the social democracy journal *Renewal*, and is an Associate Member at the Bauman Institute, University of Leeds. He writes regularly for the *Guardian* and the *New Statesman*.

Charlotte Marten has been the head teacher of Rugby High School since 2006, and Chair of the Grammar School Headteachers' Association since 2013. She was formerly Principal of Jersey College for Girls in the Channel Islands. As a Local Leader of Education, she has supported a special school and worked with the National College of Teaching and Leadership on a number of diversity projects.

Fiona Millar is a writer and journalist specialising in education and parenting issues. She writes a column in *Guardian Education* and regularly takes part in television and radio debates about education policy. Fiona is co-founder of the Local Schools Network and is a governor of two North London schools. She also chairs the National Youth Arts Trust.

Alice Phillips is former President, and currently Vice President, of the Girls' Schools Association. She is also Headmistress of St Catherine's School, Bramley, and a governor of the Yehudi Menuhin School.

Eddie Playfair has been the Principal of Newham Sixth Form College (NewVIc), a large comprehensive inner-city college in East London, since 2008. He was previously Principal of Regent College in Leicester city centre. He has taught in comprehensive schools and colleges, mostly in London, for over 30 years.

Stephen Pollard has been Editor of the *Jewish Chronicle* since 2008 and writes regularly for *The Times*, the *Daily Telegraph* and the *Express*. He is the author of numerous pamphlets and books on education and health policy, and with Andrew Adonis was co-author of *A Class Act: The Myth of Britain's Classless Society* (Penguin, 1998).

His biography of former Home Secretary David Blunkett was published in 2004.

Sally Power is a Professor in the School of Social Sciences, Cardiff University, and is Director of WISERDEducation, which is part of the Wales Institute of Social and Economic Research, Data and Methods (WISERD). She has undertaken extensive research on school choice and educational outcomes.

Jonathan Romain is a rabbi, writer and broadcaster, and minister of Maidenhead Synagogue. His books include *The Jews of England* and *Faith and Practice: A Guide to Reform Judaism Today*. He is chair of the Accord Coalition, which campaigns for inclusive education.

Neil Roskilly is Chief Executive of the Independent Schools Association, which supports the work of 350 schools in England and Wales. He advises a number of awarding bodies and government departments, including HM Treasury on the introduction of Tax-Free Childcare. He sits on the Boards of the Independent Schools Council and the international charity, Free The Children.

Gillan Scott is deputy editor at the religio-political blog, *Archbishop Cranmer*, regularly writing on the interface of Christianity, society and politics. He is also the author of the *God and Politics in the UK* blog. He has been teaching in secondary schools for 12 years, and prior to that worked for the Church of England as a youth worker, during which time he co-founded the Just42 youth charity.

Alan Smithers is the Director of the Centre for Education and Employment Research at the University of Buckingham. He has previously held chairs at the University of Liverpool, Brunel University, and the University of Manchester. As well as publishing a number of influential books, reports and papers in education, biology and psychology, Smithers has served on a number of national bodies, and is standing adviser to the House of Commons Education Select Committee.

Emer Smyth is a Research Professor at the Economic and Social Research Institute (ESRI), and Adjunct Professor at Trinity College Dublin. Her research interests centre on education, gender, school to work transitions, and comparative methodology.

Henry Stewart is co-founder of Local Schools Network and a governor of Stoke Newington School in Hackney, which his children attended. He is also Founder and Chief Executive of the training company Happy Ltd, and author of *The Happy Manifesto*.

Peter Tait is soon to retire as Head Teacher of Sherborne Preparatory School after a long career teaching in junior and senior schools in England and New Zealand. Tait has written two novels on the wives of Thomas Hardy, and numerous articles on education.

Margaret Tulloch is Secretary of Comprehensive Future. After working as a taxonomic mycologist, she became involved in parent campaigns in the 1980s. A secondary school governor for many years, she has been spokesperson for the Campaign for State Education (CASE) and Chair of the Advisory Centre for Education.

Anastasia de Waal is Deputy Director and Director of Family and Education at Civitas. A regular contributor to broadcast and print media, she is a qualified primary school teacher and Chair of national parenting charity Family Lives.

Geoff Whitty was Director of the Institute of Education, University of London, from 2000 to 2010. He currently holds a Research Professorship at Bath Spa University, UK, and a Global Innovation Chair at the University of Newcastle, Australia.

Joanna Williams is the director of the Centre for the Study of Higher Education at the University of Kent. She is the Education Editor of the online magazine *Spiked*, and regularly contributes to education debates in academic journals and the national press. Williams' book, *Consuming Higher Education: Why Learning Can't Be Bought*, was published in 2013. Her latest book, *Academic Freedom in an Age of Conformity*, will be published by Palgrave Macmillan in 2015.

Acknowledgements

Thank you to Rachel Maclean for her help on production, Lotte van Buuren for her resourcefulness, and special thanks to Anna Sonny for her tireless proofing and dedication.

Foreword

David Davis

Since the 1970s, when most local authorities closed down their grammar schools, social mobility has taken a nosedive. As a result, there are now far fewer people from state-educated backgrounds in huge swathes of society's upper echelons, whether it is in the law, accountancy, the civil service, the judiciary or even politics.

Grammar schools provided one of the best educational outcomes in the world throughout much of the twentieth century. We generated large numbers of Nobel Prize winners, and we were world leaders in science and other disciplines to a far greater degree than a country of 60 million has a right to expect.

Undoubtedly, grammar schools provided tremendous opportunities to those who could not afford private education, and I should know. I was lucky enough to benefit from just such an opportunity. I was surrounded by youngsters from deprived backgrounds, council estate children from Clapham Junction to Brixton. Every single one of them was given a decent shot at a reasonable career. Many went to top universities, a contemporary became the England rugby captain and a school predecessor became the head of the British civil service.

It was a huge tragedy when we closed off such opportunities to those that most needed them when successive governments scrapped grammar schools.

The few remaining grammar schools are nothing like the motor for social mobility that they used to be. This is partly due to the fact that their rarity has turned them into the preserves of the sharp-elbowed middle classes; but this is also due to a massive failure in public policy, a failure in confidence in high quality education for bright kids. As a result it is impossible to read too much into their impact within the current system.

Of course, the grammar school system had its weaknesses. Vitally important life decisions rested on one exam taken at age 11, and if you failed then you were out of the academic fast-stream. And a series of governments never properly invested in technical schools, the other side of the policy coin. But the problems with dividing children up according to a single academic test do not mean that the problem lies with the selective system, and to blame grammars for the failure in the other half of the school system is absurd. All these issues can be addressed within a selective education system without throwing the baby out with the bathwater.

For a start, there is no reason why selection needs to take place solely at 11, or need be so permanent. The stark choice between grammar schools and technical schools can be softened by providing a range of options, including faith schools and single-sex schools. The Coalition government's academy system and the free school system are working towards this, but far too slowly and such schools are still too constrained by the dead hand of Whitehall. What we need is a system that provides a broad array of options. Choice, for parents and pupils is the key.

The fact is that we already have a two-tier education system, one where selection is governed largely by wealth – whether through fees or covertly through house prices – rather than ability. In other words, we have a two-tier system based on injustice not justice, wealth not talent, and in the interests of the elite rather than the interests of the nation.

There is no silver bullet to reviving social mobility in Britain, but nationwide selective education is a key piece in the policy puzzle that will create a ladder of opportunity for talented and hard-working youngsters from less privileged backgrounds.

Foreword

Fiona Millar

Why do we still tolerate selection in schools? In an era of parental choice, when all major political parties want to close attainment gaps between the best and worst off children, why allow some schools to pick and choose the children they teach, and to widen rather than narrows those gaps?

There is no doubt that the case for all-ability schools has largely been won. Even the Conservative Party has dropped its historic commitment to create more grammar schools. Yet the 11-plus test – the harshest and most overt form of selection – is still being used in a quarter of all local authority areas, fifteen of which are fully selective.

The proportion of children eligible for free school meals in the remaining grammar schools is around two per cent compared to a national average of around 16 per cent.[1] Wealthy parents can trump every other child's chance of a place by paying for private tuition. Even the Chief Inspector of Schools, Michael Wilshaw, recently observed that grammar schools were 'stuffed full' of middle-class children and did nothing for social mobility.[2]

But the grammars are only the tip of what former London Schools Commissioner Tim Brighouse once described as a 'dizzyingly steep hierarchy' in which children from diverse social and ethnic backgrounds are subtly 'sorted' into different institutions as schools seek to maximise their performance in the league tables.[3] At the pinnacle of this hierarchy are the private, fee-charging schools and the grammars, where entry is determined by ability to pay, academic selection, or both. Then come the faith schools, an integral part of the English education system for over a century, yet sometimes responsible for subtle and insidious forms of covert selection. The proliferation of 'independent state schools' such as academies and free schools has led to a rapid increase in non-denominational schools that control their own admissions, when in the past they might have shared a set of common local authority admissions criteria. And at the bottom of the pile are the local community schools. But even here the local picture is distorted by residential geography and the power some parents have to worm their way, even fraudulently, into the most popular schools.

A recent internal Department for Education analysis of the top 100 non-selective schools apparently only reinforced what organisations like the Sutton Trust and the British Humanist Association have been saying for years; the highest performing schools still take relatively few disadvantaged pupils compared to their local populations.[4] Yet the OECD PISA data, so heavily used by the current government, shows clearly that the most successful systems in the world, those with good achievement across the board and narrow gaps in attainment, tend not to divide children in this way. Instead, they focus on teaching quality, strong local systems of oversight and good comprehensive schools.

We have never had a fully comprehensive system in this country, but we could, and must aspire to, if we are to join those countries where excellence is matched by equity. It would take a bold politician to champion the necessary reform, to take on the vested interests in the private, faith and selective sectors, to promote non-selective admissions and the use of random allocation, catchment areas and feeder schools to bypass the issue of selection by house price. But the education revolution in Finland, now one of the world's top-performing countries, started with far-reaching radical reform – the abolition of private and selective schools.

The latest neuroscience shows that young people's brains and intelligence continue to develop well into adolescence and beyond. Dividing children up into sheep and goats, high-achievers and low-achievers, believers and non-believers in childhood runs counter to everything the evidence tells us about outstanding, socially just school systems. Selection should be consigned to the history books once and for all.

Introduction

Anastasia de Waal

Should secondary schools be allowed to select, and if so, on what basis? These questions have been a central battleground in England's education system for many years, and the answers have often been reduced to simple dichotomies. Academic selection – selection by ability or at least *performance* – has tended to be the primary focus of this debate, polarised between advocates of the idealised grammar school and champions of the idealised comprehensive school. Both sets of advocates argue that 'their' model produces better results and greater social mobility. While useful insights have emerged, the artificial divides in this debate have masked the complexities of selection in schools today.

Who's in and who's out of today's selective secondary schools is not clear cut, and neither is the debate about whether selection should be allowed. For example, a number of the authors of the chapters that follow subscribe to a form of selection but are critical of current grammar school arrangements. A further complexity is that, while selection by academic performance is undoubtedly the central preoccupation, the selection process can also entail other criteria such as faith, gender (in the case of single-sex schools), and capacity to pay (as in the independent sector). Furthermore, these other criteria may overlap. A case in point is all-

1

ability, all-girls schools, which can still have a higher performing intake and may therefore achieve higher results despite the fact they do not actively select academically. There is also now widespread 'covert' selection, whereby some students have an unfair advantage in accessing schools, based on their parents' resources, including their knowledge of the admissions process and/or their financial means (such as their ability to afford inflated house prices within an oversubscribed school catchment area).

Accordingly, this book brings together a range of key thinkers – academics, politicians, campaigners, commentators and head teachers from different school types – to examine the evolving complexity of modern secondary school selection, and to scrutinise both reality and theory. In the process, it incorporates a rich mix of practitioners' testimony, research evidence on educational outcomes, and experience of consecutive governments' policies.

The following chapters present a broad diversity of viewpoints among the writers. But they also reflect a notable level of consensus when it comes to the bigger question of what education should strive to achieve, suggesting there is more in common between advocates and critics of selection than is sometimes acknowledged. For example, the traditionally categorised 'elitists' and 'egalitarians' are actually closer to being at one in their concern for the life chances of the poorest. As such, perhaps the most important *difference* between advocates and critics of selective secondary schools is what they consider to be the solution to addressing the disadvantage faced by poorer children. Some authors argue that not only is selection not the answer to addressing disadvantage, it is in fact furthering the problem. In this sense, perhaps an apt characterisation of the debate throughout the book is that it centres on how to make society fairer. This is a debate that asks what constitutes fairness, equality of opportunity, and/or equality of rights, and whether those values in turn are achieved by meritocratic mechanisms or equalised outcomes.

Throughout the chapters, a frequently repeated message is that much selective practice in England's secondary schools today reflects weaknesses in the wider education system. These weaknesses are cited to both lend support to, and to undermine, the legitimacy of selective practices. For instance, opponents of selection give examples of the selection process' failure to identify the 'poor bright', due to the as yet impenetrable socioeconomic achievement gap at primary school level. On the other hand, proponents of selection point to the need to apply selection criteria due to oversubscription at schools that are considered to be 'good'.

Another area of frequent agreement is that, in general, it is not the quality of education in selective schools that is in dispute. Admittedly not all of the authors hold this view (sometimes straightforward segregation is their concern), but for many of those arguing against selection, their contention is with the notion that it provides only a *'limited* good'. This point doesn't only apply to academically selective state schools. In the independent sector, for example, their smaller class sizes might be the coveted characteristic. In faith schools, the appeal often seems to be their 'ethos'. A further interesting aspect of the limited good analysis is the frequent problematising of the middle classes. Within an educational landscape of finite goods, the middle classes are often seen as disproportionate beneficiaries. A common perception is that, if middle-class parents are not paying to coach their children to get into grammar schools, then they are manipulating the allocation of school places by catchment area by buying houses near good schools. Although it is not ultimately the middle classes per se who have created the problem, their behaviour reflects a scenario where getting something good out of the education system too often demands a form of capital.

In short, unease about selection has much less to do with the fate of the *selected* but rather it has to do with the fate of the rejected. In light of this 'casualties' concern, it is perhaps worth outlining an example that illustrates the complexity of both reality and debate in the subject: in this case, the casualties of the selection process are actually those who are selected.

The 'vocational pathway' in non-selective secondary schools has long been an anomaly. When, at age 14, some students are ushered onto vocational rather than academic courses, this is a 'selection' that seems to be at odds with the guiding principle of ensuring the comprehensive level playing field. In fact, given the way that decisions have been made about the relative appropriateness of academic and vocational GCSE 'options', it would perhaps be more apt to talk about these students being *de*-selected.

A common rationale for supporting comprehensive schooling is that selection before the age of 16 is too early in a young person's development. Therefore, the selection process that has been happening within our ostensibly non-selective comprehensive schools, whereby a set of academic subjects have been 'reserved' for the higher-performing students, doesn't fit comfortably with the principle of avoiding premature selection. Providing different courses for students who show less academic promise (crucially, as gauged by their prior performance, not their interest), is a very different principle from, for example, the pragmatic acceptance of setting by performance/ability for the same course in a non-selective environment. In this respect, the vocational pathway that has been on offer at age 14 in comprehensive schools is paradoxical. In 2008, the UCL Institute of Education's Ken Spours talked about students taking vocational courses at 14 being 'refugees' fleeing from academic GCSEs;[1] perhaps they would have been better described as 'deportees'.

The relentless emphasis on GCSE performance, and A*–C benchmarks in particular, has led many all-ability schools in recent years to feel compelled to encourage certain students to opt out of academic courses when they choose their key stage 4 options. Today, league table reforms – ironically perhaps, implemented under the more pro-selection Conservative-led Department for Education – alongside a review of vocational qualifications, have significantly reduced the benefit of such a 'use' of vocational qualifications to bolster school exam results. However, the legacy of this recently widespread practice is a vital reminder of the way in which selection has existed within a purportedly non-selective system. Furthermore, although performance measures have been overhauled with a disincentivising effect, evidence suggests that the practice has not been dropped altogether.

For many years, while students were required to take a core curriculum, by Year 10 generally most of the remainder of their timetable was determined by the options they took – or rather, by which 'guided pathway' they were put on. Schools advised students about what courses they should choose, with a student's purported 'strengths and weaknesses' and 'learning preferences' being the focus. The definition of 'strengths and weaknesses' lay in the student's attainment level to date; 'learning preferences' were based on the student's demonstrated aptitude for academic subjects – again, their attainment to date. As a result, the lower a student's academic performance, the stronger the school's case for putting them on a pathway with vocational courses. Significantly, many teachers felt very uneasy about this situation but, under pressure to achieve the necessary performance targets, they felt they had little choice.

In light of the stubborn relationship between socioeconomic background and academic performance, the basis of the decision making meant that a disproportionate number of lower-income students took vocational rather than additional academic courses. For example, instead of taking history, a weaker-performing student might take a course where they learnt about the travel and tourism industry. The reality was that, in schools under pressure to deliver headline GCSE results, students who were not likely to achieve a C grade on an academic GCSE course were all too often considered to be 'unsuitable' candidates.

The corresponding justification would be that this advice was also in students' interests because better grades in vocational courses were said to serve them better than lower grades in academic courses. However, the vocational courses were frequently of dubious value. They were often only tenuously related to the area of work – hence being commonly defined as *'vocationally-related'* courses. Returning to the example of travel and tourism, one such course included a unit on learning the key responsibilities of airline cabin crew: about the tasks they perform, not how to perform them. This questionable worth reduced employers' perceptions of the vocational courses, and therefore ultimately devalued the student's grade, even if it was higher than they would have achieved on an academic course. In other words, setting aside the central contention about having a two-tiered system within a comprehensive education, the issue with these courses was not that they were vocational, it was that they were not of a good enough standard. Today, progress has been made on removing the incentives for schools to offer the weakest vocational courses, but arguably some remaining ones are still of weak quality.

In summary, the use of vocational courses to 'sort' students is significant in both principle and practice. First, it is an example of how theoretically non-selective schools have very much been in the business of selecting when it comes to secondary level course choices. As a result, the selective/non-selective dividing line is far less defined than has been assumed. Secondly, under the auspices of a broad, balanced and open curriculum, cohorts of students have in fact been deterministically directed towards futures in particular industries at the age of 14, be it hospitality or hairdressing. Finally, the nature of the selection process in this case has disproportionately impacted on students from less-advantaged backgrounds. A more equal schooling system is surely not one that strengthens the divide between what the 'haves' and 'have-nots' study.

The flawed vocational pathway that has, until recently, been widespread in our non-selective secondary schools underlines the complexity of the selection debate, a theme that is central to this book. There is of course much left to discuss and expand on in the discussion about selection in schools, from looking beyond England's borders (not just abroad, but also at other systems of selection in the wider United Kingdom), to getting a clearer picture of the practical realities of what is happening in the selection process today. There are also many more voices still to be heard, including both those who are keen to join the debate, and those found to be more reticent. This book aims to break down some of the issues that are central to the selection question and, in doing so, to add some depth to it by considering inherent overlaps between seemingly opposed viewpoints. Selection by academic performance is without doubt the mainstay of the debate. But how and where this selection criterion fits into the wider education landscape is central to our understanding of what exactly we disagree on.

Selective, Comprehensive and Diversified Secondary Schooling in England: A Brief History

Geoff Whitty and Sally Power

This chapter traces the way in which national and local policies have at different times favoured selective or non-selective admissions arrangements in English secondary schools.[1] It shows how, for most of the past century, the key issue of contention in political and educational debates was whether and how to select for a bipartite system on the basis of academic attainment or aptitude at age 11. The chapter goes on to discuss recent policies that have favoured a more diversified school system and parental choice, features that are sometimes criticised for introducing new forms of selection that may be less transparent and even more socially divisive.

The development of early state secondary education

Just as continental education systems of the nineteenth century were segmented, defining an academic and a social scale,[2] the people of Victorian England 'knew that elementary education was for working-class children and that grammar schools were for middle-class children'.[3] Following legislation of 1902, maintained grammar schools were established in almost every major centre of population, where they were seen as the symbols of educational advance and the guardians of cultural excellence. For the working-class child, the acquisition of a highly-competitive grammar school scholarship or free place represented a considerable success. From 1917, grammar school courses were linked to School Certificate accreditation, strengthening links with the universities, and reinforcing the widely-held perception that a grammar school education could open doors that would otherwise remain firmly shut. In short, grammar schools provided an academic education for a minority – predominantly middle-class – destined for white-collar work or for university, followed by a professional career. The majority of children, by contrast, received only a basic education in an elementary school, occasionally followed by a short period in a lower-status secondary institution.

It was not until after the end of the Second World War that free secondary education became a right for all children. However, the educational settlement ushered in by the 1944 Education Act did not seek to challenge the cultural status quo, and most of the post-war development plans produced by Local Education Authorities (LEAs) contemplated differentiated secondary schooling. The orthodoxy that intelligence was measurable by psychometric tests, offering 'a neutral means of assessing the aptitudes of children from deprived backgrounds and of allocating them to appropriate schools' had, by this time, dominated a generation of educational thinking.[4] A tripartite arrangement of secondary grammar, technical and modern schools was widely envisaged, but it was *bipartism* that would prevail. Properly equipped technical schools proved too expensive for more than a handful of LEAs and, in any case, there were many reservations about identifying the 'technical aptitudes' of a child aged ten-and-a-half.[5] The absence of technical schools militated against the realisation of 'parity of esteem' between all state secondary schools. Predictably, parental aspirations favoured the higher-status grammar schools, notwithstanding the fact that, on average, 75 per cent of 11-to 15-year-olds were allocated to secondary modern schools, which were merely 'an extension of the elementary school tradition'.[6]

Demands for comprehensive secondary schooling

Although the implementation of the 1944 settlement was presided over by the same Labour government that created the modern welfare state, egalitarian educational thinking was not to the fore.[7] A British multilateral (or comprehensive) school lobby, consisting of some Socialist politicians and union officials is identifiable from the 1920s, but few arguments were voiced in favour of radical cultural transformation. Grammar schools, a number of which enjoyed reputations for excellence dating back to the sixteenth century, had been successful in producing a formidable generation of Labour politicians. Moreover, they aroused sentiments of civic pride that tended to push aside considerations of the less satisfactory secondary modern experience. Multilateral schools were untried, and their anticipated size – in excess of 1,000 pupils – was a cause of concern. Some critics viewed their possible introduction as a threat to the social order; writing in the *Times Educational Supplement* (TES) in 1947, Eric James, High Master of Manchester Grammar School, expressed the fear that they might precipitate 'grave social, educational and cultural evils which may well be a national disaster'.[8]

Despite its reputation as a landmark piece of twentieth-century social legislation,[9] Kerckhoff and Trott suggest that there is 'no basis to believe that the 1944 Education Act reduced the effects of socioeconomic status on educational attainment'.[10] Indeed, by the late 1950s and early 1960s, the conclusions drawn by a number of influential research studies were already being used to challenge the principle of selective secondary schooling. As Harold Silver notes, Floud, Halsey and Martin's 1956 work on the relationship between social class and educational attainment 'was followed by a considerable literature which analysed the nature of existing secondary school provision, the factors militating against working-class children gaining access to and succeeding in grammar school education, and pointed to the solution that was gaining political and educational ground – the comprehensive secondary school'.[11] Selection, it was argued, was a major cause of 'social waste', as it advantaged the children of middle-class parents and was an impediment to equality.[12]

Selection tests were also reported to be unreliable indicators of children's potential. In 1957 a committee of leading psychologists, headed by P.E. Vernon and including Hans Eysenck (who was later to adopt a very different position), challenged the disciples of psychometric testing in arguing that human intelligence could be influenced by environment and by upbringing. The report concluded that 'any policy involving irreversible segregation at eleven years or earlier is psychologically unsound, and therefore… in so far as public opinion allows – the common or comprehensive school would be preferable, at least up to the age of thirteen'.[13] In the same year a major National Foundation for Educational Research (NFER) report noted that in some LEAs as many as 45 per cent of 11-year-olds proceeded to a grammar school, while the figure was as low as 10 per cent elsewhere.[14] Even the most carefully devised selection procedures, it was maintained, had an error margin of 10 per cent. This pointed to the conclusion that around 60,000 children per annum were allocated to the 'wrong' secondary school.[15] Additional pressure came from the many middle-class parents whose children failed to pass the 11-plus.[16]

From the late 1950s a handful of local authorities began to establish 'experimental' comprehensive schools, and by 1963 a clear trend had developed – driven in part by mounting concerns that the rationale for and methods of psychometric testing were flawed. Originally, support for comprehensive schools was mostly to be found among individuals and groups associated with the Labour movement, but by the early 1960s it had become more widespread. In some localities Conservatives were content to support the removal of the 11-plus in order to facilitate the development of carefully-planned comprehensive schemes.[17] Others revealed more audacious agendas, hailing comprehensive education as a panacea that might forge a less divided society and achieve cultural unification.[18]

Labour and Conservative policies 1964-79

The Labour government that came to power in 1964 sought to accelerate the drive towards comprehensive education. In keeping with the tradition of decentralised policy-making, it issued a non-statutory circular, requesting that LEAs provide comprehensive plans.[19] Yet, while grammar schools and secondary moderns each had a clear sense of identity, the essential character of a comprehensive school proved more difficult to define. The 'experimental' comprehensives, built during the late 1950s in such places as London, Coventry and Bristol, had overwhelmingly been purpose-built institutions, catering for the full 11 to 18 age range and serving areas of new housing. While some of them had introduced innovative curricular features, their pupil intakes were characteristically similar to secondary modern schools.[20] By the mid-1960s, the comprehensive movement could only proceed if LEAs were willing to close, merge or re-designate their existing selective institutions. A lead had been provided by such LEAs as Bradford, Croydon, Leicestershire and the West Riding of Yorkshire. The three latter LEAs each developed non-selective tiered patterns of secondary education that departed from the original conception of a very large comprehensive school. Others took a more piecemeal approach. As Labour's policy accepted diversity as the price for rapid change – at least presentationally – the Department of Education and Science (DES) accepted a number of secondary reorganisation plans that sought only to soften selection, rather than remove it altogether. Though sometimes described as 'interim' solutions, a number of approved LEA proposals contemplated the preservation of at least one grammar school to cater for the most academically-able children of the district.

Where state grammar schools continued to operate, comprehensives were ultimately 'comprehensive' only by aspiration. Some such institutions were, in fact, simply re-designated secondary modern schools. However, even where an LEA chose to adopt a 'fully comprehensive' solution, vestiges of the former selective system could sometimes be identified. For example, according to National Child Development Study data from 1974, comprehensive schools that had formerly been grammar schools were considerably more likely to have a sixth-form than ex-secondary modern comprehensives.[21] Clear statistical linkages were found between students in ex-grammar comprehensives having relatively high prior academic achievements, following a more traditionally academic curriculum, obtaining more public examination passes, proceeding to university and obtaining high-status jobs.[22]

There followed several years of conflicting policy direction. In 1969, Secretary of State for Education and Science, Edward Short, introduced a Parliamentary Bill requiring those LEAs that had not put forward plans for a comprehensive system to do so. This Bill was lost, however, when Harold Wilson called a general election the following year. As Secretary of State for Education under the 1970 Conservative government, Margaret Thatcher withdrew Labour's circular (though famously presided over more comprehensive school designations than any of her predecessors or successors) – only for Labour to reinstate the request for comprehensive plans on returning to office in 1974. By this stage Secretary of State Fred Mulley no longer shared the view of several of his predecessors that the remaining un-reorganised LEAs would fall into line.

A survey in 1975 indicated that only 20 LEAs were 'truly comprehensive', and that a quarter of 10-year-olds still sat the 11-plus.[23] Following the decision of seven LEAs to defy the government's policy, and the decision of the Law Lords that he had acted unlawfully in attempting to abandon a scheme to end secondary school selection, Mulley introduced a Bill along the same lines as the abortive legislation from 1969-70. By the time this reached the statute book, in 1976, however, Shirley Williams had succeeded Mulley in James Callaghan's government and the 'Great Debate' about the future of education was underway. The continuing economic crisis, industrial unrest and doubts about the effectiveness of comprehensive education, including at Cabinet level, made it very difficult to enforce the 1976 Education Act.[24] Significantly, a 1978 DES report was more retrospective than forward-looking – confirming the Labour government's unwillingness to differentiate between genuinely comprehensive arrangements and the partially comprehensive solutions adopted by a number of LEAs.[25]

Conservative policies 1979-97

Following the Conservative general election victory of May 1979 under the leadership of Margaret Thatcher, the 1976 Act was repealed by new legislation. In spite of this, the early 1980s witnessed a number of LEA secondary reorganisations along comprehensive lines, including Bolton, Tameside, Cornwall and Cumbria.[26] However, academic selection at 11-plus was once again officially sponsored at the margins via the new government's Assisted Places Scheme, which funded academically able pupils to attend academically selective private schools.[27] More generally, over the course of the following decade the principle of comprehensive education was subjected to significant redefinition as a result of central government policies designed to promote 'choice' and 'diversity' under the banner of improving standards. In particular, the landmark 1988 Education Reform Act sought to promote two new types of self-governing secondary school, the city technology college (CTC) and the grant-maintained (GM) school. In some areas the GM school initiative proved to be a vehicle for the partial reintroduction of selection.[28] In the wake of the 1992 White Paper, 'Choice and Diversity', and further legislation the following year, an increasing number of specialist secondary schools emerged.[29] These schools were permitted to select according to pupil aptitude in such areas as technology, languages or music, rather than by ability.

During the early 1990s a small number of comprehensive schools introduced grammar streams, while in 1994, the Queen Elizabeth GM School, Penrith abandoned its comprehensive status to become a fully selective grammar school. No groundswell of support for these initiatives followed, but those who wanted to see more selection received an unexpected boost when in 1996 the Labour Party Shadow Health spokesperson, Harriet Harman, opted to send her son to a grammar school outside her immediate locality.[30]

A White Paper published in June 1996 had been widely expected to make provision for a GM grammar school in every town. Instead, however, the document focused upon increasing the number of specialist schools and on permitting existing schools greater freedom to select. The White Paper proposed that GM schools should be able to select up to 50 per cent of their pupils, specialist schools 30 per cent and LEA comprehensives 20 per cent.[31] These thresholds featured in a Parliamentary Bill, published in October 1996. The Bill was before Parliament at the time of the Wirral South by-election of February 1997, during which the respective political parties' policies on selective and comprehensive education received close media examination. Six grammar schools were located within the Wirral South constituency, including one attended by the former Labour Prime Minister, Harold Wilson. However, plans for Secretary of State Gillian Shephard's Bill to extend selection were sacrificed in the early spring when a general election was called and on 1 May the Conservatives lost power to a new Labour government, led by Tony Blair.

The approach of New Labour, 1997-2010

For the Labour Party, comprehensive education had been a vexing issue throughout the 1990s. Party sound bites from the 1992 general election suggested a renewed commitment to the abandonment of selection within the state education system and the reassertion of LEA control over maintained schools.[32] Following their fourth successive general election defeat, however, the party moved towards a position that accepted, and then embraced, diversity and choice. It was in the name of parental choice that the party side-stepped the grammar school question. As Blair told an audience in Birmingham during the 1997 general election campaign:

> I have no intention of waging war on any schools except failing schools. So far as the existing 160 grammar schools are concerned, as long as the

parents want them, they will stay… We will tackle
what isn't working, not what is.[33]

Accordingly, immediately after its election victory, New
Labour published proposals to allow parents to decide
the fate of existing grammar schools or of area-wide
selection where it still existed. The 1998 School Standards
and Framework Act thus included provisions by which
local communities could petition for a ballot to end
academic selection.[34] Several petitions were launched but
only one received the signatures of 20 per cent of eligible
parents, the threshold needed to trigger a ballot. In this
ballot, which was for Ripon Grammar School, parents
rejected an end to selection by a ratio of 2:1. There
therefore remain 163 grammar schools in England,
located in 36 of the 150 local authorities; of these 36, only
the 15 fully selective local authorities have substantial
numbers of pupils attending grammar schools.

In power, New Labour's position on selection
remained ambiguous – certainly in the old terms of the
debate. Although it did not support the creation of new
state-funded grammar schools, and abolished the
Assisted Places Scheme, it implicitly endorsed the
principle of selection by other means. The 1997 White
Paper, 'Excellence in Schools', and the 1998 School
Standards and Framework Act that followed it,
continued the previous administration's support for
specialist schools;[35] while there was rather less emphasis
on these schools' selective character, the Act
nevertheless permitted any school to select 10 per cent
of pupils on aptitude if the governing body was
satisfied the school had a specialism.[36]

There were continuing calls from organisations like
the Campaign for State Education (CASE) and

Comprehensive Future throughout the period of New Labour government – and indeed beyond – for the Labour Party leadership to tackle the remaining grammar schools. However, Labour chose to operate in the more ambiguous territory of 'choice and diversity'. Some in the party went so far as to dismiss the comprehensive school altogether as 'an institution of the past – part of the social democratic agenda of the sixties and therefore of no relevance to the world of the nineties'.[37] Contributions to the debate about selection by centre-left writers at this time included one by Adonis and Pollard, who argued that 'for all the good intentions, the destruction of the grammar schools... had the effect of reinforcing class divisions'.[38] Nevertheless, when Andrew Adonis became a policy adviser to the prime minister, and later an education minister, he chose not to take on the residual social democratic wing of the Labour Party over grammar schools but rather to pursue his ambitions for the reform of state education through other means – most notably, using 'academies' to tackle failing local authority run schools. The main aim behind these schools was to increase diversity and choice and thereby raise standards across academies' local areas, which (under New Labour at least) were typically deprived areas.[39] Some academies were new schools, whereas others were existing schools deemed to be failing under local authority supervision, and that had not responded to earlier 'turnaround' initiatives. It was to academies (and later, under the Coalition government, free schools) that the vestiges of the comprehensive school lobby now turned their attention – and, specifically, these schools' alleged role in reintroducing social – if not strictly academic – selection by the back door.[40]

Selection within a diversified school system

Certainly under Tony Blair, New Labour continued to favour what it presented as the 'modernisation' of the comprehensive system through the differentiation of schools. Its rhetoric increasingly emphasised a supposed link between school diversity and higher standards for all. This is something that was made clear by Tony Blair in a 2006 speech, where he commented:

> At first we put a lot of faith in centrally driven improvements in performance and undoubtedly without that we would never have got some of the immediate uplift in results. But over time I shifted from saying 'it's standards, not structures' to realising that school structures could affect standards.[41]

Accordingly, the amount of differentiation among schools increased under New Labour. As under the previous Conservative government, the key ingredient for linking differentiation to standards and excellence remained choice, as illustrated by the 2005 Schools White Paper:

> School improvement has been helped not only by the reforms introduced since 1997, but also by published data and inspection reports, and the ability of many parents to vote with their feet by finding a better state school. There are those who argue that there is no demand for choice; but this ignores the reality that the vast majority of parents want a real choice of excellent schools.[42]

New Labour chose to maintain something of the Conservative distinction between local authority and

GM status, albeit under the new titles of 'community' and 'foundation' schools. In addition, it also retained the existing city technology colleges and greatly increased the number of specialist schools. To these were added (city) academies and trust schools. A new Schools Commissioner would act as a 'champion' of increased diversity and choice.

As Education Secretary, Estelle Morris stated that specialist schools were 'only modern comprehensive schools', implying that they had no special advantages.[43] But at least until they became the majority of secondary schools, the specialist school label clearly differentiated them from what Tony Blair's official spokesman, Alastair Campbell, termed 'bog-standard' comprehensive schools.[44] While the apparently superior performance of specialist schools added impetus to the policy of differentiation,[45] the fact that this performance may have been partly due to the nature of their pupil intakes was not always acknowledged.[46] Although it had always been the case that all sorts of schools that were nominally comprehensive lacked balanced intakes, either socially or academically, or indeed both, the charge was that school choice and school autonomy, including over admissions, would now make it possible for far more schools to select covertly as well as overtly.[47] Not surprisingly, academies became a particularly important category of school in this regard.

Thus, for a time, the debate about overt academic selection took second place to a debate about whether covert social selection, and by implication covert academic selection, was taking place in the new diverse school system.[48] A major issue of contention between the proponents and opponents of diversity was the effect of some but not all schools being their own admissions authorities. For example, Tough and Brooks found that schools that were their own admissions authorities had intakes that were far less representative of their surrounding areas than schools where the local authority was the admissions authority.[49] In 2005 and 2006, the Sutton Trust looked at the social composition of the 'top 200' comprehensives in England and identified a group of high-attaining schools that were more socially exclusive than the national average and other schools in their areas.[50] This mismatch may be explained by a number of factors, including covert social selection.[51]

Such covert selection was an area of concern for the House of Commons Education and Skills Committee in its review of the 2005 Schools White Paper, and its report to government prompted some significant concessions on admissions policy, mainly around the status of the admissions code.[52] In an attempt to address covert selection (whether intended or unintended), the new code prohibited schools from giving priority to children on the basis of their interests or knowledge, and this was combined with free school transport to open up choice to less-advantaged families and 'choice advisers' to assist these families in negotiating their child's transition to secondary school.[53] Later research by Allen *et al.* has suggested that the 2003 and 2007 admission codes did reduce social segregation between schools to a limited extent.[54]

Nevertheless, left-of-centre opponents of New Labour continued to argue that such measures would not be enough to overcome covert selection and 'playing the system' by knowledgeable middle-class families, so they united around a call for 'good schools in all areas, for all children'.[55] However, any attempt to return to traditional catchment areas after two decades of choice was unlikely to be attractive politically. An attempt by one local authority, Brighton, to run admissions lotteries as an alternative way of dealing with covert selection proved even more contentious,[56] although the Sutton Trust has recently suggested that ballots and banding arrangements are now becoming more acceptable to parents.[57]

The Coalition government, 2010-

The Conservative-led Coalition government that replaced New Labour in 2010 has maintained an emphasis on school autonomy, competition and choice as its driving force for school improvement, closing the socioeconomic achievement gap and enhancing social mobility. Whereas the academies policy of the Blair government used academy status mainly to prioritise the replacement or improvement of failing schools in disadvantaged areas, the Coalition invited all schools highly rated by the schools inspectorate, Ofsted, to apply for this status. As a result, at the time of writing nearly 60 per cent of secondary schools are academies or free schools. The latter are a further new form of school, set up by parents or other interested parties, and like academies they are their own admissions authorities. Although some of these schools are in disadvantaged areas or where there is a shortage of school places, others are in middle-class areas and where there is already a surplus of places. Those free schools located in disadvantaged areas have not necessarily attracted disadvantaged children.[58]

Under the leadership of Michael Gove, Secretary of State for Education from 2010 to 2014, these policies took precedence over any formal return to grammar schools, despite pressure from some of his backbench colleagues. His Liberal Democrat Coalition partners would anyway not have countenanced a return to academic selection at age 11. However, the numbers attending existing grammar schools have increased over the years and, in 2013, the government agreed to allow oversubscribed schools, including grammar schools, to set up satellite schools on separate sites. Although an initial bid by Kent County Council to open annexes to two grammar schools in Sevenoaks was rejected on the grounds that they seemed to be entirely new schools, Gove was reported to be 'genuinely open' to another application that could not be dismissed on such grounds. Those close to Gove were also reported to be critical of a strong attack on grammar schools by Michael Wilshaw, Her Majesty's Chief Inspector, who argued that 'demands for more grammars should be ignored, as they serve the top 10 per cent of the population at the expense of the poorest'.[59]

Reflections and conclusions

Can we draw any conclusions from this history about which type of school system – selective or comprehensive or diversified – is most effective? While this appears to be a straightforward question, a succession of research studies over a period of more than 50 years has failed to produce a consensus on the selective versus comprehensive issue. This is partly, of course, because we cannot begin to answer the question without first answering a series of prior questions. The obvious one is 'effective for what'? Should we make judgements on the basis of the contribution of different types of school system to academic attainment (and then for all, for some or for 'closing the gap'?) or to well-being, employability, social mobility, social cohesion – or what? All these considerations and more have figured in debates about the policies described here.

Despite all the emphasis we hear today on the importance of evidence-based or evidence-informed policy, the policies set out in this chapter have been driven much more by social and educational aims and values that are by no means a matter of consensus. For some, of course, the right to choose – for good or ill – trumps all other considerations.

Sometimes the issues at stake are a matter of such intense emotion that an appeal to evidence may be beside the point. Certainly the language used by proponents of the different systems is hardly conducive to the careful weighing of evidence. For example, in 1991, the psychometrist and former opponent of selection, Hans Eysenck, suggested that comprehensive schools were responsible for 'millions of uneducated, practically illiterate and innumerate youngsters who are almost unemployable roaming the streets, making up the legions of football hooligans, and making Britain the laughing stock of Europe'.[60] Later in that decade, one of the most passionate supporters of comprehensive education, Labour peer Roy Hattersley, launched the CASE 'Say No to Selection' campaign in October 1998 by condemning what he called the 'educational apartheid' of selection.[61] David Willetts's careful weighing of the evidence on grammar schools and conclusion that they have not in fact been a driver of social mobility, did him few favours.[62] None of this is to say that evidence should not be part of the debate, but it is unlikely to ever be the decisive determinant of policy.

In our earlier publication, *The Grammar School Question*,[63] we reviewed what research evidence could tell us about the impact of competing systems.[64] We concluded that, overall, that exercise had been 'disappointing' for those looking for decisive evidence to support one side of the debate or the other. According to Jesson, later reviews of research evidence, such as that by Coe *et al.*,[65] also brought 'no conclusive finding justifying one position over another'.[66]

In 2000 we also suggested that academic selection had become less politically contentious than it had been ten years earlier (or certainly that the terms of the debate had changed). We pointed out that a number of influential journalists who might at one time have been assumed to be supporters of comprehensive education, including Melanie Phillips and Will Hutton, had spoken and written in support of secondary school selection. Hutton though subsequently backed the way in which comprehensive schools were being interpreted by New Labour.[67]

A key issue in recent debates has been the extent to which existing state-funded grammar schools can be justified when they recruit so few students from disadvantaged backgrounds even when they are academically able,[68] so there are currently moves to encourage such schools to change their admissions arrangements and to give priority to pupils whose record of receiving free school meals makes them eligible for payment of the pupil premium.[69] Meanwhile, no major political party has embraced a full-scale return to academic selection as part of its platform in recent times. At the time of writing, only the UK Independence Party (UKIP) is expected to include the creation of more grammar schools in its manifesto for the 2015 general election. Instead, there exists something of a consensus that diversity and choice should be the hallmark of the English secondary school system and some degree of selection by aptitude, if not academic attainment, permitted within it. In view of this, future governments may just try to tinker with the existing diverse system to encourage more or less selection within it. If a future government does actively sponsor a more overtly selective system of state-funded education, this is perhaps more likely to emerge at age 14 or 16 than age 11. A majority Conservative government might conceivably consider a return to some form of Assisted Places Scheme, along the lines of the needs-blind admissions system currently being advocated by the Sutton Trust.[70] There certainly seems to be no appetite among any of the mainstream political parties to take on the overt academic selection that remains a crucial feature of the elite private sector of education in England. That remains far too hot a political issue to contemplate.

The Twenty-First Century Case for Selection

Graham Brady

Last summer marked the seventieth anniversary of the 'Butler Act' of 1944. It was a remarkable milestone in the development of state education in England and Wales. Butler was a Tory Education Secretary but the Bill was that of a National Government, its central aims of opening fee-free access to good schools, ensuring education that would suit the aptitudes of each pupil, raising the school leaving age and tackling the wartime legacy of poverty and malnutrition, enjoyed cross-party support. As Labour's spokesman John Parker said when the Bill was introduced:

> We welcome the intention to make secondary education available to the whole people and we think it right and proper that a Bill which will give secondary education to the whole people should be brought in by an all-party National Government. We are particularly pleased to see the Tories accepting progressive ideas and I welcome the fact that the two main parties are collaborating in trying to pass this Bill as law. In all our big educational advances there has been a sharing of ideas.[1]

In setting up the tripartite system of grammar schools, technical schools and secondary modern schools, the 1944 Act was not of course creating grammar schools. Many of the grammar schools were ancient foundations (visit King Edward VI Grammar School in Stratford-upon-Avon where boys are still taught in Shakespeare's old classroom), others like my old school, Altrincham Grammar School for Boys, were barely 30 years old in 1944. What Butler did was to remove fees from the state or 'county' grammar schools, opening them up to boys and girls regardless of their means. The party political controversy at the time wasn't about the 'progressive' idea of opening up the grammar schools but about the fact that the 'great public schools' weren't brought into the same world of open access. The Fleming Report published just as the 1944 Act was about to become law pressed for boarding places to be provided for children of limited means in the great public schools. Anticipating the years of post-war austerity, Butler thought he was going far enough but it looked, as the war drew to a close, as though the education debate would be framed for years to come around how good schools and the social advantages they might bring, could be opened to more of the nation's children.

The three-legged stool envisaged in 1944 would open the grammar schools to the more academically-inclined boys and girls regardless of background; establish a tier of technical schools; and as the leaving age rose to fifteen, and then sixteen, provide 'secondary modern' schools for those whose aptitudes weren't suited to the other schools. The fee-free grammar schools did what was intended, providing new opportunities for bright children, many of whom would soon be populating the expanding redbrick universities and filling the professions with a new generation of meritocrats. By 1971 Anthony Sampson in his *The New Anatomy of Britain* described just four of the twenty-one heads of Whitehall departments as attending major public schools (Eton, Harrow, Charterhouse and St. Paul's) with the other seventeen educated at grammar school.[2] By contrast, Sutton Trust research last year showed those educated in the independent sector reasserting their dominance in the Civil Service, the law and the armed forces.[3]

The technical schools were intended to cure the British disease – already a century old – of denigrating the technical or vocational and valuing only the traditional academic classical education. The plan was to educate a cadre of engineers and technicians like that which had driven Germany's successful industrialisation. Some of the technical schools were established and did well by the (mostly) boys who attended them. All too often, however, the establishment view triumphed; whilst grammar schools thrived, few technical schools were established or properly resourced. Soon the three-legged stool was looking pretty lopsided. If you went to grammar school you were OK, if not, then an uninspiring secondary was all too often the alternative. Faced with this reality, the common-sense approach would have been to preserve the best of the system and seek to raise the standards of the other schools. Instead, the idea took hold that removing the grammar schools would create a 'fairer' system, without selection, in which Labour's Hugh Gaitskell's fatuous phrase 'a grammar school education for all' could be achieved. By the late 1950s the Left was abandoning its goal of opening up the best schools to people of all backgrounds in favour of an egalitarian delusion in which everyone would go to the same schools and therefore have the same opportunities. Again it is interesting to note that the new egalitarians picked no fight with the public schools of the privileged few but instead trained their guns on the state grammars and direct grant schools that were doing well by the working and lower-middle-class many. As the sociologist Frank Musgrove put it:

> The Labour Party did not abolish the great Public Schools, the obvious strongholds of upper-class privilege; with unbelievable perversity they extinguished the only serious hope of working-class parity... the upper-classes kept their Public Schools, the working class lost theirs.[4]

In *A Class Act: The Myth of Britain's Classless Society* which Andrew (now Lord) Adonis co-authored with Stephen Pollard, a former research director of the Fabian Society, they said:

> The comprehensive revolution has not removed the link between education and class, but strengthened it... In 1965, the Labour-controlled House of Commons resolved that moving to a comprehensive system would preserve all that is valuable in grammar school education for those children who now receive it and make it available to more children. Few would maintain that this has in fact been the case.

> The comprehensive revolution tragically destroyed much of the excellent without improving the rest. Comprehensive schools have largely replaced selection by ability with selection by class and house price. Middle-class children now go to middle-class comprehensives, whose catchment areas comprise middle-class neighbours, while

working-class children are mostly left to fester in the inner-city comprehensive their parents cannot afford to move away from. Far from bringing the classes together, England's schools – private and state – are now a force for rigorous segregation.[5]

It is fair to say that the Left was aided and abetted in this 'destruction of excellence' by many middle-class families who still cleaved to the idea that a child not taking the academic route had obviously 'failed'. Too many Conservative politicians went along with this approach, all too often safe in the knowledge that their own children would never darken the doors of a state school be it selective or not.

The widespread replacement of state grammars with comprehensives was compounded in 1976 when the Labour government pulled the rug from under the independent schools that were providing free places through the 'direct grant' scheme. Especially important in the North, this had opened the doors of great schools like Bradford Grammar, Leeds Grammar and Manchester Grammar to working-class children. In 1968 a remarkable 77 per cent of boys leaving Manchester Grammar went on to university.[6] This attack on opportunity for those without the ability to pay was repeated in 1997 when the vindictive measure that closed down the 'Assisted Places Scheme' became the very first Act passed by the Blair government. Advocates of abolishing the scheme claimed that it had become a subsidy for middle-class parents who could afford to pay for independent schools in any case.[7] In fact, as I pointed out in my maiden speech on 2 June 1997:

Nothing could be further from the truth. The 300 boys on assisted places at Manchester Grammar are part of a 500-year-old tradition of providing top-quality education, regardless of social or economic standing. Of the 242 pupils with assisted places at William Hulme's Grammar School, [then an independent grammar school in Manchester] 160 have their full fees paid, which means that they have combined parental income of less than £10,000 a year.[8]

The Sutton Trust has advocated a return to a version of direct grant via its proposed 'Open Access' scheme.[9] This approach has attracted support across the political spectrum, as evidenced recently by a call from Labour MP, Ian Austin, to pilot an 'Open Access' scheme with independent schools in the West Midlands.[10] Sadly, none of the main political parties at Westminster have yet responded to this demand.

The egalitarian new order of one-size-fits-all comprehensives might have gone unchallenged if Anthony Crosland (Secretary of State for Education and Science 1965-7) had succeeded in achieving his elegantly phrased goal of destroying 'every f***ing grammar school in England. And Wales. And Northern Ireland'.[11] Then there would be nothing against which to measure the all-ability comprehensives. Except the independent sector, which is easily dismissed as succeeding because of class sizes that the maintained sector will never see and the privileged backgrounds of (some of) the pupils. Fortunately, in a rare triumph of 'localism' some English counties, boroughs, or towns were able to resist the tide of modernisation. Probably most of these bloody-minded communities (like my own) were motivated more by a desire to defend some outstanding grammar schools; less by a commitment to the Butler vision of the right school for the right child.

However, having saved their grammar schools, and often faced with an ongoing battle to defend them, they soon bent to the task of raising the standard of the other schools as well. This left a wholly selective secondary provision in Northern Ireland; widespread selection in Buckinghamshire, Lincolnshire, Kent, Trafford and the Wirral; and some grammar schools scattered from Devon through parts of London to Yorkshire and Cumbria. Elsewhere there remained selection in the independent schools but generally the pattern was of all-ability comprehensives across the country. Some of these comprehensives are very good schools but comparing the overall performance of selective areas with comprehensive ones, selective areas tend to do better. Former Ofsted chief Chris Woodhead set out the evidence in *A Desolation of Learning:*

> The evidence, on the other hand, for the academic success of selective schools is very strong. I do not simply mean that grammar schools achieve in absolute terms better results than non-selective schools. They do, of course, and opponents of grammar schools retort, understandably, that, given the ability of their pupils, they should... Of the 184,000 pupils who took A-levels at schools in England in 2008, 66 per cent were at comprehensives and 12 per cent at grammar schools. However of those who achieved three A grades 36 per cent were at comprehensives and 21 per cent were at grammars.[12]

It is worth noting that those sitting A-levels at comprehensive schools have already been 'selected' post-16 on the basis of their GCSE results. Woodhead went on to debunk the myth that the success of pupils in grammar schools is in some way at the expense of those who go to secondary modern (or 'high') schools.[13] First, pupils in selective areas *as a whole* get better results than in comprehensive areas: in 2013/14, 55.9 per cent of English pupils achieved 5 A*-C GCSEs, including English and maths, compared to 65.2 per cent of Northern Irish pupils (and this could hardly be said to have been in a uniformly affluent or trouble-free environment).[14] Secondly, students in secondary modern schools perform only a little less highly than those in all-ability comprehensives. Research by John Marks found that secondary modern school students in England were only about two months behind those in all-ability schools at key stage 3 English and seven months in maths. At GCSE the secondary modern results in English and maths were on average better than for a third of comprehensive schools.[15] Similar results are seen in Trafford where, if we discount the exceptionally good exam results of the seven state grammar schools (and with them, the most academic 35 per cent of the cohort), the remaining high schools continue to produce results which are statistically comparable with a great number of comprehensive local authority areas.[16] This pattern can be seen reflected in the persistent dominance in exam league tables of selective and partially selective areas. In 2013/14 eight of the top ten local education authority (LEA) areas at A-level were either fully or partially selective when using the AAB (including at least two facilitating subjects) measure.[17]

It is common to hear selective education criticised by those who claim to have been scarred by failure at 11. In part this is the result of the entrenched British failure to give proper status to the non-academic route. As we move to a more diverse pattern of school provision in which technical, art or sports specialist colleges compete with grammars specialising in teaching the most academic, this danger diminishes. There is no reason why a child should feel a failure for attending a university technical college or any other high-performing school. Whatever the failings of the secondary moderns of yesteryear, it is the performance of the non-selective high schools in selective areas that renders this argument invalid. If those with less innate academic aptitude achieve more in a high school than a comprehensive we should recognise the success of school and student alike.

New Labour's earliest moves were to scrap the Assisted Places Scheme and reduce the freedom that had been given to good state schools under grant-maintained status. However, by the time of the 2002 Education Act, Labour ministers had come to the same conclusion as their Tory predecessors that standards could only be raised by freeing schools from excessive intervention. Labour's academies programme focused on schools that were in need of serious improvement, whereas the Coalition has used academies to free successful schools, but the broad thrust was the same. By the time of the 2010 election neither of the two main parties was advocating returning powers to the LEAs.

With regard to selection there have been minor changes since the last government. State grammar schools are now allowed to become academies; under Labour they were not. Independent grammar schools becoming academies on the other hand, are still forced to go comprehensive. Bureaucratic obstacles to grammar school expansion have been removed and in principle Education Secretary Nicky Morgan has indicated that existing grammar schools wishing to expand into 'annexes' should be able to do so. This would only be permitted, however, if the school sites share the same staff and serve the same catchment. At present the only initiative in this direction that is progressing is for an annex in Sevenoaks, a decision which is due early in 2015. In essence the policy is that if you are lucky enough to live in an area that already has grammar school places, you can have more. If, on the other hand, you think a grammar school education would be best for your child and you live in the wrong part of the country, you can whistle for it – or pay up and go private.

In another interesting development, Angela Burns AM, the Welsh Conservatives' Shadow Education Minister has indicated that a future Conservative administration in Wales would look at providing elements of selection at age 14, with selection between grammar and technical streams by preference and teachers' recommendation.[18] The Welsh Tories' policy opens the interesting question of what age is the best at which to select. Few argue that selection for university at 18 is unjust or inappropriate; or indeed that it is wrong to set an achievement threshold at 16 for those who should progress to A-level studies. The recent history of academic selection in the state sector is based on testing at 11-plus; many public schools select their intake at 13. When David Blunkett was Education Secretary he sensibly explored ways in which children not responding to schooling post-14 might follow a more vocational fork in the road.[19] Whilst the evidence of the success of selection at 11 is hard to refute, there is no reason why selection should have to take place at any one age instead of another. A truly diverse pattern of provision might allow selection for a variety of specialisms at whatever age is most appropriate for a particular child.

If we are to raise standards and extend opportunity we must be relentless in challenging under-performance and we must have the courage to allow innovation and choice. In 2007 Labour Minister for Schools Andrew Adonis set an aspiration for 80 per cent of our children to be achieving five or more good GCSEs by 2020, a standard already being achieved or exceeded in Singapore.[20] At present only just over half of children in English schools meet that target. Michael Gove maintained the momentum by raising the *minimum* expected achievement levels for schools from 35 per cent to 40 per cent en route to 50 per cent by 2015.[21] This determination to raise standards has been reflected in schools policy since the last election. Rules on school discipline have been improved, the curriculum strengthened, examinations have been made more rigorous and some limited school choice has been introduced. Academies and free schools are an important step forward but too often the policy is still held back by dogma and the opposition of the educational establishment. If we are to revolutionise educational opportunity, we need to be prepared not only to benchmark against international competitors but also to ask some uncomfortable questions about discrepancies in performance between different types of schools in different areas in the UK. For instance, why can Kingston upon Thames get 71.6 per cent of children through five or more good GCSEs including English and maths but Bristol manages only 52.3 per cent? Why does Buckinghamshire (71.3 per cent) outperform Oxfordshire (60.6 per cent)?[22] Not only is there a dramatic gap between the performance of state education in one area compared to another, there are staggering differences between schools of a similar character within the same area. This debunks the notion that educational performance is dictated by the socioeconomic profile of a locality. It is undoubtedly harder to teach children whose families are dysfunctional, who have nowhere quiet to do their homework, or whose parents have no aspirations for themselves or their children. However, there are numerous examples of schools with large numbers of children receiving free school meals and high proportions of pupils with English as a second language. At the local authority level there is substantial variation in the attainment of those eligible for free school meals and those who have English as a second language. 71 per cent of pupils eligible for free school meals in both Kensington and Chelsea and Westminster achieve five or more A*-C grades at GCSE. In Tower Hamlets the figure is an impressive 65.6 per cent. At the other end of the scale Rutland and Barnsley achieve scores of 24 per cent and 26.1 per cent respectively. Oddly, Rutland has the highest score in the country for five or more A*-C GCSE attainment for those whose first language is not English (100 per cent). It is followed by Sutton, Kensington and Chelsea, and Trafford (88.5, 84.4, and 83.8 per cent respectively). Barnsley and Peterborough score just over half as well, at 48.1 per cent and 49.1 per cent.[23]

If comparisons between state schools can be challenging, recent Sutton Trust research shows a shocking divide between performance in the independent sector, which educates only seven per cent of the country's pupils, and that of (most of) the maintained sector. Whilst progression to higher education was found to be fairly even across sectors, (non-selective state schools: 69 per cent of pupils; independent schools: 75.5 per cent; state grammar schools: 86.4 per cent of pupils), the picture for entry to the most selective universities is starkly different, with nearly a third of entrants to Oxbridge coming from just a hundred schools (84 independent and 16 state grammar schools).[24] This disparity is compounded by regional variation with only one local authority area outside the South East in the top ten for state-educated pupils gaining places at either Oxbridge or any of the 30 most desirable UK universities (such as those in the Russell Group) and that is (selective) Trafford. The Sutton Trust's analysis shows that a pupil attending an independent school is thirty times more likely to secure an Oxbridge place than one at a state school. This picture would be dramatically worse without the remaining state grammar schools. In 2012 the 93 per cent of the population educated in the maintained sector secured just 47 per cent of places at Oxbridge colleges.[25]

Table 1: Home Applications

School Type	Cambridge Acceptances 2012		Oxford Acceptances 2012	
	Total	%	Total	%
Comprehensive	675	19.6%	703	21.7%
Grammar	558	16.2%	495	15.3%
Sixth-Form Colleges	251	7.3%	232	7.1%
FE Institutions	39	1.1%	51	1.5%
Other Maintained	87	2.5%	29	0.8%
Total Maintained	1610	46.8%	1510	46.7%
Independent	933	27.1%	1118	34.5%
All Other Categories	50	1.5%	67	2.0%
Home Totals	2593	75.4%	2695	83.2%

Sources: University of Cambridge, Undergraduate Admissions Statistics, 2012 Cycle, May 2013. University of Oxford, Undergraduate Admissions Statistics: School Type, 2012, November 2013.

Of the state schools getting the highest proportion of their students into the top 30 universities in the country, four are fully selective and a further eight are partially selective. Trafford (which operates a fully selective admissions system) is the only local authority to be in the top 20 councils outside London and the South East, with the exceptions of Bournemouth and Torbay (partially and fully selective respectively).[26] The grammar schools, educating five per cent of pupils nationally, account for a third of the total of those admitted to Oxbridge; why should this be? Partly, the answer lies in the headline differences in examination performance, but there is also a more insidious reason. Increasingly, the A-level courses that might get pupils to a top university – that might open doors to studying medicine, law, sciences or classics – are absent from the curriculum in large numbers of comprehensive schools. Independent and grammar schools claim a disproportionate share of top grades at A-level, but also account for disproportionate levels of entry for the most academically challenging A-levels. The 2013/14 provisional results show this clearly, with 32.2 per cent of selective school pupils achieving AAB (or better) with at least two of those being in so-called 'facilitating' subjects. By contrast, the figure for comprehensive school pupils is 10.3 per cent. Independent schools score 34.6 per cent.[27] Research by the Friends of Classics society found that 77 per cent of independent schools offer Latin at A-level, compared with just 33 per cent of state schools.[28] So not only are students from grammars or independent schools more likely to take the most challenging A-levels, they also perform better and take a larger than expected share of the top grades. In 2013/14, 18.3 per cent of independent school pupils achieved A*s compared to just 7.4 per cent of all state school pupils.[29]

Some opponents of selection on the Left are motivated by concern that grammar schools might 'cream off' the middle-class children who are easiest to teach. In practice the comprehensive approach often achieves this by other means. Given the poor performance of too much of state education, it is unsurprising that many parents who can afford the fees (sometimes with enormous personal sacrifice) will opt out of state education altogether.

Why is it that in Camden families are so unhappy with their local schools that 29 per cent of children are sent to fee-paying schools by parents who have already paid once for the education of their children through their taxes? Or 20 per cent in Hackney? Whereas, in leafier Bromley the figure falls to nine per cent? Why is it that the proportion going to independent schools in Trafford (five per cent) is less than half that in less affluent Stockport (10.3 per cent)?[30] It is very clear that selective areas are better at keeping middle-class pupils in the state sector than comprehensive ones.

There is a lively debate about social mobility and it is all too obvious that even in a modern economy which is more concerned with merit than with social class, there are some professions and some of our elite universities which seem worryingly impenetrable to the 93 per cent of English people educated in state schools. In part this may be attributed to the stark differences in educational standards amongst schools and between different areas. In part it is the worrying poverty of ambition that leads so many schools not to offer the most academically rigorous A-level choices. The evidence of large numbers of families fleeing failing schools by paying for independent school places tells only part of the story. If nearly 26 per cent of families in Camden go private, it does not mean the other 74 per cent are happy with the schools they are offered. In most cases it is just that they must take what they are given.

Too often governments have responded to weaknesses in the school system by censuring the universities (nearly all of which put considerable resource and energy into recruiting students from 'non-traditional' backgrounds) and by interfering with their academic independence. Not only does this undermine higher education in this country, even worse, it perpetuates the culture of excuses in our worst schools. Social mobility should properly be improved not by dumbing down university education but by making sure school standards are seriously improved.

Critics of academic selection often claim that whatever the achievements of the grammar schools in the 1950s and 1960s today's remaining grammar schools have become bastions of social privilege. Much of this is based on assertions that the percentage of pupils with free school meals is far below that of the wider community. Even leaving aside the fact that most of the grammar schools in the (less affluent) urban areas were closed or forced to revert to being fee-paying independents and the remaining grammars exist in areas of lower free school meal eligibility, this analysis is flawed. If 14.5 per cent of children receive free school meals, at first sight it seems wrong that a much smaller percentage of grammar school pupils are from that income bracket (roughly two per cent).[31] This is often held out as proof that these schools are socially selective more than academically. This argument gets weaker under closer inspection. Fundamentally the problem is that too many schools fail disadvantaged pupils before they get to secondary school. At key stage 2, (between the ages of seven and 11) there is a substantial attainment gap between those pupils who are eligible for free school meals and those who are not, but it also makes it less surprising that they are under-represented in grammar schools. Those in receipt of free school meals are significantly less likely to achieve level 5 than their peers at the end of primary school, the attainment scores being 32 per cent and 53 per cent respectively.[32] It is likely that this disparity continues into the higher reaches of level 5. Given that grammar schools tend to recruit roughly the top 25 per cent of students (lower than the proportion who achieve level 5 at key stage 2), and given that prior attainment is likely to have some impact on performance in admission tests, it is likely that a lower percentage of free school meal pupils will be recruited.

Analysis of the educational performance of ethnic minority groups under comprehensive and selective areas makes further uncomfortable reading for opponents of selective education. Pupils of every ethnic group perform better at GCSE in wholly or partially selective LEAs than they do in comprehensive ones.[33] It is ironic that some of the politicians who are keenest to improve their appeal to minority audiences have the least understanding of the policies that might help to secure their support.

Although the evidence above demonstrates that we would expect fewer free school meals eligible pupils to be entered into grammar schools, there may well be other factors which deserve further investigation. Fundamentally, however, it cannot be fair to blame grammar schools for disparities in *prior attainment* of the children in their catchment area. Improvements in primary education must also be made to address the attainment gap in later life. This is not to say grammar schools cannot do more, and it is notable that 32 grammar schools have recently altered their admissions procedures to prioritise disadvantaged children, while another 65 have told the Department for Education (DfE) that they intend to consult on doing so.[34] Efforts to ensure entrance tests are less susceptible to coaching and that children from less privileged backgrounds are encouraged to apply are welcome, and a more level playing field can also be achieved by ensuring that children are offered familiarisation with entrance tests where they might otherwise encounter them 'cold'. In any case the Sutton Trust research in 2010 found that of the 100 most socially selective schools in the country, 91 were comprehensives, eight were grammars and there was one secondary modern.[35] More recent research by the Trust also found that around one in three (32 per cent) professional parents with children aged between five and 16 now move to an area which they believe to have the best schools, and 18 per cent have moved to live within a specific catchment.[36] Concern about this selection by house price leads the Sutton Trust to favour moving to a system of balloting to allocate places in oversubscribed schools. I suspect that doing so would simply increase the number of parents opting out of state education when they have the means to do so.

What should the future look like? If we really believe in giving more autonomy to schools and more freedom to parents and communities, it follows that we should allow the creation of selective or partially selective schools where there is local demand for them. We should end the 'Henry Ford' approach to school choice by which we allow parents to have whatever kind of school they want as long as it is a comprehensive. Michael Gove sensibly allowed existing grammar schools to expand, a policy continued by Nicky Morgan, but this will benefit only those areas that already have selection. These opportunities should eventually be available wherever parents want them and should be available within the state sector – not just for those who can afford to pay. We should have the confidence to give genuine freedom to successful schools, judging them by their outputs not by how they achieve them. Research shows that academic selection can raise standards in both selective schools *and* in neighbouring non-selective schools. Within the non-selective secondary moderns it is possible to focus resources and bring substantial benefits to those not receiving a grammar school education. Northern Ireland has made great progress recently, closing the performance gap between the pupils at secondary moderns and those at grammars from 53.2 per cent in 2005/6 to 26.6 per cent in 2013/14. This was achieved without reducing the level of performance at the grammars.[37]

We now have 40 years of evidence showing that while it is possible to achieve good results in comprehensive schools, selective areas as a *whole* tend to perform better. It is now widely accepted that teaching by ability works, so it is unsurprising that schools that can specialise in teaching a more or less academic cohort typically achieve better results. A start should be made by giving those academy schools that wish to have it, permission to select (on criteria including academic ability) up to 20 per cent of their intake and the right to petition the Secretary of State for 30 per cent, 40 per cent, 50 per cent of intake at her/his discretion. In addition, now the first free schools are up and running, we should trial wholly selective free schools in some urban areas where existing state provision is most deficient. Not only is it intrinsically easier to offer greater choice in more densely populated areas where there are more schools, this approach would also bring the benefits of selective schools to some of the most deprived communities. If the result of reorganisation in the 1960s and 1970s was that remaining grammar schools were pushed into the suburbs and shires, reducing their traditional role as ladders of opportunity for the working classes, these new selective schools would begin to reverse that process. Not only would some of the more academically gifted youngsters from poorer areas find new opportunities, it would also challenge other local schools to raise their game in preparing pupils for entry to university or other advanced learning.

Too often in the past selection was seen as 'pass' or 'fail' and focused only on those who are most academically inclined: selection should be viewed more broadly. Most effectively it should seek to match a child to the best school to develop his or her talents to the full. This is already evident in many areas where there is a real choice of schools with a genuine specialism. Lord Baker's initiative to develop a network of university technical colleges is an important step in this direction.[38] Alongside this, new academically selective schools in our major cities would provide opportunities for young people in communities where aspirations are often too low.

In 2005 Tony Blair extolled the virtues of school choice:

> Many other countries have successful experience with school choice. There is increasing international evidence that school choice systems can maintain high levels of equity and improve standards...

In Florida, parents can choose an alternative school if their school has 'failed' in two of the last four years. Again, studies showed test scores improved fastest where schools knew children were free to go elsewhere.[39]

If Blair aspired to emulate the success of school choice in the United States, David Cameron and Michael Gove started to make it a reality. Pioneer founders of free schools, like Toby Young tell us, however, that they have faced endless bureaucratic obstacles. Communities should be given real freedom to establish new free schools and a commissioning body should be put in place to facilitate the process. It may be that we can learn from some of the most effective Charter School models such as that in Arizona where a separate Charter School Board had responsibility for driving the process forward.

Nicky Morgan is consulting on the creation of a per capita National Funding Formula which will bring more transparency and equity to school funding. At the moment one can walk out of a school, drive five miles up the road to an exactly comparable one in another local authority and it could receive several hundred thousand pounds more each year. Massive efficiencies could be achieved if all funding came via the direct per capita route, appropriately but clearly weighted to reflect factors such as deprivation or large populations with English as a second language. A National Funding Formula will be beneficial in itself but will also provide a mechanism to allow a massive further expansion of school choice. Once the per capita funding for each pupil is transparent, it will become much harder to resist demand from parents or providers who believe that they can offer better alternatives. A world of transparent funding will inevitably create pressure for a return to the 'direct grant' model: if an independent school can educate your child better for the same price why should you be denied the right to take that opportunity?

We should embrace the opportunity created by the move to a National Funding Formula, to end the educational apartheid between state and independent schools. If the last Labour government was happy to buy services or beds in private hospitals as long as they were offered at the NHS tariff rate, why shouldn't state places be available in independent schools? Direct grant was an educational success but also broke down social divisions. A greater expectation of real choice in school provision will also highlight the absurdity of claiming that parents and communities can choose the kinds of schools that they want – and then telling them that they can't have it. As Michael Portillo wrote in the *Daily Mail*:

> The paradox today is that no major political party would dare to bring back grammar schools, yet where they still exist, such as Kent or Buckinghamshire, no front-rank politician would dare to advocate their abolition, because they are so cherished by parents.[40]

This paradox is all the greater in the light of an ICM poll in 2010 that found 76 per cent support for more grammar schools to be created.[41] The answer is to take this power away from politicians and put it in the hands of parents. As more state schools operate autonomously, they will share many characteristics in common with independent schools: they will employ, and if necessary dismiss, staff, negotiate terms and conditions on site, transfer funds amongst budget headings, own or have long leases on their land, choose their own service providers, and control their own curriculum and methodologies of teaching. In fact the priorities of the school will be set by the professionals on the spot. The new academies have freedoms unknown outside the independent sector of education for decades and the two sectors will move closer together. Already some independent schools have assisted with the creation of academy schools by supplying governance advice and help with curriculum and staffing; a handful have, with varying degrees of success, actually sponsored new academies. Many have expertise which could be extremely valuable to state schools; indeed their association with them can bring many benefits to both sectors and is much to be welcomed.

Already some independent schools are choosing to adopt 'academy' status, allowing them to stop charging fees. So far some excellent schools such as Bradford Grammar have taken this route but the driver hasn't been the attraction of the academy model but rather the harsh economic climate making it harder for parents to afford fees. One of the impediments to more independent schools taking this route is the excessive prescription that the DfE insists on, regarding the ethos and admissions policy of the school. Whereas independent schools such as St. Ambrose College and Loreto Grammar School in Altrincham chose to become state schools under the freedoms of grant-maintained status in the 1990s, the present government would have forced them to adopt comprehensive admissions were they seeking to make a similar transition today. Even though the Coalition has legislated to scrap a Labour prohibition on state grammar schools becoming academies, absurdly it still won't allow a selective school in the independent sector to become an academy *without changing the nature of the school*. If this were changed a number of the former direct grant grammar schools might once again become available free of fees. Access to capital funding might be tied to the provision of state-funded places for a given period.

It is easy to see a future when a per capita funding formula would allow parents to use the sum of money available for the education of their child in *any* school of their choice, be it a free school, an academy or an independent school prepared to offer a place at the same cost. With this transfer of power to parents it would be ridiculous for the man in Whitehall to maintain the current level of petty prescription as to the types of school that parents should be *permitted* to choose. Taken together, allowing independent schools to enter academy status and allowing parents to take 'free' places at independent schools would effectively rebuild the direct grant model that was such a motor of social change and opportunity in the decades after the Second World War.

Seventy years on from the Butler Act, few would wish to try to prescribe a blueprint for state education across the country. We can see some successes in maintained schools and some failures. There are some outstanding comprehensive schools and some very poor ones. There are some stand-alone state grammar schools and there are a few areas that still have a wholly selective pattern of provision. There is a vibrant and highly successful independent sector educating around seven per cent of the population but dominating our elite universities and some of the professions. Looking at educational outcomes in England (or Britain) today it would be hard to say that we have a more equal society than thirty or forty years ago. Good comprehensives are often the most socially exclusive: selection 'by class and house price' as Andrew Adonis put it all those years ago. This has led some to think that the only fair way to allocate places would be by random ballot. Where the state schools are comprehensive (and especially where they are not very good) there is a flight of middle-class families, not just those who move to areas with better schools but the very large percentages in some areas that feel the need to go private – paying a second time through fees for the education they have already funded once through their taxes.

Politicians across the political divide largely agree that schools should have more freedom and autonomy. They agree too that parents should have greater choice in the kinds of schools that should be available. But even though 76 per cent of the public say they want more grammar schools, all the main political parties are determined not to allow them that choice.[42] The exception is in the areas which still have grammar schools where they are invariably so popular with parents that politicians of all parties are happy to leave them be.

The results achieved by selective areas (taking grammar schools and high schools together) disprove the old arguments that grammar schools in some way damage the quality of the other schools nearby. If anything, they seem to raise the standards of the other schools. There is no viable argument that selection leads to bad educational outcomes. Almost everyone now accepts that teaching is best done by ability groups: some people think this must be done within the same school, some of us do not. Essentially though, that is an argument about the effects of selection on society – not on educational outcomes.

Those who think that selection between schools leads to greater social inequality, or reduces opportunity, have to confront the inconvenient truth that forty years of the comprehensive revolution has increased, not diminished, the grip of the independently educated on our best universities and the professions that recruit from them. In all of this debate, politicians have not covered themselves in glory. Now we agree that good schools should be free to thrive; outcomes matter more than structures and parents should call the shots; it is time for the man in Whitehall to bow out and allow real freedom, choice and diversity.

The Case for Comprehensive Schools

Henry Stewart

Over the last forty years, since the widespread introduction of comprehensive schools, there has been a huge improvement in educational achievement and a five-fold increase in the numbers of young people reaching higher education. In contrast, the selective system, even in the heyday of grammar schools, was not popular and generally did not help children from poorer backgrounds. In 1963 only one per cent of the children of unskilled workers, and just two per cent of skilled, went to university.

In the remaining selective areas, the 11-plus results in great stress at an early age. Children from a disadvantaged background are a fifth as likely to get into a grammar school as others in the local area. Overall, grammar schools help the richest five per cent of the population but the poorest 50 per cent do less well in selective areas. It is time to celebrate the achievements of comprehensive schools, while looking at how to improve them further. There is more to learn from the best, at home and abroad, to help all children to achieve – rich or poor, and whatever their level of academic ability.

The reality of selection for 11-year-olds

The long-term effect of failing the 11-plus was described by John Prescott: 'The message was that suddenly you are less than they are. It tends to leave you with an inferiority complex.'[1] Research by Love To Learn, a website offering courses for those aged over 50, found that this effect is common even 40 years later; of those who failed the 11-plus, over one in three said they still 'lacked the confidence' to undertake further education and training courses, while one in eight reported that it had 'put them off learning for life'. Almost half reported that they still carried negative feelings with them into their fifties, sixties and beyond.[2] The stress associated with the 11-plus seems even greater today and success is arguably as much about parents' ability to pay for tutoring as any innate ability. One report describes how some children attend 11-plus coaching from 5am in the morning and parents pay as much as £5,000 in tuition to get their children through the exam. It found that more than six out of ten children received some form of tutoring.[3] Of those parents using the website elevenplusexams.co.uk, almost two in three agreed that private tutoring 'significantly enhanced' their child's chances in the exam. In contrast, in comprehensive areas it is rare for any tutoring or extra stress for children at the age of 11. My children were educated in Hackney. As well as the national SATs, they took one banding test, which is used by all secondary schools in the borough to ensure a fair spread of ability in their intake. This is not prepared for, no tutoring is involved and they were not even made aware of their results. Children are not divided and nobody is made to feel a failure because of how they did in an exam. They are able to continue to enjoy their childhood, with serious exams still five years away.

Comprehensive education: forty years of progress

Comprehensive schools were introduced in England and Wales principally between the mid-1960s and mid-1970s. From less than 10 per cent of secondary school students being in comprehensive schools in 1965, the numbers rose to 68 per cent in 1975 and 90 per cent by 1980. This laid the groundwork for the expansion in achievement that has taken place since, and the move from education beyond the age of 16 being for a minority to it being the norm.[4] The proportion of young people achieving five O-levels or GCSEs has risen from less than one in four in 1976 to more than three in four by 2008. The proportion in education at the age of 17 rose from 31 per cent in 1977 to 76 per cent in 2011, even before it became compulsory. While some argue there is an element of 'grade inflation', there can be no dispute about the increase in students going onto higher education. The number achieving a degree has gone from 68,000 in 1981 to 331,000 in 2010, an almost five-fold increase.[5]

Comprehensive schools come in for frequent criticism in Parliament and the press. However satisfaction among those who actually use state schools, both students and parents, is high. By far the most extensive survey of parental views is carried out by Ofsted, who receive responses from over 300,000 parents a year. The 2011 Ofsted Annual Report revealed that 94 per cent of parents completing their questionnaire agreed that they were happy with their children's education, up from 93 per cent the previous year.[6] Later Ofsted Annual Reports no longer include this statistic. However, a Department for Education survey of over 11,000 Year 9 parents in 2014 found that nine in ten thought their child's school was 'good' or 'very good'.[7] The education system is not perfect. There are still schools that are not providing the standard of education that our young people deserve, and the increased focus on the achievement of those from disadvantaged backgrounds is vital. However, the big picture is one of educational progress and satisfied parents.

The selective education system: never popular

The 1944 Education Act embedded a tripartite system of education with what were called 'academic', 'technical' and 'functional' strands. Whatever the intention, the technical colleges never became a major element (peaking at around five per cent of students) and the issue became whether students 'succeeded' and went to grammar schools or 'failed' and went to a secondary modern.[8]

The first comprehensive schools were established as early as the 1940s. London County Council set up five experimental comprehensives in 1946, and Anglesey followed with one in 1949. Contrary to popular myth, it was not entirely politically partisan. Around 1950, J. Thompson was able to write that: 'the four counties with most of the secondary school places in comprehensive schools are Caernarvonshire, Cardigan, Westmoreland and the West Riding, and the first three were not Labour-controlled, while the West Riding was'.[9] The desire for change from a selective system was clear by the end of the 1950s. The Crowther Report, commissioned by Conservative Secretary of State David Eccles, stated in 1959 that the rapid rise in school rolls after the war 'has largely increased public clamour against a competitive element in grammar school selection, which seems to parents to be contrary to the promise of secondary education according only to age, aptitude and ability'.[10] While grammar schools were popular with those parents whose children succeeded in entry to them, the system was not popular with those whose children had failed the 11-plus. A policy that was disliked by three in four voters was clearly not a clever electoral strategy. Simon Jenkins recalled the climate at the time:

> At political meetings at the end of the 1960s, Edward Boyle [Minster of Education from 1962 to 1964] was torn limb from limb by conservative voters, infuriated that their children who had 'failed' the eleven-plus were being sent to secondary moderns, along with 70-80% of each age group. They had regarded the grammars as 'their schools'. The eleven-plus, they said, lost them the 1964 election and would lose them every one until it was abolished. Margaret Thatcher recognised this as has every Tory party in practice ever since.[11]

The incoming Labour Secretary of State for Education in 1964, Anthony Crosland, was a supporter of comprehensive education and issued Circular 10/65, a request to local authorities to plan for conversion of their schools. This policy was not reversed when the Conservative Party achieved office in 1970. It has often been observed that more comprehensive schools were established while Margaret Thatcher was Education

Secretary, from 1970 to 1974, than under any other Secretary of State.[12] Of the 3,612 applications she received from local education authorities or schools to abandon selection at 11 and introduce comprehensive education, she approved more than nine in ten of them.[13]

There can be few proposals more likely to win the support of the *Daily Mail* and the Conservative Party rank-and-file than the reintroduction of grammar schools. However, there was no move during the eighteen years of Conservative government from 1979 to 1997, or during the current administration, to reintroduce grammar schools. Education Secretary Kenneth Baker commented, in the period after her death, that while he was encouraged to think radically by Mrs Thatcher, 'she at no time asked me to create more grammar schools'.[14]

The 1979 Conservative government did give local authorities the power to hold a ballot on reintroducing selection at 11. Only one borough, Solihull in 1984, tried to do so but abandoned the idea in the face of what David Willetts described as 'a parental revolt'. As he said, 'we did have the opportunity to create more grammar schools and it did not happen'.[15] The only general election in the last forty years which the Conservatives went to the electorate with a promise to increase grammar schools was that of 1997. John Major promised 'a grammar school in every town'. While this may not have been the cause of what was their worst result of the entire twentieth century, it clearly did not have the desired effect of winning back Conservative voters. The return of grammar schools was not to be Conservative policy at the 2010 election and Michael Gove, while embarking on what he has described as a 'cultural revolution' in education, did not choose to expand grammar schools.[16] His focus was on academies and free schools, on the basis that they can succeed as all-ability institutions.

Advocates of grammar schools claim that opinion polls show that a majority support them. This seems to depend on how the question is asked. Grammar schools do have a positive image for some, but most people do not like the idea of the selective and divided school system that grammar schools result in. A 2004 opinion poll in Northern Ireland captured this contradiction, with a majority supporting grammar schools, and a majority of the same respondents opposing selection by 11-plus.[17] In one debate on the website Conservative Home, a contributor succinctly expressed this confusion by stating 'Every child should be able to go to a grammar school'. The nature of grammar schools is that every child cannot attend one. Grammar schools are based on selection, on a minority gaining access and a majority failing to do so. Many on the right, including supporters like the *Daily Mail*, are puzzled by the failure of the Conservative Party to back an expansion of selection. However, for most of the last fifty years, the party leadership has been consistent in not advocating its return. Leading Conservatives understand that grammar schools bring no benefit to the most disadvantaged and those politicians may well carry the political memory of the electoral effect of support for selection in the early '60s.

The comprehensive ideal

The comprehensive ethos expressed a positive alternative that was embraced by all political parties. With selection seen as divisive and unpopular, the idea of comprehensive education offered a chance for change. Instead of children being divided at 11, with the majority having failed the 11-plus exam, the intention was that all our young people would be educated together. Every child would have the same opportunity to learn, to develop their skills and to fulfil their potential. In the words of Robin Pedley, in 1963:

> Comprehensive education does more than open the doors of opportunity to all children. It represents a different, a larger and more generous attitude of mind… the forging of a communal culture by the pursuit of quality with equality, by the education of their pupils in and for democracy, and by the creation of happy, vigorous, local communities in which the school is the focus of social and educational life.[18]

We cannot claim that Robin Pedley's vision, where all students attend their local school and learn together, has been completely achieved. Private schools create one level of segregation. In addition, there are now foundation schools, faith schools, academies, free schools – all with some level of control over their own admissions, and some with an element of selection. And we still have grammar schools. While only four per cent of secondary children attend grammar schools, many more are affected by them. In fully selective areas, around a third of students attend them. This means that up to 8 per cent of all children are in what used to be called secondary moderns, made up principally of those who have failed the 11-plus, even if some are now inaccurately termed comprehensives. Even in some generally comprehensive areas, like London and Birmingham, there are a number of grammar schools that select from the very top of the academic range – often from the top two per cent. Other schools are affected by not having these children.

In the grammar school era, it was widely believed that intelligence was fixed and could be fairly accurately measured at the age of 11. That idea has now been widely refuted and replaced with concepts of flexible intelligence and the recognition that people's ability can continue to develop.[19] Most teachers can tell you stories of young people whose ability became clear long after the age of 11. One example is a student I know who would not have got into a grammar school at 11, at 14 or even at 16. Yet he suddenly found his passion and academic ability at sixth form and, from the all-ability comprehensive he attended, was able to go on to Oxford University at the age of 18. Selective education was designed seventy years ago for a world in which only a small minority were expected to go to university, join the professional classes or, in any sense, be a 'knowledge worker'. It was felt that intelligence was innate and could be accurately judged at the age of 11. All this has changed and society needs an education system that reflects the social values of today, and enables all our young people to thrive at any age.

Grammar schools in their heyday

The fact that selection was seen as unpopular by electoral strategists of the 1960s is itself an indication that the golden age of grammar schools is somewhat mythical. It was certainly not a system which gave easy access to those from more disadvantaged backgrounds, and did not make the contribution to social mobility that is often claimed by advocates of selection. The

Crowther Report in 1959, using the results of a national service survey, found that 'a majority of the sons of professional people go to selective schools, but only a minority of manual workers' sons do so', and 'a non-manual worker's son is nearly three times as likely to go to a selective school as a manual worker's'.[20] The Robbins Report in 1963 showed that, based on a survey of undergraduates born in 1940, there was a stark disparity between the chances of success in going to university, dependent on what your father did (no data being available on mothers' professions). While one in three of those with fathers in 'higher professional' jobs went on to degree-level higher education, it was just under one in eight for those whose fathers who were in managerial positions, one in fifteen for clerical, one in fifty of those whose fathers were skilled manual and just one in a hundred of those in semi-skilled or unskilled occupations.[21]

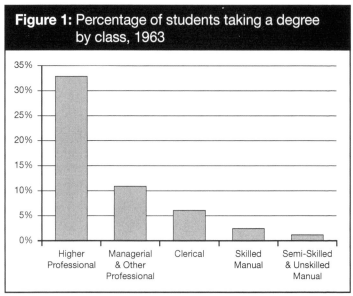

Figure 1: Percentage of students taking a degree by class, 1963

Source: The Robbins Report: Higher Education, 1963, p.50, Table 21.

It is common to hear those who went to grammar school arguing that it was a route to advancement for the poorest. Viewers of BBC One's *This Week* will be familiar with this argument from Diane Abbott, Michael Portillo and Andrew Neil. There is a reason for this misperception. The manual workforce represented such a large part of the working population (almost three in four of the entire workforce at that time) that the tiny proportions of their children that got to university added up to significant numbers. Even though only one per cent and two per cent of the children of the two manual groups reached university, those children would have represented just over one in four of all students taking degrees at the time.[22] The impression would have been of many students of working-class origin, even though very few from this background did succeed.

Previously, the Gurney-Dixon Report, 'Early Leaving', identified that even if children of semi-skilled and unskilled workers got into grammar schools, they were more likely to leave early without gaining qualifications. Two thirds of the children of those unskilled workers who did attend grammar schools left without three O-levels.[23] In the early 1960s, according to the Robbins Report, 26 per cent of children were from the 'unskilled working-class'. Yet they represented just 0.3 per cent of those achieving two A-levels at grammar schools.[24] A widely used measure of performance is five or more passes at A*-C at GCSE, the equivalent of the O-levels of the 1960s. But in the mid 1960s, only 16 per cent achieved that benchmark. By 2011 the proportion had reached 79 per cent.[25]

Few of the poorest children, or of those from the manual classes, went to grammar schools and only a tiny percentage of these children went to university.

However, this tiny minority still represented a substantial number of students overall. The one per cent of children from unskilled and semi-skilled family backgrounds make for very visible success stories that give the appearance of a level of social progression far greater than was actually the case.

The fall in social mobility

Advocates of grammar schools have claimed that they enabled greater mobility. The principle evidence is a 2005 London School of Economics (LSE) report for the Sutton Trust. This compared two cohorts, one of boys born in 1958 and one of boys born in 1970. (Sadly, data is not available to give similar analysis for girls.) Two different LSE publications, both written by the same authors, give different results for this study. The 2005 report suggests that, from the poorest quartile, 40 per cent reached the top half of earners by age 33 for the 1958 cohort compared to just 37 per cent of the 1970 cohort.[26] However, a 2007 report by the same authors suggested that 42 per cent of the earlier group reached the top half and just 35 per cent of the later group – a more substantial fall in social mobility.[27] In neither report do the authors make any suggestion that the cause of this change had anything to do with grammar schools. They do suggest that educational attainment is more closely related to income in England than in other European countries and give credit to Sure Start, Excellence in Cities and the Education Maintenance Allowance in helping to close the gap. Despite this, the idea that the phasing out of grammar schools and the rise in comprehensive education has led to a dwindling of social mobility has passed into popular mythology.

This change has been described (for example, by John Major) as a 'collapse in social mobility'.[28]

If the argument is that selection enabled bright children from lower income backgrounds to be upwardly mobile, it would need to be the case that most of these children benefited from selection. Advocates of selection argue that the upward mobility of 40 per cent of the poorest students in the 1958 cohort, outlined above, was due to the opportunities provided by grammar schools. The suggestion is that poor students were able to attend grammar school, succeed there, go onto university and then move into high-paying jobs. However, it was never the case that anywhere near this 40 per cent proportion went to grammars. The Crowther Report of 1959 found that only 7 per cent of the children of unskilled manual workers, those who would be in the bottom income quartile of the population, attended grammar school.[29] If only 1 in 14 of the poorest students went to grammar schools, and only a minority of these went on to university, it is hard to see how such schools could be responsible for the upward mobility of 40 per cent of that population. With few of those attending secondary moderns even taking O-levels, it seems that most of that 40 per cent were then able to succeed without strong educational qualifications.

Others have commented that the 1960s and 1970s, with the expansion of white-collar jobs, provided opportunities for social mobility that had not existed before and have not existed since. There are also new barriers like the requirement in some sectors to start work in an unpaid internship, generally affordable only by the better-off whose parents can support them. However, there is another important if often overlooked factor in making social mobility harder. In the 1960s and

1970s, it was far easier to rise up the career ladder without having a degree. While it was always the case that a few specific professions (such as medicine) required specific degrees, it was relatively unusual to advertise a job as 'degree required' without specifying what that degree should be. During the great wave of social mobility in the 1950s and 1960s, for example, journalists might have worked their way up through the local newspaper, lawyers through the article route, or accountants by starting out as a bookkeeper. Such opportunities have diminished in recent decades and a degree is now commonly a minimum entry requirement to a job.[30] The numbers of those from the poorest background attending university have increased markedly over the last fifty years, with evidence of a six-fold increase, but are still well below those from more prosperous backgrounds.[31] If it is harder for those without degrees to get into professional careers, then this will have the effect of reducing social mobility. If the government genuinely wants to increase social mobility, one approach is to find ways to encourage more of the poorest to attend university. However, another approach would be to deter employers from requiring degrees and explore ways of opening up the alternative routes that used to exist.

In fact, a recent study at the University of Bristol found that grammar schools *increased* social inequality. They found that the gap between 'top earners' and those at the bottom was £24,000 for those who grew up in selective schools, compared to £20,000 for those from the comprehensive system.[32]

With so few of the poorest attending grammar schools, or going onto university, it does not seem to have been education that was responsible for the bulk of any past mobility. Instead we need to look at wider changes such as the greater academic requirements now required to progress.

Grammar schools today: not a path for social mobility

The English educational system is not fully comprehensive. Of the 151 local education authorities in the country, 36 include at least one selective maintained school. There are 17 authorities that can be defined as principally selective, taken as those where at least 15 per cent attend grammar schools. An examination of Department for Education 2012 data reveals that, in every single selective authority, the proportion of disadvantaged students in grammar schools is far below the overall level locally.[33] There is not a single grammar school in England where the

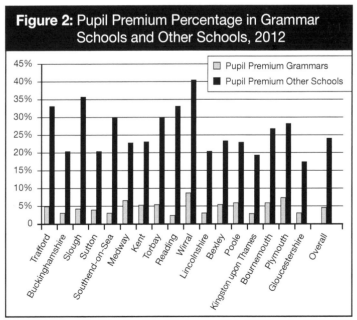

Figure 2: Pupil Premium Percentage in Grammar Schools and Other Schools, 2012

Source: Department for Education, School Performance Data: 2012 Download Data, 2012.

proportion of disadvantaged children is above the national average. Across the country, 42 per cent of schools have fewer than one in five students from a disadvantaged background. However, 98 per cent of grammar schools have this lower level of disadvantage.[34] Overall, across these authorities, fewer than one in twenty students in grammar schools are from disadvantaged backgrounds. In contrast, in other schools in those areas, almost one in four come from these backgrounds. That is a five-fold difference between the proportion of the disadvantaged in grammar schools and other local schools.

The above graph illustrates the disadvantage level in schools, using the 'pupil premium' measure. This is a Department for Education measure of students eligible for the pupil premium, based on the proportion of students who would have qualified for free school meals at any point in the last six years (plus any students in care).

Can grammar schools be a path towards social mobility? The argument in favour is that grammar schools provide a path for bright students from disadvantaged backgrounds to succeed. For this to be true, there would need to be a large proportion of disadvantaged students going to grammar schools. The under-representation of poor children applies even to those of the highest ability. Researchers Adele Atkinson, Paul Gregg, and Brendon McConnell, found that poor children in selective areas were only half as likely to attend a grammar school as other children with the same underlying ability (as measured by their key stage 2 test scores).[35] They found that of those in the top three groups at age 11, just 32 per cent of those eligible for free school meals attended grammar schools, compared with 60 per cent of children from better-off backgrounds. This pattern is also true of children with special needs and those for whom English is a second language.[36] The Sutton Trust found the same bias in entry: 'children who are not eligible for free school meals have a much greater chance of attending a grammar school than similarly high achieving children who are eligible for free school meals'.[37] They found that, amongst those that achieved level 5 at age 11 in their SATs, only 40 per cent of children eligible for free school meals go to a grammar school compared to 66 per cent of children not eligible.[38] They also found that grammar schools have lower proportions of black children, and that children are less likely to go to a grammar school if they attend a primary school with a high proportion of pupils from deprived backgrounds. They noted one of the reasons as being that 'more affluent, middle-class families are coached to pass the entrance exam'.[39]

Grammar schools are aware of the problem that fewer students from disadvantaged backgrounds pass their entry exams. In 2014, Buckinghamshire introduced what it hoped would be 'tutor-proof' tests. However, the first indications are that the effect has been the reverse of that intended, with a lower proportion of children from local state schools getting into the county's grammar schools.[40] Rebecca Hickman, who carried out the research, commented:

> What we are seeing now is that it is impossible to devise a fair test of ability to divide children at 11 which will not discriminate according to social background, race and prior opportunity. Those with superior resources to start with will still come out on top. [41]

The evidence is stark. In the remaining selective areas, children are far more likely to go to a grammar school if they come from a prosperous middle-class background and far less likely, by a factor of five, if they come from a disadvantaged background.

How well do selective local authorities perform?

Many claims are made for the performance of selective areas. Conservative MP Graham Brady found that seven of the ten top-performing local education authorities (LEAs) at GCSE also had grammar school places available to some or all of their pupils.[42] It sounds an impressive statistic. However, it is explained by examining the academic ability at age 11 of those students in schools in selective areas.

Of the top-ten LEAs, in terms of the ability of students entering their schools at age 11, eight are in selective areas.[43] On the basis of their higher ability at the start of secondary school, selective areas should also be responsible for eight of the top-ten areas for GCSEs. That they only provided seven of the top-ten represents a lower level of value added than could be expected.

There are two key reasons for this higher achievement at age 11. First, grammar school areas are likely to be consistently Conservative and in turn, therefore, more affluent than the average. There is a clear link, unfortunately, between affluence and exam results. All the principally selective areas in Graham Brady's list have proportions of disadvantaged students that are well below the national average, ranging from just 13.5 per cent in Buckinghamshire to 20.6 per cent in Trafford (the national figure is 26.3 per cent).[44] In addition, one effect of grammar school areas is that they attract some of the most academic children from other areas while some of their own less academic children often have to cross borders to schools in neighbouring boroughs. As the Sutton Trust commented: 'Stand-alone grammar schools often draw large numbers of their pupils from outside their local authority.'[45] They found, in selective areas like Kingston upon Thames, two thirds of students attending grammar schools lived in a different authority area. Another example is Reading. A Freedom of Information request, for this publication, revealed that only 26 per cent of the pupils in Reading grammar schools also live in the Reading area. In 2013, the proportion of pupils in Reading schools achieving the GCSE benchmark was 64 per cent, above the national average of 59 per cent. However, once the figures are adjusted to reflect those living in the area, the figure for Reading falls to 58 per cent - just below the national average.[46] Thus, the nature of a selective area will tend to create a group of students with higher potential, not because of the schooling, but because the system has attracted higher ability students to those schools.

Example: Trafford

Trafford is one of the selective areas whose GCSE results are sometimes quoted to support the case for grammar schools. In 2013, it was indeed the 10th-best LEA for the GCSE benchmark, with 70 per cent of students achieving 5 A-Cs including English and maths. However, when those students entered secondary school at age 11, Trafford had the lowest proportion of 'low attainment' students in England, and the third highest proportion of 'high attainment' students.[47] The question that should be asked is why its GCSE achievement was not higher.

For those entering Trafford schools with 'low attainment', only 4.6 per cent went on to achieve the GCSE benchmark, placing it in the bottom 25 per cent of LEAs for this statistic. This is well below the 7.5 per cent figure for England as a whole. In neighbouring Manchester, almost three times as many of these students (12.6 per cent) achieve the benchmark, and the best London LEA does six times better than Trafford. Trafford schools do marginally better for those entering with strong results at age 11 (96 per cent against a national figure of 95 per cent), but much worse for those who arrive with weak results.[48]

Selective LEAs generally appear to do well for GCSE results. This is to be expected given their stronger intake at age 11. However, for those most in need of support, the disadvantaged and those with low attainment at age 11, the best performing LEAs are generally fully comprehensive. In 2013, eight of the top-ten LEAs for the GCSE performance of disadvantaged students - and ten out of ten for students with 'low attainment' at age 11 - were fully comprehensive.[49]

Analysis by local authority is inexact, especially because the population of the schools is not the same as the population of the local area. What is needed is analysis that compares the performance of individual students in selective and non-selective areas. Fortunately, one journalist has had unique access to pupil-level data and has carried out analysis, which we now examine.

Grammar schools do not help social mobility now

Chris Cook, while at the *Financial Times,* gained unique access to student-level data for the entire cohort taking

GCSEs in 2011. He took Kent, Lincolnshire, Medway and Buckinghamshire – the larger and more distinct authorities where parents were unlikely to skip across boundaries – and created the new region of 'Selectivia'.[50] Using his access to individual student records, he has created a score for each student based on English, maths and their next three best GCSE results (resulting in a figure for each student of zero to 40, 40 representing five A* GCSEs). Creating a graph of what per cent of students get each point score, he compared Selectivia to the rest. A more successful system would have more students with higher point scores and fewer with lower ones. The reverse was true of the selective areas: for the poorest students, those on free school meals, more were getting lower GCSE results and fewer getting good results. Cook observed:

> You can see that poor children do dramatically worse in selective areas. There is an idea out there in the ether that grammar schools are better for propelling poor children to the very top of the tree. But, again, that is not true. Poor children are less likely to score very highly at GCSE in grammar areas than the rest.[51]

The results are clear. The most disadvantaged students are less likely to get the top scores and far more likely to get low scores than in areas of comprehensive education. Cook went further and analysed performance by background. He found that, for the very richest in society, there was a benefit to attending grammar schools. Those in the top five per cent by income did better than those in non-selective areas. However, those in the bottom 50 per cent for income did, overall, worse in selective areas.[52] Grammar schools do not increase social mobility. Few of those from disadvantaged backgrounds get into them and, as Chris Cook has shown, they do worse in selective areas than those in comprehensive areas.

Oxbridge and university entry

The claim that 'the percentage of state school students at Oxbridge has actually declined since the decimation of England's grammar schools in the 1960s and 1970s' is a common one, in this case made by Toby Young.[53] The House of Commons Library has analysed this question in papers titled 'Oxbridge "Elitism"', the most recent published in June 2014.[54] It found that the proportion of state pupils at either Oxford or Cambridge was 26 per cent in 1959 and 37 per cent in 1964. This rose to 43 per cent in the early 1970s, when the majority of students would still have taken the 11-plus. By 1981, when two-thirds of students overall would have started in comprehensive schools, it jumped to 52 per cent.[55] In 2012, the *Daily Telegraph* reported that 55 per cent of admissions at Oxford and 66 per cent at Cambridge were now from state schools, though the Cambridge figure did slip in 2013.[56] In terms of the selection debate, readers may wonder if those state school Oxbridge entries came from grammar schools or comprehensives. The 2011 Sutton Trust report 'Degree of Success: University Chances by Individual School' suggests that at that time, 85 per cent of state school Oxbridge entries came from comprehensive schools.[57] The report comments: 'Given their selective intake, grammar schools would appear to be underrepresented among the most successful schools for Oxbridge entry.'

Researchers at the University of London, using a 1970 cohort of children (who would have applied to university around 1988), came to a similar conclusion: 'there was no statistically significant advantage in the chances of accessing a top university for people who had been to grammar schools compared to those who had been to comprehensives'.[58]

It is still the case that the proportion of Oxbridge students coming from state schools is well below the numbers in UK schools (93 per cent). Oxford and Cambridge Universities would argue that this is down to attainment levels in the state sector. But it is also the case that this proportion is below the numbers achieving three A/A* A-level grades that are from state schools (68 per cent in 2012/13).[59]

The belief that fewer state school students go to Oxbridge than in the heyday of grammar schools is simply an urban myth. State school entry to Oxbridge is still not in line with their proportion of the population, but it is at an all time high and well above the levels of the grammar school era, and the vast majority of those come from comprehensives.

International evidence: how comprehensive and selective systems compare

Speaking in the House of Commons in 2012, Finnish schools expert Pasi Sahlberg described the origins of the country's educational success as being the decision in 1970 to abolish both selection and private education. With a completely comprehensive education system, Finland has famously been the top country in the international PISA comparison tables in 2003 and 2006 and the top in Europe in 2000, 2009 and 2012. (PISA is the Programme for International Student Assessment and, every three years, attempts to measure and compare student achievement across different countries.[60]) Indeed, from the year 2000 up to the latest PISA results, of those countries with selective educational systems, only the Netherlands has ever been listed in the top 10 in any of the PISA listings.[61]

The first PISA release, for 2000, came as a major shock for Germany where schools use a tripartite system with students being selected between the ages of 10 and 13. German students came below the OECD average for reading and literacy, resulting in a national debate on how to improve. As a Pearson report commented: 'After extensive debate, education experts concluded that the tripartite school system was one of the main reasons for Germany's weak overall performance.'[62] The figures made clear that there was a high correlation between socioeconomic background and achievement, and the channelling of children into three types of schools from as early as age 10 was seen as limiting achievement. Looking into the detail of PISA performance, in this case the 2006 science results, the OECD stated that 'a clear cut finding from PISA is that early differentiation of students by school is associated with wider than average socioeconomic disparities and not with better results overall'.[63] Analysing 2009 PISA performance, the OECD went on to note:

> School systems that track students early into different educational programmes show lower levels of equity but do not achieve higher levels of average performance than systems that track students later in their school careers. This finding is consistent with

prior research showing that inequality is higher in more differentiated school systems.[64]

These conclusions are backed up by research by Eric Hanushek and Ludger Woessmann, who carried out a thorough review of the effect of selection in educational systems around the world. They found that it not only increased inequality, but also tended to lead to reduced performance.[65]

Taking comprehensive education forward

The evidence is clear on selective education. In its heyday, the selective system was neither popular with the general public nor successful in helping poorer children to succeed. In the grammar school areas that remain, it is still the case that students from poorer backgrounds are less likely to attend grammar schools and do less well overall. The international evidence backs this up, with all the most successful education systems being non-selective. The first step to school improvement would therefore seem to be to find a way to integrate the remaining selective schools into the comprehensive system. If a way could be found to achieve that, it would be likely to lead to improved results and to greater social mobility in those areas. A return to selection would be a return to a system that did not work for most children in the '50s and '60s, and does not work for most children, especially the most disadvantaged, where it remains. Instead, let us work to further improve the comprehensive approach that has delivered improvements across all ability ranges over the last forty years.

Free to Pursue an Academic Education

Joanna Williams

The long history of grammar schools can make both their continued existence and the recurring controversies which surround them, take on a magnitude that is at odds with the more mundane reality of people's lived experiences. Although I attended a comprehensive school in the north-east of England in the late 1980s, later, as an English teacher, I taught at both a selective independent school and a secondary school which, despite carrying the title comprehensive, competed for pupils with neighbouring grammar schools. Today my own sons, having passed the 11-plus test, now attend a local boys' selective school. In this chapter I argue that although selecting children deemed suitable for an academic education is problematic, there is little to be gained from abolishing grammar schools now. In a period when low expectations of children are rife, and teaching academic knowledge is too easily replaced by time spent developing skills or emotional wellbeing, grammar schools serve as a reminder of what children are intellectually capable of achieving when suitably challenged. Likewise, when it can appear as if picking a grammar school for your child is the least socially acceptable parental choice there is, I defend the rights of parents to exercise the freedom to choose any form of education they want for their children, even schools that offer an unashamedly elitist knowledge-driven curriculum.

A history of controversy

Many of the grammar schools around in England today were established in the sixteenth and seventeenth centuries, and some date back much further. The strong affiliations schools shared with local churches influenced the curriculum which was dominated by Latin, and later Greek and English, grammar. Church funding enabled some talented boys from poor families to have school fees subsidised or even waived altogether. Following the 1944 Education Act, grammar schools either became fully independent or incorporated into the state education system. The implementation of a 'tripartite' secondary school system placed children at age 11 into grammar, technical or secondary modern schools, depending upon their performance in a selection test. Technical schools never took off to any great extent and the reality of the post-war educational system for most was a binary division of children with roughly the top 20 per cent of the ability range earning a coveted grammar school place and the vast majority of children being allocated to secondary moderns. At present there are 163 grammar schools in England with a majority concentrated in small geographical pockets mainly in Kent and Yorkshire.

Campaigns against grammar schools, and more specifically the process of selection, began almost as soon as the 1944 Education Act was passed and have continued ever since, taking quite distinct forms in different political eras. Right from its introduction, the selection test, or '11-plus' as it came to be known, stood accused of selecting children on the basis of social class rather than raw intelligence. It was argued that a disproportionately high number of middle-class children were chosen for grammar schools with the associated promise of educational and social advancement, usually starting with a university place.

The political war against grammar schools gathered momentum in 1965 with the Labour Party's Anthony Crosland appointed Secretary of State for Education and Science. Crosland considered, perhaps rightly, that the education system in the UK, from the division of pupils aged eleven to the wealth and autonomy of the universities, was elitist and socially divisive, serving only to confirm the status of the middle and upper classes. However, rather than seeking to drive up educational achievement in schools and enabling more working-class children to access a high-quality academic curriculum such as on offer in grammar schools and subsequently universities, Crosland decided to abolish the entire tripartite system. He saw his first priority in office as the dismantling of the grammar schools. Crosland, and others, argued for comprehensive schools on the egalitarian grounds that all children were equally deserving of access to the same curriculum. Real growth in the numbers attending comprehensive schools took off in the first half of the 1970s when Margaret Thatcher was Secretary of State for Education. Since that time successive governments have sought to garner electoral support through either, like John Major, calling for a grammar school in every town, or like Labour's Charles Clarke, demanding their final abolition. In reality, the last two decades have seen a political compromise where the remaining grammar schools continue to sit, perhaps somewhat uneasily, within their local communities. While the existing grammar schools are oversubscribed and many parents invest considerable resources in attempting to secure a place in them for their child, at the same time, they can seem to represent everything loathed by a more politically correct educational establishment. The unabashed competitive entry process and teaching of a predominantly academic curriculum is out of kilter with a therapeutic promotion of wellbeing and a more general focus on developing pupils' functional skills.

In this chapter I make the case for the continuation of grammar schools in England. This is not an argument based on an ideological commitment to selection of pupils aged eleven, or the notion that only certain children are either entitled to or capable of mastering an academic curriculum. Rather, my arguments for keeping grammar schools today are a response to the objections levelled by campaigners for their abolition. There is a danger that scrapping high-performing schools could lead simply to an unhelpful promotion of mediocrity and low expectations for everyone. From a parent's perspective, it can often seem that any school choice is more socially acceptable than arguing you would like your child to receive a challenging induction into the best that has been thought and said. Yet a positive case for grammar schools can be made on the basis of their pursuit of academic excellence and the right of parents to enter their children into an intellectual competition for access to such an education. I begin by exploring what's different about the curriculum of grammar schools and why it is important to defend the teaching of specialist subject knowledge. I then look at the issue of parental choice and the freedom parents have to choose a particular type of education for their child. In the final section of this chapter I consider recent arguments against selection which focus upon the psychological damage done to children through the pressures of taking tests often aged just ten-years-old. I will suggest that often the perception of the 11-plus as harmful is an adult response and children, in turn, react to this interpretation of events. Further problems are created by some non-selective schools offering even very bright pupils a curriculum that is not only less rigorously challenging but covers fundamentally different subject matter to that on offer in grammar schools. This means that differential life chances are exacerbated by school selection aged eleven.

An academic curriculum

In the 1960s, when political opposition to grammar schools first began to gather momentum, it was based on the egalitarian premise that every child should be entitled to the educational opportunities that were, at the time, available only to a few. The pre-Second World War assumption that intelligence was fixed, measurable and determined a child's future role in society, had been replaced by a more progressive belief in the general educability of all children. The proposal for comprehensive schools was driven by an understanding that all children could benefit from access to a knowledge-based curriculum. The comprehensive ideal was less about dumbing down and more about levelling up academic standards. Unfortunately, with the possible exception of a small historical and geographical blip, the aims of the comprehensive experiment were never fully realised. There were many social, political and economic reasons for this failure, only one of which was the survival of a rump of grammar schools.

The introduction of the National Curriculum to all state schools in England, Wales and Northern Ireland in 1988 represented a further attempt by government to ensure all children had access to a balanced academic curriculum. For the first time it was written into law that all state-educated children were entitled to provision in specified subject areas. The founding principles of comprehensive schools and the implementation of the national curriculum lessened the perceived threat of the minority of remaining grammar schools. The educational establishment could just about tolerate comparing grammar schools with comprehensives when both sets of schools followed the same curriculum leading to the same set of public exams. It was always possible for bright, hard-working pupils in the comprehensive sector to leave school with the same subject knowledge as their grammar school contemporaries, and perhaps with even better exam results.

Despite being elected with the slogan 'education, education, education', Tony Blair's Labour government set in place a series of measures which ended the comparability of the educational experience of children throughout the country. Of major significance was the decision by New Labour to introduce a new range of vocational qualifications that children could take while still at school and to declare them, for the purposes of league tables, the equivalent of GCSEs in more traditional academic subjects. The political emphasis placed on league table positioning meant schools were incentivised to find the easiest route for pupils to achieve as many qualifications as possible, irrespective of the subjects studied. The effect of this change was to go some way towards re-introducing the academic and vocational divide that comprehensive schools had been intended to end. It meant that while 16-year-old grammar school pupils were able to take GCSEs in French, history and biology, many of their comprehensive counterparts were too often offered courses in combined science, leisure and tourism, or health and social care. From this point, grammar and comprehensive schools began to move further apart, with grammar schools serving as an unwelcome reminder of the education bright pupils at non-selective schools no longer received. In 2011 Secretary of State for Education Michael Gove announced plans to introduce an 'English Baccalaureate' which would emphasise academic subjects and prevent vocational qualifications from counting towards a school's ranking in league tables but this met with vocal opposition from some secondary school head teachers.[1] One problem for Gove was that many of those involved with schools had accepted the argument that the purpose of education is to prepare children for the world of work. This runs counter to the liberal, knowledge-based academic curriculum of the grammar schools. In reality, comprehensive school pupils are no less capable of mastering an academic curriculum than their grammar school peers.

The most recent calls to close down grammar schools come from campaigners who argue academic selection contributes to a socially unequal society because ex-grammar pupils go on to earn higher than average salaries.[2] Obviously it is very hard to know whether what is measured in such statistics is causation or correlation. If we accept that grammar schools have an intake dominated by the middle classes then there may be many personal and social reasons for their number going on to the top jobs, schooling being just one of these. Even if it is true that grammar school alone gives children a competitive advantage in later life then surely this would be an argument for expanding grammar schools and making the type of education they offer available to as many children as possible. Instead, in 2013, as Chief Inspector of Schools, Michael Wilshaw urged against expanding grammar schools which he derided as being 'stuffed full' of middle-class children and failing to improve social mobility.[3]

To argue that social mobility is the purpose of education is to fundamentally miss the point of a liberal academic curriculum where learning, as the pursuit of knowledge, is undertaken as an end in itself. When social mobility, or put more crudely, job prospects and earnings potential, are made the goal of education then arguments for teaching knowledge as opposed to work-based skills are more difficult to justify. Currently, some children get access to a knowledge-based curriculum while others are expected to make do with generic functional skills and job training. *This* is where the gross inequality lies at the heart of our education system. Making the case for academic knowledge for all, however, requires a genuine understanding of what a liberal education is about and also a belief in the ability of all children to access and benefit from such a curriculum. Unable to do this, Wilshaw and others taking the same position instead seek to abolish grammar schools and limit the expectations of all children. Patronising youngsters with subjects deemed relevant for their assumed lot in life is retrogressive and degrades the whole concept of education.

Under the previous Labour government, time for academic, knowledge-based education was further squeezed from the school day to make room for a preoccupation with children's physical health and emotional wellbeing, alongside the promotion of selected values such as encouraging recycling, healthy eating and good citizenship. With the exception of classes in citizenship, it was not so much the case that new subjects entered the curriculum, although the teaching of personal, social and health education took on a new status at this time, rather the content of traditional academic subjects was altered to include the discussion of topical moral issues. Science and geography lessons increasingly became an arena for the promotion of environmentalism, population control, sustainability and fair trade. Teachers in other subject areas started teaching gradually more and more on healthy eating, anti-bullying initiatives and emotional literacy. Comprehensive schools providing children with a broad-based liberal academic education were rare.

And so the gap between the learning experience of pupils at grammar and comprehensive schools widened under the last Labour government and although Michael Gove, despite heavy criticism from many in the educational world, attempted to reintroduce a more knowledge-driven curriculum for all pupils, still the differences exist. Today, many grammar schools enter pupils for international or IGCSEs despite the fact that a number of the most popular subjects are not recognised in GCSE league tables.[4] IGCSEs are not modular, contain little if any coursework and are generally considered more challenging than traditional GCSEs and better preparation for A-level. Increasing numbers of independent schools also enter pupils for IGCSEs. In addition, grammar schools are more likely to teach a more traditional academic curriculum than non-selective schools, offering separate science subjects rather than combined science; history and geography rather than humanities; modern foreign languages rather than travel and tourism.[5] They are unlikely to offer 'equivalent to GCSE' vocational courses.

There is a problem for the educational establishment if grammar schools opt out of vocational qualifications and regular GCSEs because they are not seen as being rigorous enough. It raises questions in the minds of parents about the quality of these exams. Attempts at equalising opportunities have, until relatively recently, tended to focus upon bringing grammar schools in line with the rest of the education sector. Yet having equally low expectations of all children will not raise standards for anyone. Michael Gove's recommendations that schools and exam boards should demand more from children were often met by howls of protest yet they would provide a more secure foundation for narrowing the gap in children's educational opportunities. Abolishing grammar schools would concentrate rigorous knowledge-based education in the hands of an even smaller proportion of the population – those who can afford to pay for it.

Parental choice

The comprehensive ideal was undermined by the teaching of different subjects to different groups of children which created unequal access to types of knowledge. While some children were offered liberal academic content, others were expected to make do with vocational skills. Rather than tackling such disparities through arguing for a rigorous knowledge-based curriculum for all, discussion focused on the structures, rather than the content of schooling, and the education sector became increasingly fragmented. Following the 1944 Education Act, the majority of children were allocated a place in a selective or non-selective school and then attended the nearest state-run school to their home. The wave of comprehensivisation which took place from the mid-1960s onwards saw a divide between 'all-in' schools and a rump of remaining grammars, though arguably schools in areas that retained selection were comprehensive in name alone and remained effectively secondary moderns.

The days of the 'bog standard' comprehensive have long since been numbered. Since the mid-1980s, the educational landscape has become far more fragmented. Margaret Thatcher's political dislike for the power wielded by local educational authorities (LEAs) led her to introduce grant-maintained status through which schools could opt to receive funding directly from central government rather than the LEA. The Conservative government at this time also established city technology colleges, new schools which were under direct government control, although only fifteen such schools emerged. Diversity of provision continued under Tony Blair who introduced foundation schools as a successor to grant-maintained provision, and 'specialist' schools which would receive an increased budget in return for focusing upon a particular aspect of the curriculum. Local grammar schools were no longer set in opposition to a secondary modern or a comprehensive but rather to a specialist sports college or performing arts school. The current Coalition government continued with academies and introduced free schools, and on top of this there exists an array of church schools and fee-paying independent schools.

For the differences between schools to be meaningful, parents needed increased freedom to choose which school they would like their children to attend. The 1988 Education Reform Act enshrined in law a parent's right to choose by stipulating that up to the point at which its physical capacity was filled, a school was obliged to admit any child whose parents applied. By the late 1990s parents in some areas of England had a number of potential schools to choose from and today it can no longer be assumed that children go to the school which is closest to their home. Such a degree of parental choice is surely to be welcomed if for no other reason than it serves to remind us of the warning from John Stuart Mill over one hundred and fifty years ago now, of the dangers of having only one type of school on offer. Mill argued that 'A general state education is a mere contrivance for moulding people to be exactly like one another; and as the mould in which it casts them is that which pleases the predominant power in the government... it establishes a despotism over the mind'.[6] It can only be hoped that an increase in the types of schools lessens the degree to which institutions are able to mould people in the state's image.

England's 163 remaining grammar schools provide parents with one school choice among many. Church schools, free schools, academies and specialist schools all compete alongside grammar and fee-paying schools for pupils and their associated funding. It seems to be the case that education journalists and campaigning pressure groups have, at least until very recently, had little problem with the concept of parental choice as such. They recognise that many parents go to enormous lengths to get their children into their chosen school. Some parents will move house, discover religion, undertake extra tuition, or make financial sacrifices to afford school fees all in the name of securing a prized school place. Likewise, today's educational establishment have little problem with the notion of selection it seems. We already have specialist schools that can select a proportion of pupils by aptitude, religious schools that select by church attendance and devotion, schools in wealthy catchment areas that select by postcode, fee-paying schools that select by income and schools that select on the ability of middle-class parents to play the system and make a convincing appeal. Given the decades-long promotion of parental choice and the evident desire of many parents to exercise this choice, the recurring attacks on grammar schools suggest not all choices are considered equally valid. For parents to choose, or schools to select, on the basis of academic standards is, it seems, just not politically acceptable in today's climate. John Stuart Mill suggested one justification for the existence of state-run schools:

> An education established and controlled by the state, should only exist, if it exist at all, as one among many competing experiments, carried on for the purpose of example and stimulus, to keep the others up to a certain standard of excellence.[7]

The danger today is that rather than grammar schools being celebrated for reminding us of a certain standard of academic excellence, they are derided as socially and academically elitist. Every child should be entitled to a broad-based knowledge-driven education. In the absence of such schools for all, the right of schools to pursue such a curriculum, and the rights of parents to choose to enter their child into the competition for a selective place, should be protected. No choices should be stigmatised as less politically correct, or socially acceptable, than others.

Pushy parents

One reason for grammar schools providing a less socially acceptable choice is changed attitudes towards the processes of selection and getting young children to sit competitive intelligence tests. Preparing a ten-year-old for an academic test suggests a degree of parental ambition and aspiration that is less apparent in those who opt for comprehensive schools. Parents who choose to move house, pay for a private school or take up church attendance are not castigated to quite such an extent because the sacrifices and pressures are placed on them rather than their children. It is assumed by many nowadays that psychological harm to the child will result from the experience of being prepared for and entered into a competitive test with the resultant chance of failure. Such increased sensitivity to the potential for the grammar school entry test to cause emotional damage in children can be seen on a continuum of changed attitudes regarding children, competition and broader perceptions of risk. Children are viewed as uniquely vulnerable and more in need of protection today than at any other period in history. Mindfulness, meditation and happiness classes have replaced competitive tests and sports. Teachers and parents alike are encouraged to seek opportunities to boost a child's self-esteem. The word 'fail' is banned from the classroom, red pens for marking have been replaced by green, and crosses next to wrong answers have been replaced by tiny dots. In this light, the 11-plus does begin to take on a greater significance. For many children it will not only be the first pass or fail test they have taken but will perhaps be the only such test they take during the course of their school careers. Furthermore, whereas GCSEs and even A-levels contain coursework, are modularised or can be re-taken, none of this currently applies to the 11-plus.

Much of the stress experienced by children taking a test for selective school is a reaction to the process being so out of kilter with current social and educational trends. In addition, children are aware of the increased stakes put upon test success by parents and teachers. Rightly or wrongly, many of today's parents have a heightened sense of the importance of secondary school in determining life chances. When this is conveyed to children, either explicitly or through emphasis placed upon extra tuition and practice tests, they react to these projections of adult anxiety. Whereas the grandparents of today's 11-year-olds recall having sat grammar school tests 'unawares', few children are afforded this luxury nowadays.

Certainly abolishing grammar school entry tests would alleviate any stress experienced by children taking them. However, the best way to remove *parental* anxiety from education is surely to make the education offered in non-selective schools more equivalent to that currently available to those who clear the hurdle of the test. If all children were offered access to the same curriculum then the opportunity costs of failing the 11-plus test, and attending a comprehensive school, would be reduced. This would not only lessen the anxiety projected by well-meaning parents but it would also reduce any disadvantage experienced by those attending non-selective schools later in their adult lives.

One argument campaigners frequently level against grammar schools is that they depress educational standards in a community by creaming off the most able pupils. This suggests that the mere presence of academically able, often middle-class, children in comprehensive schools will automatically raise standards. Rather than looking to teachers, school managers or teacher-trainers to raise standards, responsibility is abdicated and children themselves are expected to play this role. Ironically, this expectation that bright children will raise the educational standards of a whole school or even community is rarely perceived as anxiety-inducing or unnecessary pressure. In addition, the view that schools need a particular intake to have high educational standards is patronising to both teachers and the children who do attend non-selective schools. What's being said is that those who fail a test aged eleven cannot be expected to go on to do well at school and their teachers cannot be expected to get good results with such children. There are many factors that account for low standards in schools, but, it seems, grammar schools are a much easier target than poor quality teaching, low aspirations and a badly designed curriculum which focuses on functional skills, moral values and emotional wellbeing rather than academic knowledge.

Final thoughts

There is a need to defend the unashamed academic elitism of the grammar schools. A curriculum that offers children access to the best that has been thought and said, and expects them to be able to master this knowledge about the world is jettisoned at huge cost to society as a whole. Standards in all schools will not be raised by abolishing those performing well. This is not, however, an argument for the social elitism of selective schools. On the contrary, access to a knowledge-driven curriculum should be available to everyone with the interest and determination to pursue it. Ideally, all schools would offer children an entitlement to knowledge, but this is the rarely realised comprehensive ideal. With the vast array of school choices on offer today, there is little prospect of a comprehensive ideal being achieved in the short term. Rather than focusing upon scrapping the 163 remaining grammar schools, a better proposal might be to increase the grammar school intake rather than reducing it. Why should only 20 per cent of children be deemed suitable for grammar schools? Why not 30 per cent or even 50 per cent? Another proposal might be to consider the age at which selection takes place. The public schools select through a common entrance exam sat when children are thirteen. An extra two years prior to the selection process might allow for candidates to have greater emotional and mental maturity, in which case test results might act as a better predictor of interest and effort rather than just an ability to cram from tutoring.

Abolishing grammar schools will not solve any of the problems currently facing England's schools. Grammar schools are needed to remind society what an academic education actually is, and what it means for a pupil to have acquired a certain level of knowledge. Parents need the freedom to enter their child into the competition for a place in such a school, and those who choose this option should be trusted and not castigated as inflicting psychological damage upon their children. Abolishing selective schools will only deprive more children of the chance of a decent, broad-based, academic education.

Education for New Times

Neal Lawson

Education is our most vital social act. Why, what and how we teach has the most profound implications for what sort of society we are and in whatever form, private or public, education is an undeniably social act. We can never learn alone. Whether through the book, the class or even today the 'MOOC' (massive, online open courses), education is collectively created between learner and the learned. Indeed, the very concept of the hermetically sealed individual denies the very possibility of education. We learn together, or not at all.

But how we educate today, given the context of education, we can see not just a new purpose for education, but a way of conceiving education that unites means and ends. Here I will argue that 'New Times' provide the context in which the desirable is not just made feasible but necessary. In so doing a new model of education begins to emerge and a way we can begin to transform from the rather confused way we educate today to one that is aligned.

The context of education today

Compare and contrast the essentially Victorian structure of established education with the emerging world; a world of hierarchical structure in which the expert imparts their knowledge to the passive recipient learner. From the top down and the centre out – the essence of education is and has been elitist, something that is linear, controllable and measurable. In the last 30 years this essentially technocratic view of education has been bent towards the dominant globalised/free-market economic model. The purpose of the educational hierarchy was to equip people with the individual tools to survive and maybe for a few to thrive in the global race. As the state withdrew from a host of social security functions, the prominence of education came to the fore as the means to equip some of the people to be winners and learn the culture of life in a consumer-driven global economy; that is, to maximise earning potential and become imbued with key notions of modern survival – such as debt. Along the way parents, students and teachers became immersed in an essentially competitive culture whereby education becomes a positional good – not valued because of what it teaches us but because of what it teaches us above and beyond what it teaches our neighbours. Education has become a race – not for knowledge and understanding – but simply to win in terms of pounds, shillings and pence. And likewise the relationship between schools and all educational establishments is essentially competitive – the free market, aided by the bureaucratic state, would sort the wheat from the chaff, the survivor would by definition be the best and all would be dragged towards improvement or pay the price.

The jarring system of secondary selection points out the outmoded nature of the arrangement. We have an essentially closed and segregated system – that erects barriers at key intervals that can either be gamed or overcome with sufficient competitive resource. Policy makers on the Left and Right can't seem to be able to think beyond the Soviet Union or Serco as models for reform. In these liquid modern and open times of fluid movement socially and culturally, the stark rigidity of these old hierarchies could not be more apparent and irrelevant. There are many telling critiques of this model – both moral and practical – some of which will be dealt with below. But it is the charge that this model is simply out of its time that begins to force us to think about the future of education in different and incredibly exciting ways. Once we have dispensed with the last century constructs of the market and the target, or to put it another way, the Soviet Union and G4S, as the models for educational production, where does that leave us?

New Times

It's been a while coming but we are now going through a paradigm shift in the way things are governed; the driver is largely technological but the implications for education, and much else, are profound. Slowly, but now at a quickening pace, the century of the big bureaucracy, the top-down hierarchy, the expert and an elite view of the teacher and the taught – the world in which our view of the education system was formed – is giving way. It is giving way to a world that is much flatter. Technology is now connecting everyone to everything. We can speak to whom we want and know whatever we want in a networked world that is fast destroying old hierarchies and sources of power. The notion that education can survive this revolution is a non-starter. The implications are profound in terms of why and how we educate. Not least because the world of work is changing as a result of this revolution in two ways: the way we work with each other but also the precariousness of work. In this more horizontal world the notion of the labourer as a worker ant, which takes orders from above, is fading in the rear view mirror. How can you be a deferential robot at work but an online, informed and opinionated citizen when you clock off? Efficiency, productivity, creativity and innovation will come from networks, not command and control or competition. People will increasingly collaborate, cooperate, share, experiment, learn, fail and try again – together. Power and decision-making will be dispersed and pluralised. And on these emerging flat planes where everyone's voice counts and everyone can be heard there is an egalitarian and democratic potential. In this many-to-many world the skills of the future will be relational, emotional and empathetic.

But just as the quality of work will increase, for many life will become more uncertain. Clearly the world of a job for life has long gone but the world of eight jobs in a lifetime is being replaced by eight in a year as technology replaces many previous work functions. The mix of algorithms, big data, sensors, 3D printing and Wi-Fi will see widespread disruption of which Uber and its devastating effect on taxi drivers is just an outlier. Machines have long been replacing labour and will go on doing so. By 2030, predicts the Oxford Martin School, 47 per cent of US jobs will be automated.[1] But software is already replacing brainpower. Traditional knowledge learned at school will become redundant as professional judgement is replaced by decisions that come from mass collaboration or are technologically determined. As the notion of 'zero marginal cost' kicks in, the fact that much we now value is replicable at no or little additional cost because of the abundance created by digitisation, wages could stay stagnant or even continue to fall with inequality increasing still further. Given the existing model of economy and society being a never-ending race to acquire, the prospects for most of us in these new times do not feel great. That is unless we change the terms of debate and have a different conception of a good life and a good society. This is partly why we need to move beyond a model of life as material consumption and towards a life of creation, caring, learning and leisure. Whether forced or voluntary, full-time employment and full-time spending is going to be a thing of the past. Work and money are going to be in shorter supply but time outside work can be hugely expanded. This can either be achieved via market allocation – whereby the already powerful and wealthy become even more powerful and wealthy – or it can be planned and organised on a fairer and more sustainable basis via concepts such as the shorter working week. As such, education has to be about preparing people for more than work but also for the civic, the social and the family. And of course there is a further imperative that will change dramatically the life/work imbalance we currently suffer from: the sustainability of the planet and the ecosystem on which all life forms depend. We simply cannot go on as we have, consuming without end. Education is going to have to help prepare us for the infinite abundance of ideas and the finite limits of the planet.

So what now?

Given all of this, the nature of current educational debate seems remarkably narrow; small and backward looking, limited to the extent of free schools and academies and the nature of inspection and not very much else. The war of words and policies we hear between the parties seems rather phony – designed to mask the fact that the debate is over small differences at a time when so much else is changing. Ken Spours reminds us that organised universal education is very new in terms of our development as a species, barely 125 years old.[2] And yet it is feeling woefully out of date. We are educating for a world of twentieth-century work, using largely nineteenth-century customs and hierarchies just when the twenty-first century is finally kicking in and leaving the old world behind. Surely it is a moment to pause, reflect and think afresh?

Given the analysis above, how should and could we educate for a world in which we can be defined not just by what we produce or consume, but as active, engaged citizens? The answer lies much less in the predictable agenda of syllabus, curriculum, testing and auditing, although all will undoubtedly play their part even in new times. Rather the answer lies much more in making our education system look and feel more like the future – the shadow of which we already live in – so that future can be both evenly distributed and caught, not just taught. So the way we educate must be open, inclusive, permeable, experimental, democratic, participatory, relational, empathetic and respectful. Changing a culture is much harder than changing a structure. That's why politicians opt for the short-term win at the cost of long-term failure. But this paradigm shift is too big and too obvious to be ignored. We don't all feel it or know it all, but we sense and experience enough of it to know something big is happening. Of course the technological and cultural trends can be pushed in different directions, towards more surveillance and greater isolation and inequality despite all the virtual connections. But a different future is now not just desirable or even feasible – it's essential. A good society was never fully or genuinely possible via the top-down bureaucratic and remote systems of the twentieth century, despite all the good they did. Neither will the free market deliver the levels of equality and opportunity necessary to fulfil our lives. But the peer-to-peer, networked-citizen world we see emerging is different because it offers the chance to unify means and ends. The more just, democratic and fulfilling world we want to see is created through cultures and structures that are themselves more just, democratic and fulfilling. And this is no longer just an aspiration or a dream, it's a world that is fast being created in reality.

Now let's be clear. Education cannot build a good society, that places too much burden on the system. But everyone should experience a good society in the education system. What does this mean in practice? Education must be a lifelong endeavour for all of us. We all have a part to play and we all have a life to fulfil. And over the lifespan we are going to have to keep developing and adapting – not to be bent to the modernising will of corporations that are too free or states that are too remote – but because we want to and need to develop as human beings. Institutions, argues the social theorist Roberto Unger, shape us but are finite – we are not.[3] We have an infinite ability to develop and create. It is the capability to learn, develop and adapt that must now be enshrined throughout life, not as a temporarily time-limited chore but as a joyful and never-ending journey of self and mutual discovery. Education institutions must be both porous and democratic. In a networked world the idea of going to school in the traditional fashion will soon seem quaint. With every fact, every great lecture and every new idea available instantly, anytime and anywhere, the notion of learning solely in a fixed place will become impossible to sustain. Schools will become hubs of learning – for guidance, prioritisation, coaching and development. The education institution will be a platform rather than a set of walls that bound knowledge and capacity. Primacy will lie not with the sole institution but with the locality, as institutions share and collaborate, as they specialise and support each other. No one will go it alone because no one goes it alone in a networked society. If they do, they fail.

So it's not different schools for different abilities we need but different schools for different specialisms which then interact and support each other. The rigid social hierarchies of the twentieth century will no longer hold in the twenty-first. It is fluidity not rigidity that will mark success, teamwork and collaboration over command and control. Classes will be created for and by learners under the guidance of their teacher because it is the practice of creating lessons that will provide the best grounding for future life. Teachers' professional standing will be enhanced through this system of co-production and their professional development will be continuous and progressive. Students will be expected to take democratic responsibility for the running of the school, in tandem with professionals and the community. And by democracy, this does not mean the dry and desiccated model of Westminster, but an engaging and enriching form of everyday democracy where decisions are debated and complexity negotiated. This democratic spirit will be the guiding principle of accountability and innovation. The institution, its fellow institutions, the community and the local politicians will hold to account and be held to account for performance. Governors in particular will be supported and trained to play a leading role in the development of the institution and they will be highly regarded in society and their community for the responsibility they take. A Local Education Board comprising all key stakeholders will help determine a local education plan. Yes, there will be disappointing results and failure but learning from them will be key. Repeated failure will trigger central state intervention via an expert HMI-type approach that emphasises improvement over punishment. What will be measured is the capability of learners to be relational and adaptable as workers and citizens. The goal will not be to compete with each other, be it fellow learners or other learning institutions, but competition to deal with problems society faces. The curriculum will be more open and local with greater emphasis on collective problem solving. A new independent National Education Council would oversee the long-term development of the system, free from the tinkering of a Secretary of State whose job will be to ensure the platforms of education have the resources and support they need.

Is the desirable feasible?

Why might any of this be impossible? The main argument against such a system is that we are in a global race which we either win or lose. But globalisation can unite as much as it divides. Just as we can share, collaborate and learn locally, so we can across borders. The context described above is not particular to the UK. The same paradigm shift is happening the world over. It will be interpreted and directed in different ways – which just proves that we have choices. But more than anything the feasibility is proven by the fact that the collaborative and capability building approach is happening in schools and colleges despite the system not because of it. Cooperative schools in particular are growing strongly, as is interest in democratic schooling. The adoption of lifelong learning is happening informally on and offline – again *despite* the system not because it – as people look to develop new knowledge and skills. People are participating in civic organisations, brought together by the power of digital connections, and making places more liveable or shared interests more attainable. Self-help and development books are flying off the shelves and being downloaded as e-books. The Confederation of British Industry talks enthusiastically about emotional intelligence being taught in schools, and places as diverse as Finland and Canada show us what is possible.[4] What is more, the promise of success by working hard and playing by the rules no longer holds and everyone knows this. As Simon Jenkins has written:

> Britain's economy is in a mess not for a lack of maths but for a lack of ethics and common sense. Being top of the world in science did not save the Soviet Union from collapse... the academic terrorism of tests and league tables has made Gradgrind's rote-learning seem almost liberal.[5]

There are two options we can take, to carry on tinkering with the old system or to face new times and bend modernity to the values of a new education system in which we each succeed because we all succeed. The selection debate infers some are more select than others.

How We Got Into This Mess

Stephen Pollard

On 12 July 1965, the English state education sector was injected with a dose of poison. The system then was far from perfect; there was a long tail of underperforming schools. But on that day, the British government pledged its official commitment to the end of all that was good about state education to that point.

It was not, of course, presented like that. Rather, as the Department of Education and Science put it, it was simply complying with a motion passed by the House of Commons on 21 January 1965:

> That this House, conscious of the need to raise educational standards at all levels, and regretting that the realisation of this objective is impeded by the separation of children into different types of secondary schools, notes with approval the efforts of local authorities to reorganise secondary education on comprehensive lines which will preserve all that is valuable in grammar school education for those children who now receive it and make it available to more children; recognises that the method and timing of such reorganisation should vary to meet local needs; and believes that the time is now ripe for a declaration of national policy.[1]

And in doing that Circular 10/65 was issued:

> The Secretary of State accordingly requests local education authorities, if they have not already done so, to prepare and submit to him plans for reorganising secondary education in their areas on comprehensive lines. The purpose of this Circular is to provide some central guidance on the methods by which this can be achieved.[2]

It might have used the word 'requests' but in practice the Department used its power not merely to request but to require such a change, refusing to pay for any new school or improvements to existing schools that were not comprehensive. And with that came the end not merely of grammar schools, which had had a transformational impact on the lives of so many poor but bright children. It also hailed the end of what has come to be known as traditional education, replaced by so-called progressive methodologies which spread the anti-education virus throughout the system.

If it was not so awful it would be hilarious – the idea that the single greatest act of educational vandalism in British history was meant to raise educational standards. For all that there were problems with two legs of the old tripartite system (the technical and secondary modern schools), one wing of British state education, grammar schools, did a fine job of lifting children out of poverty and giving them opportunity. Yet today, our system still has some of the worst rankings in the developed world and opinion polls show that a majority of parents would pay to escape the state system if they could afford to do so. There was, however, nothing inevitable about this. There is no comparable problem in the rest of Europe, where academic and vocational selection have remained widely practised and state schools have, in the main, succeeded in the task of offering decent opportunities to children. The responsibility for our failure lies with the comprehensive ideology which gripped first the education establishment and then politicians in the 1960s.

Although the arguments for comprehensive schooling had been floated since the 1950s, they were initially regarded as merely one option – and a decidedly politically partisan one at that. Had Tony Crosland not been Education Secretary, and had he not issued Circular 10/65, education would almost certainly have looked very different today, as this near-compulsory shift to the comprehensive system would not have happened. The story of how selection went from being regarded by the opinion-forming classes as the engine of social mobility to its enemy is one of the most fascinating tales of twentieth-century political history. The transformation – first on the Left and then by much of the Right – occurred within a few decades. This chapter seeks to describe and explain that transformation.

The key event behind the change, as in so much of post-war British history, was the Second World War. The social levelling it brought about had a profound effect not just on those directly involved but across the upper and middle classes, from the old aristocracy to the 'backbone' of the country, the professional classes. All underwent a crisis of confidence – not least around the future of the public schools which had served them almost exclusively. The public schools' demise was widely prophesied, even before the 1945 election swept a socialist government to power. In 1940, Churchill himself had told the boys of his alma mater, Harrow, that after the war the social advantages of the public schools must be extended on a far broader basis.[3]

As Michael Young, author of Labour's 1945 manifesto, wrote:

> It was feared that impoverishment of the middle classes would remove their capacity to pay fees, and some of the strongest supporters of the public schools looked to the State to prevent catastrophe. They were not only ready to accept a proportion of poor pupils, they pleaded with the State to pay for their places.[4]

But the fears proved groundless. Nicholas Timmins, in his *A Biography of The Welfare State*, describes the 'great lost opportunity' of R.A. Butler's wartime failure to reform the public schools in his 1944 Education Act:

> The combination of financial crisis in the public schools themselves and widespread criticism of their role and performance in the early 1940s provided the only time in the twentieth century when the political will and political votes to integrate them into the national education system just might have been assembled...[5]

Butler appears to have been ready to contemplate doing so, establishing an official inquiry into the subject which, like the Beveridge committee on national insurance, was given a brief to produce a grand plan if it so chose. But Lord Fleming, its dour and unimaginative chairman, was no Beveridge: he deliberated for two years, issued his report a matter of days after the passage of the 1944 Act, and produced a damp squib of a scheme for uniting the state and private sectors. As Butler put it: 'the first class carriage had been shunted on to an immense siding'.[6] It might easily have been hauled back onto the main line by the post-war

Labour government, with its landslide majority and reformist mission, but Clement Attlee, Haileybury boy and proud of it, attached no urgency to the issue. In the public schools, as in the army, Whitehall, the House of Lords and the Monarchy, the old elite behaved with enough circumspection to keep socialist agitation at bay, while sustaining its collective confidence sufficiently to want to keep its old institutions intact. The moment for transformation from above had passed and by the early fifties it had passed irrevocably.

As Michael Young continued:

> The middle class proved as tough as ever; they survived high taxation and high prices and went on sending their children to the same old venerable schools. In the middle 1950s, of people with more than £1000 p.a. – a miserable enough sum by modern standards – nineteen out of every twenty sent their children to private schools.[7]

But it was a very different story in the state sector with the wholesale egalitarian educational reforms of the 1960s. For all the reforms introduced by Tony Blair and subsequently Michael Gove aimed at reducing the divide between state and private schools, and for all the once unimaginable cooperation, that divide remains wide. It is not, as the educational reformers of the 1950s and 1960s promised, narrowing, but widening as those at the top still perform better in their private and selective state schools, while the mass of white working-class males continue to languish in an almost anti-education culture in under-performing comprehensive schools. Indeed, the comprehensive revolution has not removed the link between education and class but strengthened it.

In 1965, the Labour-controlled House of Commons resolved that moving to a comprehensive system would 'preserve all that is valuable in grammar school education for those children who now receive it and make it available to more children'.[8] Few could seriously maintain that this has in fact been the case. Far from ushering in an era of levelling up, the comprehensive revolution set in chain a form of unilateral educational disarmament in which the real victims were the defenceless poor. The words of Chris Woodhead, the former Chief Inspector of Schools in 1996, remain horrifyingly true:

> The failure of boys, and in particular white working-class boys, is one of the most disturbing problems we face within the whole education system. Research shows that white working-class boys are the least likely to participate in full-time education after the age of 16, and that white boys are the most likely to be completely unqualified on leaving compulsory education... The fact is that our most disadvantaged children, especially boys, remain disadvantaged at the end of their schooling.[9]

So what went wrong? Grammar schools, put on a formal footing and opened to all who were bright enough by Butler's Act, enabled working-class children to mix with their similarly able middle-class peers. That is why the 1944 Education Act, which enshrined the idea of a grammar school place for the intellectually able rather than the socially well-connected, was the culmination of the arguments of socialists such as Sidney Webb and R.H. Tawney. The challenge for the next generation should have been to build on the success of grammar schools, extending their ethos and emphasis on qualifications and standards to the secondary modern sector, emulating the achievement of Germany and the Netherlands in particular, with their vocational schools. But the comprehensive revolution, tragically, simply destroyed much of the excellent without improving the bad.

The comprehensive revolution had two goals: one educational, the other social. Many of the most influential educational theorists in the 1950s and 1960s genuinely believed that mixed-ability teaching and comprehensive schooling 'gives all children a fresh start in the secondary school... The expectations which teachers have of the majority of their pupils are better – and their pupils, sensing and responding to this higher regard, in turn achieve more', as Robin Pedley, one of the leading advocates, put it at the time.[10] He went on:

> Comprehensive education does more than open the doors of opportunity to all children. It represents a different, a larger and more generous attitude of mind... the forging of a communal culture by the pursuit of quality with equality, by the education of their pupils in and for democracy, and by the creation of happy vigorous, local communities in which the school is the focus of social and educational life.[11]

There was also a more profound objective underlying the reform: 'In spite of the virtual abolition of poverty, in spite of the rise there has been in the rewards of labour, in spite of the fact that... the great bulk of the nation now regards itself as middle class, Britain is still a jealous and divided nation', argued *The Times* in 1961.[12] Education, which was seen by the advocates of comprehensive schools 'as a serious alternative to nationalisation in promoting a more just and efficient society' (as Tony Crosland, the Education Secretary who would not rest until he had 'destroyed every f***ing grammar school', put it), was thus to be a vital step in moving towards a classless society.[13]

In January 1965, Crosland was moved from his role as George Brown's deputy at the Department for Economic Affairs and promoted to the Cabinet, at 46 its youngest member. As his biographer writes of his initial months at the Department for Education and Science (DES):

> What impressed civil servants and political colleagues alike was the minister's clarity and sense of purpose. In subsequent ministerial posts, Crosland usually took time to settle in and he believed it required at least six months to get a sound grasp of how a department worked. But at the DES he had already written extensively on the subject before he arrived and felt confident of the issues requiring his early attention.[14]

The problem was that his focus and determination were fundamentally misguided: 'He soon made it clear to officials that top of his list was one aspect of education that had figured prominently in Labour's election manifesto – secondary school reorganisation.'[15] As Crosland put it in his seminal 1956 book *The Future of Socialism*, the tripartite system separated 'the unselected goats and the carefully selected sheep on the basis of tests which measure home backgrounds as much as innate ability'.[16]

For all that the proponents of comprehensive education had been gathering converts, by the time Crosland arrived at the DES in January 1965, very few of the 6,000 state secondary schools had been converted or were even scheduled to convert. And the House of Commons resolution cited above was intended by the Prime Minister, Harold Wilson, simply as an expression of hot air to shut up the more driven Labour backbenchers – indeed, in 1963 Wilson had said: 'The grammar school will be abolished over my dead body.'[17] In 1957, a Labour Party opinion poll had found that a majority of the population was happy to continue with selective education and only 10 per cent thought it undesirable. As George Tomlinson, Labour's Minister of Education in 1947, put it: 'The Party are kidding themselves if they think that the comprehensive idea has any popular appeal.' Looking back in 1971, Dennis Marsden wrote in the Fabian pamphlet *Politicians, Equality and Comprehensives:* 'Claims of a mandate for comprehensives were so much eyewash.'[19] Indeed, the old and successful notion of the grammar school that emanated from the same liberal or Whig intellectual well as the Northcote-Trevelyan civil service reforms in the nineteenth century was enthusiastically adopted by Fabian socialists such as Sidney Webb and, later, R.H. Tawney. They saw grammar schools (because they were forced to select on the basis of ability rather than class) as the apotheosis of a socialist meritocracy, opening up opportunities to all on the basis of ability rather than parental wealth.

Crosland's appointment, however, changed everything. His predecessor, Michael Stewart, had gone through the motions of drafting a circular but with limited enthusiasm and even more limited effort. The real work started when Crosland took over, with discussion – or, to be more accurate, argument – centring on whether to 'require' or 'request' local education authorities (LEAs) to reorganise their schools. For all Crosland's determination on the issue, he himself had argued in *The Future of Socialism* that the immediate abolition of grammar schools would produce too great a backlash and that only a voluntarily brought-about system would last. As he put it in a speech in January 1966, Britain's education system was 'educationally and socially unjust, inefficient, wasteful and divisive... True equality of opportunity cannot be accomplished in one generation, or by education alone; it needs a wider social revolution'.[20] But the circular gave LEAs a year to draw up their response, which meant, in some cases, a year of resistance. *The Times*, for instance, attacked the 'unrealisable ideal of equality'. Some LEAs, such as Bournemouth, made it clear that they were having none of it. So the argument within the DES was over how to respond to this. In March 1966, Crosland issued a further circular stating that no building projects would be approved unless they fitted in with a comprehensive system. With the baby boom necessitating large building projects for schools to cope with the demand for places, this was not so much bribery as downright blackmail, given that Circular 10/65 was a supposedly voluntary request. It was not surprising that by the deadline there were fewer than 20 LEAs which had not submitted the 'requested' plans. Counties such as Bromley and Surrey, which would ordinarily have had no truck with comprehensive schooling, caved in to financial necessity. As the *Times Educational Supplement* concluded when Crosland left the DES in September 1967: 'A great shove towards comprehensive schools has been given.'[21]

Not that one should misread the situation. When the political establishment – let alone the educational establishment – is solidly agreed on a received wisdom then it is almost always wrong. And make no mistake: even without the financial penalties, there was an overwhelming chattering class consensus behind comprehensive schooling, although much of the support was based on ignorance, with some people thinking that somehow comprehensives would exist alongside grammar schools. And Butskellism – the *de facto* fusing of Labour and Conservative policy that characterised the 1950s – was, by the 1960s, fully at work in education. In 1963, the then Conservative Education Secretary, Edward Boyle, said that: 'none of us believes in pre-war terms that children can be sharply differentiated into various types or levels of ability'.[22] Margaret Thatcher, appointed to the DES after the Conservative victory in June 1970, withdrew Circular 10/65 and replaced it with Circular 10/70, allowing each authority to decide its own attitude; but even she nonetheless closed more grammar schools (3,286) than any other education minister before or since. The Conservatives' 1970 manifesto expressed the party's pride that 'many of the most imaginative new schemes abolishing the 11-plus have been introduced by Conservative councils'.[23]

The few grammar schools which still exist today had councils which placed the value of education higher than political and ideological dogma. And that is the tragic irony. For all the good intentions, the destruction of the grammar schools – the one undoubted social success of English state education – had the precise opposite effect to that which was intended. Those who can afford to flee the system now desert it for the private sector, those who have the money to escape to a leafy middle-class catchment area leave the inner cities, and those who can't are left to fight to improve their lot – if they have the wherewithal, or are lucky enough to live in an area with other parents who do. As A.H. Halsey, one of the leading egalitarian theorists of the 1960s, put it: 'the essential fact of twentieth-century educational history is that egalitarian policies have failed'.[24] In some cases these parents literally took their schools with them, as the leading direct grant schools (which were self-governing but state funded in return for taking scholarship pupils from state primary schools) left the state sector in the seventies rather than abandon selection. In the post-war decades direct grant schools such as Dulwich College provided a far more structural bridge between the state and private sectors even than the old Assisted Places Scheme.

The direct grant scheme achieved, without any fanfare, the simple aim of opening up many public schools to ability rather than wealth. It is a sad irony that in destroying the direct grant schools on the altar of equal opportunity, the 1974-79 Labour government succeeded only in denying opportunity to many poor children and increasing the number of fee-paying parents. From then on, for any parent concerned to secure a particular type of education for their child, there was generally little choice but to go private. Thus, while the total school roll fell during the eighties, the number of children in private schooling rose. Hand in hand with this went a change in teaching. Supposedly 'bonding' theories of progressive teaching, exemplified by the Plowden report in the 1960s, were similarly toxic. 'The progressive classroom', writes Adrian Wooldridge, 'was a laboratory of the classless society – an idyllic place in which cooperation flourished and competition was unknown. Nothing angers progressive teachers quite so much as testing, which, they argue, measures little more than social background and so simply perpetuates and justifies social inequalities. Children who are labelled as failures at primary school are likely to go on to fulfil their own low expectations. The yobs on the football terraces were venting their anger at those nasty spelling tests.'[25]

For all the improvements and changes, the state school classroom in many instances still resembles an unfamiliar environment to those who work on the basis of fact and reason. As an infamous 1990s guide for trainee teachers published by the London University Institute of Education – home of many of the country's most influential educationalists – asserted, schools are guilty of too often 'legitimising one popular view of mathematics' – arithmetic, algebra and geometry – and so devaluing 'the students' informal mathematical experience and skills... which are equally, if not more, valuable to the individual'. Maths is oppressive, it should be replaced by 'ethnomathematics', since 'the view that "official" mathematics dominates "ethnomathematics" is consistent with that of Western cultural/educational imperialism in mathematics education'.[26] Our everyday experiences are what maths is really about, not the pedagogic instructions of a teacher. As the headmaster in Lambeth who appointed an expert in Nigerian cooking, with no experience of maths, to teach maths in his school put it: 'It is real life maths with Ibo cookery – transferable maths.'[27]

The comprehensive disease was able to take hold because of the British private school phenomenon, which effectively removed the upper tier of the professional class from any stake in state schools and so meant there was no influential protest as the ideologues tightened their grip. With their professional classes still involved, other countries were not afflicted by the disease which took over the British education establishment after the Second World War, which viewed education not as the passing on of knowledge and the skills required to think but as a key battleground in the process of transforming society. This led to a blueprint being drawn up which would impose the mechanism of that social engineering – comprehensive education to achieve equality – across the country. When a similar contagion threatened to envelope the French state system, politicians of all parties were motivated to mobilise to prevent any damage because they all had a stake in the system. And it was a left-wing politician, the Socialist Jean-Pierre Chevènement (dubbed France's Tony Benn), who as Minister of Education in France led the fight against these 'progressive' notions through his policy of '*élitisme republicain*' (elitism for all).

The British attitude was typified by Michael Young's *The Rise of the Meritocracy*, which argued that a country in which meritocracy was the determinant of social mobility would be profoundly unequal because it would simply lead to a new elite, leaving others to fester behind; thus, equality of opportunity should be replaced with equality of outcome – a line that Crosland swallowed hook, line and sinker. Comprehensive schooling would be the first line in that battle and would force children to be equal. This went hand in hand with the sociological analysis which gripped the educational establishment during the first half of the twentieth century, which held that everything boiled down to class: educational failure was determined by schools' class bias. Ridiculous as it may seem now, there was a widespread view that if working-class children failed grammar or maths tests, they were simply resisting middle-class control. As one perceptive historian of the subject puts it:

> For both intellectual and practical reasons many educators were convinced that the solution to apparently intractable educational problems lay not in perseverance and meritocratic classification but in the abandonment of the syllabus and the celebration of working-class culture. And sometimes even of counter-cultural rebellion.[28]

Melanie Phillips points out in *All Must Have Prizes* that the impact of the First World War had been profound. Just about everything in society was thrown open to question. Anything which resembled Prussian attitudes was viewed as dangerously militaristic – and elements of education, with orderly rows of desks and multiplication tables, were thus viewed as suspect. Books such as *What Is and What Might Be* by Edmond Holmes, published in 1911, which argued that education was simply about fostering growth rather than imparting information, moved from being seen as wacky notions unfit for serious consideration to forward-thinking analyses of the mistakes of society. Holmes put it thus:

> The process of growing must be done by the growing organism, the child, let us say, and by no one else ... The forces that make for the child's growth come from within himself; and it is for him and him alone, to feed them, use them, evolve them.[29]

God forbid that the teacher should have such a role. By 1938, the Spens Report on elementary education was able to cite with approval an earlier report's demand that the curriculum 'should be thought of in terms of activity and experience rather than of knowledge to be acquired and facts to be stored'.[30] The sentiments in that one sentence embody the ruin of education which has followed. The watershed for these developments was the Second World War, after which ideas that had merely been gaining piecemeal adherents became the norm. Why did it all come together then? Melanie Phillips explains:

> The war had created a new sense of social solidarity. There was the desire to create a new society, a new social order based on fairness and social justice, accompanied by a deep sense of guilt among the middle classes that social class had deprived working-class children of their chance of success. There was the increasingly widespread impact of psychological theories of child rearing which inspired deep guilt among adults about the harm done to children by repressing their personalities. There was the increasing influence of teacher training colleges as teaching struggled to give itself higher professional status. There was the panic among teachers at having to control classrooms of children who didn't want to be at school at all but were captive pupils courtesy of the raising of the school leaving age, a panic that made the teachers receptive to any suggested techniques that claimed to hold children's attention.[31]

The culmination of this was the Plowden Report into primary education, published in 1967. This report has come to be regarded as the foundation of progressive education; in truth, it simply drew together ideas which had already seized control of teacher training colleges. Plowden put it thus:

> The school sets out... to devise the right environment for children, to allow them to be themselves and to develop in the way and at the pace appropriate to them. It tries to equalise opportunities and compensate for handicaps. It lays special stress on individual discovery, on first-hand experience and on opportunities for creative work. It insists that knowledge does not fall into neatly separate compartments and that work and play are not opposite but complementary.[32]

All that mattered was freeing the innate creative imagination of the child. As for imparting facts, other people's experiences were a waste of time. Only if a child had experienced something for itself or learned to empathise could it be said to understand something or be educated. Worse still, imposing facts – other people's experiences and assertions – was a deliberately destructive act, since it fettered a child's creativity. Take the writings of Caroline Gipps, former Vice Chancellor of the University of Wolverhampton and previously one of the most renowned educationalists in the land. In 1993, she informed us that learning 'is a process of knowledge construction, not of recording or absorption'.[33] So no multiplication table tests for her pupils then? This guff – today's received wisdom of educational theory – is absorbed at teacher training colleges and then regurgitated in the classroom, condemning generations of pupils to ignorance of basic knowledge and failure in life. No child must ever be told he or she is wrong. Every experience is by definition correct, because it is the child's own experience that matters. Literacy – being able to read and write in what was traditionally regarded as the proper manner – is merely an imposition on a child's creativity.

As Peter Traves, a one-time English adviser with Shropshire Council, put it in a paper in 1991, such a definition of literacy was actually damaging. 'Proper literacy' involved bringing 'your knowledge and your experience to bear on what passes before you'. 'Improper literacy' was simply letting your eye look at the words on the page and your brain translate the symbols. 'Mere reading... is a reductive and destructive state of being in which the illusion of achievement is substituted for the genuine article, where the potential for power has been thwarted and channelled'.[34] But, as Melanie Phillips shows, what turns this into something truly memorable is Traves's remarks about his son, Richard:

> Richard's pre-school and nursery experience of reading was a very positive and fairly rich one. Although he went to school unable to 'read' in the sense of being able to decode the print of books, he behaved as a reader in almost every other respect... He enjoyed being read to, talked about the stories and wanted more books. He memorised stories and large chunks of the phrasing from books and then delivered them back enthusiastically in a readerly tone of voice.[35]

It is difficult to know whether to laugh at the sheer idiocy of this man's supposedly serious views or to cry for poor Richard for being brought up by such a father. It gets worse when he describes Richard's school experience: 'Richard started at the bottom of the scheme and stayed there... He had seen himself as a reader. He now described himself not only as a non-reader but as generally stupid'.[36] Poor Richard had no chance. Readers in Staffordshire will no doubt be delighted to learn that Traves went on to become Corporate Director of Children and Lifelong Learning for Staffordshire County Council.

Wrapped up in this issue is the so-called debate between advocates of phonics and 'Look-and-say' – in reality no more of a debate than that between those who argue that 2 + 2 = 4 and those who say that 2 + 2 = 5. Phonics is the label given to learning how to read through recognising and sounding every letter and then reading them together to form words. 'Look-and-say', on the other hand, requires children to recognise entire words from their context. The difference is that phonics works and 'Look-and-say' doesn't, a fact which at last appears to have dawned on enough people to force the hands of educationalists who had rejected phonics. A seven-year study of schools in Clackmannanshire demonstrated conclusively – as if there were any doubt – that pupils taught to read through phonics were, by the age of eleven, on average three-and-a-half years ahead for their age in reading and one year and eight months ahead in spelling. Boys outscored girls and there was almost no difference between pupils from different backgrounds.[37] As one of the proponents of phonics, Ruth Miskin, showed when teaching in East London, even in a school where almost every pupil was Bangladeshi, and for whom English was a second language, by the age of six every one of them could read fluently.[38]

For the 'paradox of Plowdenism', as Wooldridge calls it, is that it strengthens the class divisions it is supposed to tear down.[39] Poor children simply cannot adjust to the unstructured, loose environment of such schools – unlike their middle-class peers whose confidence typically sees them through alien experiences, and whose parents compensate for the failure of teachers and schools to do their job. And when teachers are recruited to teach knowledge in schools which place a value on high standards, their influence can be worse than useless, since many teachers themselves suffer the consequences of their own education. Martin Stephen, former High Master of St Paul's School, relates that: 'Subject knowledge has become the poor relation of teaching, a once elemental requirement that for several years has been kicked into touch'.[40] He describes what happened at recent job interviews:

> At my school, we make all teaching job applicants teach a specimen lesson. They are given details a week in advance, and the topic is deliberately simple and straightforward. Twice recently, we have been thrilled to interview candidates for science teaching posts with a 2:1 in their subject from a highly regarded university, and five or six years' experience. The lessons were catastrophic, riddled with basic factual errors. The head of department, observing the lessons, confiscated the pupils' notes, for fear they might regurgitate them at GCSE.[41]

There were, of course, those who argued that comprehensive schools and progressive teaching methods were a good thing on their own educational merits; that the way to overcome the failure of the secondary modern schools was to destroy the grammar schools, force high achievers into mixed-ability classes and schools and watch the less academic pupils improve. But we are still waiting for that to happen.

Will Selection at 11 Ever End?

Margaret Tulloch

Many English children face selection at 11. Soon another government which has done nothing to end selection will come to the end of its term of office. So it is perhaps worthwhile to ask why no government so far seems willing to grasp this particular nettle. Is ending selection the vote loser it is claimed to be? How many votes would be lost – has there ever been a real analysis? Even if on first analysis it was shown to be a vote loser because change is always unpopular, surely a responsible government should provide the evidence and support needed to encourage voters to see that change is needed?

That selection at 11 is a major factor affecting English education should not be in doubt. Any government concerned about raising standards, extending opportunity and using the talents of all young people should not ignore the effects of selection. Yes, only around five per cent of children have 'passed' the test to get to a grammar school but for every one of those 'successes' around three times that number are likely to be told they have failed it. In other words more than one in ten English children are given this message when less than halfway through their education. This is unnecessary and damaging when we all agree that we must encourage young people to aim high and stay in education or training until 18. Surely what a significant number of young people do not need is official confirmation that they have not made the grade at 10? In some areas where selection is the overriding influence on the education provision, this message goes down the generations. 'Education did nothing for me' will be the message children get from their 11-plus-failure parents, 'so why should you expect anything different?' One hears from Open University (OU) tutors that adults embarking on new qualifications will preface their comments by 'I failed the 11-plus but...'. One Comprehensive Future supporter did her OU dissertation interviewing fellow OU 11-plus failures 35 years on. As one said in 2002:

> Whilst it, as an event, in a sense is less immediate … the waves spreading out from the ripples that it created are still very much there… This is an old wound and most people tend to leave old wounds alone, they may walk with a limp, but they've got used to it... even though it has all sorts of ramifications in their present lives.[1]

Head teachers of non-selective schools in selective areas know that the first task they face is to raise the self-belief and motivation of their intake of 'failures'. As one Head of a non-selective school in a selective area said to Comprehensive Future in 2006, 'In any other another context we would be guilty of child abuse.'[2] An education system which is based on the rejection of the many is not fit for the twenty-first century. How can a modern economy continue to waste talent like this? But, some say, children need to learn to face and cope with failure. Yes, of course they do, and failure happens to all children to varying degrees: but it need not be the educational one-off decision that selection at 11 causes. There is no need to put children through this when comprehensive education avoids the pass or fail cliff-edge of the 11-plus. Now as perhaps never before, education must be about opening doors not closing them.

To believe that selection at 11 should be a necessary part of the education system requires belief in two propositions. One that ability is fixed and unchanging – it isn't. Second, that even if the first were true, that it is necessary on the basis of a test of ability to divide children up into different institutions at 11 when they leave their comprehensive primary schools. Across the world education systems which are successful do not track children so early in their careers. Time after time international evidence shows that early differentiation into different schools is associated with a wider gap in achievement between rich and poor.[3]

Any article calling for an end to selection will provoke comments and letters to letters pages from those who believe that grammar schools offered them a chance in the 1950s to make the progress which they assert comprehensives cannot offer. These contributions need to come with a health warning: these are the successes. The failures don't speak up much about how failing the 11-plus was the best thing that could have happened to them.

It is very unfortunate that comprehensive education is seen by many as a left/right issue. In the 1960s many Conservatives supported the introduction of comprehensive education. It was an educational issue then as it should be now. Much of the debate now is about achievement and social mobility. There is convincing evidence that selection widens the gap in achievement between rich and poor and does not encourage social mobility. However there are many other considerations which should be taken into account. Children need to learn to live and work together. This is not to say that special provision is not needed, but rather that it can be provided within a comprehensive school. Entry into this world is fully 'comprehensive' and schools should reflect that. In later life the benefits of being at a comprehensive show themselves. Benefits which are a preparation for adult life are not easily arranged in league tables but are valuable nonetheless. We also know that motivation affects achievement; being rejected at 11 *must* have an effect on motivation.

The effect of selection is very little reported outside the areas where it is found. Yet over the years Comprehensive Future has heard about some of the other issues not often mentioned, such as the effect on primary schools, the environment and on families. Sometimes comprehensively-educated parents moving into a new area are amazed to find that selection still exists. A parent of a five-year-old wrote to us and said:

> We were both comprehensive educated children who went to university and gained a lot from our mixed schooling… [Here] children are pushed hard and I feel that consequently this has a knock-on effect even on the infant school, not least because it causes parents to start stressing out about their child's progress even at Reception stage! I find the whole situation uncomfortable and deeply worrying.[4]

A parent in Kent wrote about the effect on transport, and as a result on the environment:

In my local authority, we have daily traffic congestion chaos in many ways caused by selective schools with their pupils travelling into the town by car, bus and train. Some pupils travel up to 20 miles each day![5]

A Kent Head Teacher wrote:

The 11-plus causes social and family division. Curiously in selective areas non-selective schools have a very high incidence of twins, because parents want them to go to the same school, and often with identical twins one is likely to pass the 11-plus and the other not, and with non-identical twins of different sex, coeducational non-selectives are the only option as most grammar schools are single-sex. Many families are torn apart by different siblings passing and failing the 11-plus. In my own village the grammar schools are in one direction and the main secondary moderns are in the other. Thus youngsters wait on different sides of the road for buses to their schools, on the one side in their blazers and ties, and on the other in their polo neck shirts and sweat shirts, often hurling insults at each other.[6]

It has been said to pro-comprehensive activists that there is more chance of ending selection if we could find another word about non-selective schools than 'comprehensive'. The comprehensive aim, that schools are open to all without an entry test, seems to have been unfairly lumped with concerns about spelling, grammar, the use of the apostrophe and other countless issues of standards arising from the educational policies of the '60s, described in 2007 by David Willetts as 'progressive teaching fads'.[7] Ending selection is not about mixed ability versus setting or having good provision for all abilities within the school, including very able and those with special needs. The debate about selection is about whether it is right to set a test for 10-year-olds to decide their educational futures.

Less concern is expressed now about the word 'comprehensive' since the recent Education Secretary Michael Gove seems to have been willing to use the word more often than some previous Labour politicians. Indeed along with him saying his foot was hovering over the pedal to allow more grammar schools he also said that selection was not a silver bullet. Ofsted chief Michael Wilshaw has spoken up for comprehensive education which is a welcome change from one of his predecessors, Chris Woodhead, who often espoused the incorrect claim that grammar schools had been the route for the working class out of poverty.[8] Advocates of selection often claim that grammar schools offer a route out of poverty. It is doubtful if that was ever true to any significant extent. Again as David Willetts said in 2007, we just have to recognise that there is overwhelming evidence that such academic selection entrenches advantage, it does not spread it.[9]

The fact that selective schools have far fewer children on free school meals and a significant proportion of children coming from prep schools is now undeniable. To combat this the Sutton Trust and the Grammar School Heads' Association have been working with the Department for Education to find ways to get more poor bright children into grammar schools.[10] Tests claimed to be 'tutor proof' are being used by grammar schools. Most grammar schools are now academies and are allowed by the School Admissions Code to prioritise entrants eligible for the pupil premium if they wish. Surely these efforts would be better spent working to ensure poor children do not fall behind in their early years? This is when the gap in attainment begins. Whilst some are making these efforts to encourage poor bright children not to go to comprehensives others are working to bring all schools up to the level of the best comprehensives recognising that excellence is possible without selecting the intake first. This is where efforts should be concentrated instead of trying to find what seems to be seen as escape routes for a few. We need an education system which serves all young people.

So what have elected governments done about selection? Before the 1997 election many of us who wanted to see an end to selection hoped that an incoming Labour government might take action to end it. Those hopes were quickly dashed by the introduction of the School Standards and Framework Act (SSFA 1998) and the grammar school ballot regulations. With David Blunkett as Education Secretary, we were told that his lips should have been read as 'no more selection' not 'no selection under a Labour government'. It is sad to look back and think that if the New Labour government with their massive majority had been bolder and brought selection to an end in 2000 for the Year 7 intake onwards those 11-year-olds would now be in their early 20s. In England the 11-plus would be a faded memory. Such a lost opportunity is hard to forgive.

The legislation introduced by the SSFA 1998 allowed selective entry into grammar schools to remain unless a majority of local parents eligible to vote voted for it to change or grammar school governing bodies decide to change their admission policies to admit children of all abilities. No governing bodies did so. Before a ballot could be held the rules required 20 per cent of eligible parents in the areas concerned to sign a petition calling for a ballot.[11] To require all of the then 164 grammar schools in England to take children of all abilities would have required 48 petitions and ballots.

Crucial to the legislation was the definition of an eligible parent.[12] This differed depending on whether the ballot would be an area or feeder ballot. Area ballots would have been needed to end selection in the ten local authorities defined by the regulations as fully selective (Bexley, Buckinghamshire, Kent, Lincolnshire, Medway, Slough, Southend, Sutton, Torbay, Trafford). Here all parents living in the area would have been eligible to sign a petition and ballot, including those with children below school age or those living outside the area but with children in the schools within the local authority. For the 38 ballots in the other 26 English Local Education Authorities with grammar schools only parents who had children in the feeder schools to the grammar schools would have been eligible. Feeder schools were defined as those which have sent a total of five or more pupils to the grammar schools in question over the year when the signatures are being gathered and the preceding two years.

Only one local campaign achieved a petition and thereby a ballot, this was in Ripon where the numbers required for a petition were achievable. This was a feeder ballot. As the then Secretary of the Campaign for State Education (CASE) I was in close touch with the campaign by Ripon CASE. In the ballot two-thirds of eligible parents who took part voted to keep the status quo. Although selection was not ended at least the campaign showed up the bizarre effect of the feeder school ballot regulations. Private school parents made up a quarter of the electorate, although a parliamentary question at the time revealed that only 4.6 per cent of primary children in North Yorkshire were in private education.[13] This was inevitable as many private schools coach pupils to pass the entry tests to grammar schools. The second largest group of the Ripon electorate were the parents in a school 10 miles away, while some Ripon parents were ineligible because they sent their children to infant schools or their schools did not send many children to the grammar schools.

To achieve an area ballot would have required thousands of signatures on petitions. For example, 18,000 signatures would be needed to trigger a ballot in Buckinghamshire. There were many other complications, not least that all signatures had to be collected in one petition year. Petition signatures could not be carried over from one petition period to another despite that fact that only one cohort of parents becomes ineligible each year and a new one eligible. There were many reasons why change was not possible under these arrangements. The rules dictated that the ballot asked only if named grammar schools should change their admission criteria to admit children of all abilities. A fundamental difficulty was that, even before signing a petition to trigger a ballot parents wanted to know what their local comprehensive system would look like – a question campaigners could not answer. For example, some parents in Ripon quite reasonably asked if they voted to end selection would the secondary modern and grammar merge or would there be two schools. The Ballot Information Code was interpreted by bodies such as local authorities and primary schools as forbidding them from providing information, for example how a local comprehensive system might come about or the effects of selection. So selection supporters could exploit any uncertainty by merely defending the status quo. In contrast, any other school reorganisation plans produced by local authorities at that time would have had detailed proposals and required local consultation.

Over the years I have been assured by many that these complications were entirely aimed to ensure there would be no change. After introducing the legislation on petitioning and balloting at national level the Labour government provided no leadership, funding or supporting evidence to encourage an organised change to a local comprehensive system. This was even more galling when at the same time this government was turning schools into academies and therefore into a new legal status without any parental petitions or ballots. Also schools were being encouraged to specialise without any real evidence that this would raise standards.

Is it too much to expect that a government should bring about change by commissioning research about a concern then take the action needed? In 2000 the Northern Ireland Department of Education published research commissioned by Martin McGuinness about the effects of the selective system there. The ensuing Burns Report stated that:

> We have been left in no doubt that the Eleven-Plus Transfer Tests are socially divisive, damage self-esteem, place unreasonable pressures on pupils, primary teachers and parents, disrupt teaching and learning at an important stage in the primary curriculum and reinforce inequality of opportunity. [14]

After extensive consultation it was agreed that selection should end but be replaced by parental choice based on pupil profile. In 2006 a draft Northern Ireland Order included the provision to 'abolish academic selection, and confer powers to enable the Department to make regulations about the admissions criteria for post-primary schools'. However complications and concessions arising during the St Andrews Agreement meant that the implementation of this became confused. Nevertheless the decision was made that the November 2008 state-sponsored 11-plus tests were to be the last. What then happened seems to be that Northern Ireland ended up in the English situation where the majority of grammar schools set their own entry tests. Although the outcome has not been as decisive as many might have hoped, this action by government – review followed by legislation – does perhaps represent what a government should do. Interestingly now in terms of how we might move forward is that some Catholic grammar schools in Northern Ireland have decided to phase out selection. Perhaps some English grammars might follow suit?

The evidence that selection at 11 is harmful to children and the education system as a whole is surely overwhelming. Comprehensive Future believes that with governmental support the transition to a fairer non-selective system in England could be done smoothly and gradually. There is no need to close schools, primary numbers are rising. Selective schools could begin to phase out selection from Year 7 onwards. No school should close and no existing pupils or staff in the schools need move but over a number of years the schools would become comprehensive. If there is a wish to retain the idea of a ballot of parents to require change then a more logical approach would be for a government which recognises the educational benefits of ending selection at 11 to require this to happen in the gradual way described but to allow local primary parents (which would be those most likely to be affected) to petition and ballot to keep selection if that is what the majority wish. Government should not stand by and look the other way but support change with resources and evidence. Surely that is what any responsible government concerned with raising standards should do?

Not long ago at a meeting, a primary head from Kent, incensed by the effect of selection, invited the then Shadow Education Secretary Stephen Twigg to come to his school when the 11-plus results came out. I am not sure if the visit happened but it should be a diary date for any new Secretary of State for Education after May 2015. The conclusion must be that selection at 11 is a damaging and unnecessary feature of English education. Across the country there are successful comprehensives which were grammar schools years ago. There is no reason that the 163 selective schools in England could not become successful comprehensives. What is needed to end selection is the political will to move forward.

The Case for Grammar Schools

Charlotte Marten

Were grammar schools a species of flora or fauna they would be on the list of critically endangered species. Survivors of an earlier education system, some of England's remaining 163 grammar schools can trace their roots back to the late middle ages, to an era when education was the privilege of the rich and when monarchs and other wealthy benefactors, keen to ensure that poor boys had access to learning, could establish schools without reference to anyone. The educational landscape has developed considerably since then. Should grammar schools be consigned to the museum of educational history? It is my contention that the remaining grammar schools have a continuing and vital role to play in twenty-first century England's education system.

The educational landscape of England today is highly diverse: the creation of city technology colleges (CTCs), the specialisms, academy and free schools movements have created a richness of provision unthinkable in the 1960s and 1970s. This diversity is enriching and stimulating, something to celebrate and to treasure. I claim that there is a strong case for retaining and supporting the existing grammar schools as a part of this modern provision. In addition, I would argue that it is time to remove grammar schools from 'the political deep freeze' and consider planning a specialist provision for the most academically able in areas where there is a shortage of secondary places.[1]

One only has to open the newspapers in August the day after GCSE and A-level results are released to see evidence of how highly the 160,000 children who attend grammar schools achieve. Selective state schools dominate the results tables. The government's analysis of 2012 GCSE results shows that grammar school students are more likely to get five A*-Cs including English and maths than students in any other sector including the independent sector.[2] They are also much more likely to achieve the English Baccalaureate: in 2012, 68.2 per cent of grammar school students did this compared to 48.9 per cent in the independent sector and 16.4 per cent in the state sector as a whole, suggesting that the grammar school sector is adept at providing a broad academic curriculum.[3] Analysis of the government's 2013 key stage 5 (KS5) Performance Tables reveals that the average points score per entry at grammar schools was 233.5 QCA points. In England's state schools as a whole (including grammar schools) it was 211.3, more than two-thirds of an A-level grade lower.[4]

Of course, it could be argued that grammar schools start from a higher level of prior attainment so it is not surprising that students perform well. However this is not what the evidence suggests. Researchers from the University of Durham's Centre for Evaluation and Monitoring concluded that students in grammar schools achieve up to three-quarters of a grade more in each GCSE subject than peers with the same prior attainment in non-selective schools.[5] Analysis of the KS5 progress data for grammar schools for 2013 shows positive value-added scores for 81.1 per cent of selective schools demonstrating that in the vast majority of grammar schools students are not just achieving some impressive raw results but are making better progress than might normally be expected based on their prior attainment. Even opponents of selection acknowledge that the areas of the country which still have grammar schools have better A-level results than those that do not. Ironically, it is data like this which leads opponents of selection to argue that 'we need as many of our pupils as possible to benefit from a grammar school style education' whilst simultaneously arguing that the remaining grammar schools should become comprehensive.[6]

Grammar school students are the only category of school in the state sector that can challenge the independent sector when it comes to admission to Britain's most prestigious universities. It is still the case that many grammar school students are the first in their family to attend university. A Sutton Trust report on entry to Britain's 30 most prestigious universities published in 2011 showed that 48.2 per cent of students attending independent schools were accepted by these universities, as were 47.6 per cent of students attending state selective schools and 18 per cent of students attending non-selective state schools.[7] This is a much greater share than might be attributed to the selective nature of grammar schools given that they educate a mere five per cent of the secondary population. This success is due partly to the aspirational culture that exists in grammar schools; a culture which leads high-achievers attending grammar schools to be *five* times more likely to make two or more applications to a highly selective university compared to similarly high achieving students in the non-selective sector being three times more likely than other students to do so.[8] Access to the broad range of sources of careers advice and guidance that many grammar schools provide may also be a factor in students' decision making.[9]

Are the needs of our country's most able students being met in its non-selective schools? Ofsted suggests that they are not. Almost two-thirds of the primary students who attained national curriculum level 5 in English and maths at the end of their primary careers and who went on to attend a non-selective state school did not attain A*or A at GCSE in 2012. Twenty-seven per cent of these students scored less than a grade B.[10] Ofsted's 2013 survey 'The Most Able Students: Are they doing as well as they should in our non-selective secondary schools?' attributed this to poor identification of the most able students, poor support for the most able in four-fifths of lessons leading to a lack of challenge, irregular progress checks, a focus on C/D borderline students at GCSE and a failure to prepare well for the transition to A-level.[11] Critics of grammar schools would argue that Ofsted's sample (41 schools visited and data gathered from inspection of a further 109 schools) is too small to be representative. However, whilst the practices of only 150 non-selective secondary schools come in for detailed scrutiny, the headline data that was reported represented the 11-18 non-selective sector as a whole. This catered for 529,041 GCSE students in 2012 as opposed to 22,556 in the selective sector.

Our country needs all of its young people, including the most able, to achieve as well as they possibly can if we are to remain competitive in the global economy of the twenty-first century. Grammar schools have a long tradition of doing this successfully. Part of the reason for their success may lie in the impact of young people being with other high achieving students. The work of economists Damon Clark and Kirabo Jackson suggest that there are positive effects simply from attending a selective school. Jackson argues: 'The school selectivity effect can be directly attributed to the incoming achievement level of the peers.'[12] This would seem to conflict with Ofsted's 2013 findings which imply that the difference in outcome is connected to classroom practice. Clark, in turn, identifies long-run impacts as a result of attending a selective school, for example, on courses taken and the probability of university enrolment.[13] Newer research suggests that 'the selectivity effect is larger for girls than for boys' and that this may be because girls may be more responsive to peers than boys are.[14] Damon Clark and Emilia Del Bono identify positive impacts for women in particular in attending a selective school. In their longitudinal study focused on men and women born in the 1950s, they show that women who attended selective schools were more likely to get A-levels, have a higher income and a lower rate of fertility.[15] These findings are corroborated in a research paper by Simon Burgess, Matt Dickinson and Lindsey Macmillan.[16] However, longitudinal studies should be treated with some caution in the context of educational structures. In 1947 38.7 per cent of the population attended grammar schools, by 1975 that had shrunk to just 9.8 per cent. What was true of a much larger sample in 1960 may not be true of today's young people. But, given the liberating effect of grammar schools in the past, it would seem foolhardy to discard them without a much more careful look at their role in transforming the lives of the nation's women and (by extension) the lives of the nation as a whole.

Critics of grammar schools argue that some of the underachievement of students in *non*-selective state schools must be laid at the door of selective schools who cream off the most able students. However, only 36 of the 152 local authorities in the country actually contain a grammar school. Even allowing for the magnetic effect of some 'super selective' schools, this means that large swathes of the country are entirely untouched by state school selection. The Sutton Trust's 2008 report 'Social Selectivity of State Schools' concluded that there was 'little evidence of significant "collateral harm" – at least academically – suffered by other schools because of grammar schools'.[17] The findings of Adele Atkinson, Paul Gregg and Brendon McConnell support this.[18] They found that students educated in grammar schools do substantially better than students with the same prior attainment in non-selective areas. Furthermore they claim that the disadvantage to children in the selective areas who do not attend a selective school is slight (half a GCSE grade point).[19] The researchers noted that there was a considerable benefit for poor children who gain a place at grammar school, and noted that if access to grammar schools could be widened then the case for keeping selective education would be greatly enhanced.[20] The National Foundation for Educational Research's Ian Schagen and Sandy Schagen, in turn, argue that there is a particular advantage gained by 'borderline' students (those of average ability and those just above average) in attending a grammar school.[21] Schagen and Schagen's analysis shows that borderline students performed at a higher level in key stage 3 tests than their peers in comprehensive schools; they also found that these students were more likely to be entered for higher-tier papers.[22] As the authors note, their findings pose an interesting challenge to all schools. How can we extend the benefits of the grammar school effect not only to other schools, but also to a wider ability range?

So, if there are tangible benefits for students in attending a grammar school in terms of raised attainment and aspiration, conferring long-term economic and social advantages, why is it that grammar schools form such a small part of the English education system? The answer lies in the politics of the 1960s and 1970s and in the argument that grammar schools are socially divisive.

One of the key arguments put forward by supporters of grammar schools for their retention is the contribution that grammar schools have made to social mobility. Writing in the *Guardian*, novelist D.J. Taylor described grammar schools satirically as 'a rope ladder' providing 'an escape route from the swamp' for the likes of Professors John Carey and Malcolm Bradbury.[23] Until the late 1960s grammar schools provided access to the academic education, essential for university entrance and for the glittering careers that lay beyond. All five of the British Prime Ministers who served between October 1964 and May 1997 were grammar school educated. In their heyday, when they educated nearly 38 per cent of the population, it was rather easier for grammar schools to make a contribution to social mobility.[24] Today's rising stars are less likely to have attended a grammar school: in 2012 just five per cent of secondary-aged students attended a grammar school.[25] Opponents of grammar schools argue that whilst grammar schools may have made a contribution to social mobility in the past, they now no longer do so.

Grammar schools are often accused of being the preserve of the sharp-elbowed middle classes who pay for private tuition in order to ensure that their children succeed in the 11-plus. With fees at independent day schools reaching as much as £21,000 per annum, the attraction of a free grammar school place is considerable.[26] Grammar schools have recently come in for criticism because analysis of their intakes indicates that a much lower percentage of students receiving free school meals attend grammar schools than there are recipients in the local population as a whole. This is perhaps not surprising as students in receipt of free school meals are much less likely than their peers to achieve level 5s in English and in maths (a broad proxy for the standard expected of grammar school students).[27] Liberal Democrat education minister David Laws recently challenged grammar schools to admit 'the same proportion of children on free school meals as in their local area'.[28] Whilst this seems rather unrealistic there is a broad acceptance amongst grammar school head teachers that more must be done to ensure that a grammar school education is accessible to all able children living within their catchments and not the exclusive preserve of some. Recruiting just two hundred more students in receipt of free school meals would end the bias in favour of non-free-school-meal students in grammar schools.

Opponents of grammar schools would do well to pay heed to the Sutton Trust's 2013 report 'Selective Comprehensives: The social composition of top comprehensive schools' and their 2008 report 'Social Selectivity of State Schools', which identified that just 17 of the 100 socially most selective state schools were grammar schools and that 50 of those non-selective schools were academically more selective than grammar schools.[29] The 2013 report highlights that the top 500 comprehensive schools have less than half the proportion of children eligible for free school meals than is the case nationally. The problem of social inclusion extends beyond the grammar school sector.

Grammar schools' commitment to social mobility can be seen in the changes that more than 30 schools have made to their admissions policies for 2015 in order to give priority in their oversubscription criteria to students in receipt of free school meals. Some schools have adjusted their pass marks for these students as a way of levelling the playing field. In Birmingham the King Edward VI Foundation has engaged in an extensive programme of outreach targeting primary schools in areas with a large percentage of students in receipt of free school meals. This programme has been designed to raise awareness of the whole range of schools to which students have access as well as to familiarise students with the requirements of the 11-plus examination. It is too early as yet to report on the outcome of this and other moves such as changes to tests to make them less susceptible to coaching.

Grammar schools play an important role in ensuring that the next generation of teachers is ready to enter the classroom. Schools like Lawrence Sheriff School (Warwickshire), The Crypt School (Gloucester), Dr Challoner's Grammar School (Buckinghamshire) and Sir Joseph Williamson's Mathematical School (Medway) have become teaching schools co-ordinating teacher training and facilitating the sharing of good practice across the region in which they are located. Grammar schools often provide teaching practice places for beginner teachers, helping them to develop their subject knowledge and providing an environment in which they can explore a broad variety of teaching tools. Standards of behaviour in grammar schools are frequently outstanding and this means that young teachers are able to focus on developing their repertoire of teaching techniques and their subject knowledge. The pace of learning is rapid for both students and teachers. A number of grammar school head teachers have chosen to take on a systems leadership role, becoming either a national or a local 'leader of education', helping to induct new head teachers and supporting colleagues in schools which require improvement. Elsewhere colleagues have embraced the sponsorship of a local secondary school, forming multi-academy trusts with the intention of raising standards and developing practice in both schools. The Skinners' School in Kent and Torquay Boys' Grammar School are good examples of this. Both schools have sponsored local secondary schools with the idea of providing outstanding educational opportunities to local students. With over 70 per cent of grammar schools graded outstanding by Ofsted, their leaders are well placed to contribute to the development of the system as a whole. Whilst there are not so many of these leaders that the system would collapse without them, they do nonetheless make a vital contribution to raising academic standards and challenging underachievement. Grammar schools were enthusiastic supporters of the Specialist Schools' Trust. In their role as specialist schools, they set up a broad variety of community projects designed to inspire young people about learning and to raise standards across the local area. Some of these projects have survived the loss of the funding that previously accompanied them and continue to thrive. So, for example, in my own school come summer, it is not unusual to find science labs full to bursting with primary pupils engaged in trying to solve various fictitious crimes using a variety of different forensic techniques, whilst across town, the boys' grammar school offers engineering problem-solving activities. Activities like these are important in raising aspiration and creating an awareness of new possibilities. Grammar schools are team players rather than isolated ivory towers. Quietly and unobtrusively they are making a significant contribution to the attainment of our nation's young people, making a difference, not just now but for the future.

It is unrealistic to pursue a return to the educational policies of the past. Any proposal to open a new grammar school is likely to reignite the sterile debate of grammar versus comprehensive that dominated the 1960s and 1970s, and may only result in the destabilisation of existing local provision. Instead of wasting our energies on an ideological argument in these areas, it would be much more productive to look constructively at educational provision in areas of the country where there are insufficient secondary places. A planned provision that includes a specialist provision for the academically able could be truly transformational. It might form a strand within a school (as it does in partially selective 'bilateral' schools) or it might be the product of careful setting (as recently suggested by the Conservative Party). Both planning and provision itself could benefit enormously from the knowledge and expertise that grammar schools have, particularly with regard to preparing students to make a successful transition to university.

Grammar schools have a key role to play in the education system of the twenty-first century, as part of a diverse provision. They are skilled at delivering a particular kind of academic education. They have a role to play in helping to challenge underachievement and tackling inequality. In today's global knowledge-based economy they are helping to ensure Britain's continuing prosperity. It is time to abandon the entrenched positions of the debate about schooling in the 1970s and work collaboratively for a diverse secondary provision with grammar schools included, in which there is a relentless focus on all children's achievement and which ensures that no child gets left behind.

(Un)natural Selection

Peter Tait

It is naïve to approach the subject of selection without recognising that the process of selecting the most able children for admission to high-achieving schools has long been a mainstay of our education system. The culling of grammar schools in the 1970s and subsequent fall in Britain's standing in international rankings over recent years has reinforced the views of those who feel we need to become more selective, not less. After all, the argument runs, in any society, selection by a pre-determined set of criteria is an inherent part of life's process, whether it be in determining university places or securing jobs. That journey is inevitable and happens using criteria applied competitively through some form of assessment – unless, of course, that society resorts to social engineering or giving preference to particular social or ethnic groups according to factors other than the ability to do the job (or fulfil the demands of a course). It is what we are used to.

Except that having spent half of my teaching career in New Zealand, it was not what I was used to. There, almost all schools, state and independent, are non-selective and, even though independent schools have much the same percentage of pupils as in the UK, they provide no tangible advantage in terms of future job success over their peers from state schools. Even though the first examinations that have any significance are not until Year 11, this system has produced many leaders both at home and abroad, including a significant number of prominent academics now based in this country, who have all benefited from the greater opportunities afforded from being allowed to develop at their own pace.

In addressing the subject, I will focus on three key issues. First, to ask the question as to how long the process of selection can be delayed in order to allow children to mature and develop and for other factors to even out before making the decision to divide a cohort. In asking this question, it is important to note that it is not selection per se that is on trial, for that is an inevitable and necessary part of life, but whether selective entry based on academic testing when used by schools (and especially in the primary years), best serves our children and our society or is anything other than a convenience. Second, to look at the criteria used in such selection and ask whether the end result of entrance tests caters for children and young adults who are carefully prepared and able to pass examinations, but which fail a large percentage of the population without such advantages. And third, to look at the social, emotional and physical cost of driving children too far, too soon, and the toxic underbelly that can result from early selection, something too rarely acknowledged especially by selective schools.

To address all three issues, we need to look at what passes as 'education' and what we have come to accept, often unwittingly, as a process of selection for reasons of expedience. It is not an easy argument for those used to associating selection with academic rigour and can be used to fuel our prejudice against any change by labelling it as 'dumbing down'. We all deal best with what we know which makes it difficult to consider that the system of selecting children for schools by a series of tests as young as three may be inherently flawed. Such a process is particularly widespread in independent and grammar schools, where pressure for places can mean that the level for entry can be as high as the marketplace will tolerate, (whether this is in the best interests of the child or not). Not only do we accept this as normal, but we celebrate those schools that produce the best results, regardless of how easy their journey has been. Those that defend selection use a range of arguments as to why this process is necessary, usually centred around the contention that it enables the most able to be taught at a level that maximises their natural ability and that each and every child is offered an education commensurate with their ability. Which sounds sensible at first glance, but on closer examination is anything but.

Any system based on selection presupposes that ability is fixed in time and that it can be easily measured. We therefore have the situation in London and the South East, where children are often selected at pre-school age when their abilities have more to do with the level of maturation, of readiness, and the home situation than anything else. It presupposes, amongst other presumptions, that such results wouldn't be achieved by a system of setting and streaming in otherwise non-selective schools. It also presupposes that such a system of educational apartheid produces better all-round students rather than the expected high grades and has a wider benefit for society.

In essence, the selection criteria used in almost all instances are there to help identify the brightest and most able pupils, regardless of other considerations, including socioeconomic factors, maturation or dependence on external factors such as tutoring. It is a process with no defined ceiling that ultimately produces children layered in different strata based, in the main, on examination or test results. The pressure placed on children, parents and schools at each point where selective criteria are involved is often irrational and can have little to do with education per se, but everything to do with enabling selective schools and universities to sort the wheat from the chaff. Except it doesn't. What it produces is children and young adults who have been placed in schools where expectations and the standard of teaching are high and examination results are impressive, but that often lack the ability to intellectually scrap with or learn off children with different abilities. Of more concern than those it isolates and benefits, however, is that the system rejects those whose trajectory is slower, who take longer to mature, who lack the support and preparation yet who, in time, could well be better students, given a greater opportunity and lead-in time. Children don't need to be pushed as far as they can endure at an increasingly young age since this often results in considerable collateral damage, usually not recognised until later. This is not education. This is a form of Social Darwinism in which the strongest survive, but only while they remain in the comfort zone of the like-minded. Whether these children develop the resources or resourcefulness to cope once the tutors and teachers undo the ropes is far from assured; in essence, what they have been taught is how to maximise their performance in exams whether this is healthy or not or whether it curtails their intellectual development; what they have not been taught is how to relate to a range of intelligences and abilities, to mix with those not the same as them, whether in aptitude, background, ability or aspiration. Such a process does not allow the child to show what has been learned outside academia, offers few opportunities to share any original ideas or conversational skills and only a muted ability to engage beyond the four walls of prescribed thought. George Orwell recognised such entry tests as a 'sort of confidence trick' in which the student's job was to 'give an examiner the impression that you knew more than you did' dependent as much on the skill of teachers to teach the techniques required to pass exams than anything else.[1] It was, and is, the system that favours the advantaged rather than the able, and its cull of talented children is lamentable. If we are to get the best from all our children and thereby increase social mobility and raise aspirations, we should start by fixing a system of school entry that does huge damage to the social fabric of our society and, worse, discriminates against the majority of the school population.

Selection lies at the heart of this form of education. In itself, it does nothing to encourage reflective thinking, intellectual initiative, the ability to work in teams, the need for highly developed communications skills or to learn to relate to people of different abilities. Its focus is on outcomes, on producing results, on raising standards by a very limited measure, even if such results are not enduring and divide communities. In running a school for many years, I have always had one simple premise, one overriding question I have asked myself at any point in time, viz., what is the best education my school can provide for its children (that is, each and every child)? This is distinct from the question so often asked by heads which is: 'What are the best results I can get for my school?' While the two questions are not mutually exclusive, between them there is a gulf that raises the one overwhelming question, of how we judge the success or otherwise of an education. Do we take it from grades achieved through a series of entrance exams, SATs, Common Entrance, GCSE and the like which measure a specific ability to pass tests, often under duress; or by an education that is inclusive and which produces successful, adaptable, globally aware adults committed to life-long learning? For one of the more disgraceful acts of selective education is the annual culling of students after GCSE on the grounds that either the school cannot properly cater for them (for which, shame on the school), or worse, that they will affect the school's results and therefore, its academic standing.

There are, of course, other ways to cater for a range of ability within institutions, notably by setting (placing students of similar ability in classes for particular subjects), streaming (separating students by class groups based on an average ability or predetermined criteria) or better differentiation by better trained teachers. And while I do not suggest that streaming should be seen in the same light as selection, (particularly if such systems are open, flexible and constantly reviewed), the practice does again tend to 'fix' students in bands, which directly affects progress, as research on how students and teachers respond to different expectations has clearly shown. Many of the arguments put forward in favour of streaming suggest, for instance, that children get better results in streamed schools; that they can be stretched, if able, and can be better supported if not (for instance, if they have learning difficulties); and that teachers achieve better results when teaching pupils of similar abilities. There is, inevitably, a corollary to each of these claims, but in essence the case for streaming is founded on the assertion that the process results in higher levels of achievement for all children, commensurate with their ability – which would be fine if ability was fixed, if the separation of children of different ability was proven to be beneficial to all and other factors such as work ethic, levels of maturation, attitude and background didn't tell us otherwise. And therein lies a multitude of problems, not least in determining what constitutes a good education and at what age these judgements can be made. Even as a means of producing the best academic results, it is flawed, as evidence from non-selective, non-streamed school systems would indicate. Setting, in turn, has the merit of not separating students from their peers across the board, while allowing for specific abilities and talents to be nurtured. Unlike streaming, setting is more likely to be fluid, especially with common assessment across the entire cohort and has much to commend it as a way of meeting children's educational needs although, again, it should not be introduced too early in a child's schooling where separation can have a generally deleterious effect.

If we take a closer look at the process of selective schooling, which can start as young as age three, what we find is that selection usually reflects the degree of parental attachment and support rather than academic potential. Sadly, once these very first decisions are made which result in divisions being made between cohorts of children, it is hard to alter the template or reverse the process. These decisions could, in future, be aided and abetted by planned baseline tests in numeracy and literacy for four-year-olds which is no doubt why they have received so much comment from the teaching profession. Tests and assessments that focus largely on targets and attainment at such a young age can have a huge impact on establishing the corridors of learning for children which will determine the rest of their lives. Yet the validity of this data is very questionable. With SATs tests the pressures are similar although the older the child is, the less impact the process is likely to have. This is even more so at age 13 when entry tests are widely used for gaining admission into many independent schools. The question, however, is not whether segregation works or is fair, but whether it is actually necessary. The rationale for many independent and selective state schools is simple: by demanding that pupils are at a high level prior to entering their schools, their schools are able to secure a disproportionate share of Oxbridge and Russell Group places by which measure they can actively market themselves. As a business case for schools, it is hard to dispute, even ignoring the obvious caveat that pupils need to have been extended through the early years even to be accepted by such schools. As a result, entry levels are at record levels, especially in London and the South East, leading to a boom in tutoring and a commensurate rise in emotional and physiological problems amongst children as they strive to compete out of their comfort zone to achieve a measure that, sadly, has less to do with education than securing a place at an oversubscribed school.

So attached are we to league tables we often avoid asking the obvious questions about whether the process actually works. Does the business case, for instance, override the moral responsibility of schools to provide an appropriate level of education? What happens to those children who happen to reach their potential later in life? Is there any social fall-out caused by the separation of students based simply on their ability to pass examinations? What is the value-added measure of students at highly selective schools over less selective or even non-selective schools? Does selection produce better students – or better adults? Or is our examination system producing clones for the sake of expediency? Apart from the obvious flaw of using data based on examination results to determine what is a 'good' school for a particular child, league tables often show no more than how selective a school is. When schools advertise themselves by their results with no reference to their selection process, therefore, they are complicit in a process that serves to deceive. Of course, selective schools will do well, and the more selective the better. This is what selection delivers. Which is why they should not be judged on the number of places they obtain at Russell Group universities or the like, but how many graduate, how many go on to get jobs, and how many have the emotional intelligence to match their academic achievements to bring to their future relationships and families.

Schools use a variety of increasingly sophisticated tests to select their pupils although a few, such as Eton, now rely on interviews or other more appropriate means of assessment as much as data. Durham University's Centre for Evaluation and Monitoring has become associated with many of these often bespoke tests, but too often their services are sought by schools as a means of convenience because other measures would take more time and effort, even though using such data alone is fraught with danger. Looking at early attempts to measure intelligence, the widespread use of the IQ test in the first half of the twentieth century came about for a variety of reasons, including the need to identify mental retardation in children. One of the pioneers, French psychologist Alfred Binet, a key developer of what later became known as the Stanford-Binet Intelligence Scales, however, came to the conclusion that intelligence was multifaceted, but came under the control of practical judgement 'otherwise known as good sense, practical sense, initiative, or the faculty of adapting oneself'.[2] Intellect on its own is not a measure of potential success; sadly, it is often the opposite, as Binet was to evidence himself when his tests were used by the eugenics movement in the USA as a proof of intellectual disability, resulting in thousands of American women, most of them poor African Americans, being forcibly sterilised based on their scores on IQ tests.[3]

The reliance on data and results without placing them into a proper context is undoubtedly one of the problems. I have been in education long enough to regard IQ scores with caution. I am even reluctant for teachers to know the IQ of their pupils and most certainly parents. This isn't some form of denial, but simply the effect that data has on the way we judge people, creating a glass ceiling of expectation. IQ taken on its own is a poor measure of ability or future success. I have known too many people with high IQs who achieved nothing of note, who lacked any sense of purpose or responsibility and whose emotional intelligence quotient (EQ) was sadly deficient. Indeed there is evidence that very many 'intelligent' people are deficient in other areas of life, particularly those who have had their education in the narrow corridor of academia, who struggle in relationships and in making moral judgements and who end up in positions of power and influence. Invariably, such people are the product of selective schooling. On the other hand, I have also known a similar number whose IQ was in the average band, or even below, but who more than compensated for a lack of IQ points by displaying Binet's 'practical judgement' who overcame whatever number was attached to them. They are often the high-achievers, achieving the balance between intelligence and the ability to do something with it.

One of the arguments put forward for selection is that it promotes academic excellence, that any deviation from such an approach would result in a drop in standards and that departure from selection is an example of the liberal approach to education that has ruined the country's schools. That is simply not true. There is no reason why education should not be every bit as rigorous in non-selective schools, especially with a judicious use of setting and streaming. It is not lowering standards and expectations, but the opposite. It is, however, likely to be more challenging for teachers who are not equipped to teach a wider range of abilities, who can only operate in the closeted world of selective schools and whose strengths are, sadly, restricted to teaching to the test. The training of teachers to improve the differentiation of their lessons by employing the different abilities and intelligences of their pupils to complement, create and enhance the learning of all, is still given too little place in teacher training. If we want to improve our schools, improving the craft of our teachers is a good place to start.

So much of current practice is based on the assumption that by selecting children earlier, we end up with better educated – not just more knowledgeable – adults. Hand in hand with the disquiet caused by league tables, the competition for places at top schools and universities, the calls to start formal education earlier and the referred pressures placed upon teachers and schools to deliver, however, has come an epidemic of stress-related diseases, eating disorders and mental illness. We ignore the statistics at our peril and the fact that an estimated 80,000 children in Britain suffer from severe depression,[4] that the number of children with sexually transmitted diseases has nearly doubled in the last decade,[5] and that the number of teenagers who self-harm has increased by 70 per cent in the last two years, should be of paramount concern.[6] Add to that, children struggling with eating disorders and body image and with the residue of family breakdowns, and the priorities change, along with our definition of what constitutes a balanced and successful education. Is this reality really any surprise when we have an approach to education that is focused on driving up standards without ever appearing to consider how such a thing might be best achieved or even the fundamental question of what, in this day, represents the best education for our children? How do we go about building character and resilience, growing aspirations, and having less emphasis placed on summative exams which can stifle curiosity and independent thought? What place does discipline – including self-discipline – have in learning? What is the best mix of knowledge and skills? Naturally, we should insist on excellence and try to improve examination results – but not at any price. Instead, we should be looking at how we measure children – and why.

In evaluating whether we are placing our priorities in the right areas, we should look at the disjoint between what schools are producing, often by placing children under duress, and what employers, universities and, dare I say, society wants. We should focus on addressing key issues like class size, classroom discipline, teacher training (and re-training), as well as the amount of funding lost to bureaucracy, and look to move the focus in education from demanding more from children in the way of time and tenuous results to asking more of them as people. We need to give our schools some social capital. At present, it appears there is no time for deviation in our quest for better exam results, no time for exploration, no time for the commensurate social development that needs to take place, no time to allow for readiness or for challenging the scurrilous idea that education is confined to the walls of a classroom. Parents and children are weary of hearing comments about how initiative, curiosity and time for collaborative learning are all sacrificed because 'they are not being examined'. And for what? Are our children at 18 better motivated or better educated? Or just better drilled and tutored, but in fact, less-rounded, less resilient, less inclined to want to keep learning? As a consequence, we have children being blamed for not working harder, cynical about what lies ahead for them; teachers being lampooned for the lack of effectiveness in raising performance and aspirations; and schools sacrificing children on the altar of league tables for their own ends. All of this is a disaster. We seem to be looking everywhere and nowhere: the Far East, Australasia, Finland, as if there is some trick to it. There is not, for we know that education is simple: it is about the effectiveness of the engagement; developing attitudes and a good work ethic; raising expectations; inspiring and facilitating ideas; and setting students new challenges and the intellectual freedom to deliver. It is about engendering self-discipline; it is about the quality of what is delivered and acquired, not the quantity; it is about starting children on a lifelong journey, not subjecting them to a marathon, before their brains and bones are set. We should focus more on character and values, nurturing creativity and initiative and less on prescribed knowledge if we are really wanting to get the best from our children.

Academically the early pressure placed on children raises several issues and it is right that we question the presumption that early selection benefits children and is a requirement for later academic success. In a novel based on the life of Katherine Mansfield, C.K. Stead wrote in the person of Bertrand Russell: 'People of my sort… have a lot to unlearn. Too much is laid on us too early. We grow up fettered'.[7] There is much to be said for not cluttering the mind, for not forcing the excessive acquisition of knowledge and encouraging children to think and question rather than to putting children under pressure at a young age simply to provide a mechanism for selection. There is considerable evidence from very successful school systems, such as in Sweden, Finland, Denmark, Belgium, Canada, New Zealand and Australia that less selective systems work at least as well as a more rigorous selective system, in academic terms alone as well as producing a more cohesive society.

And finally, what are the lessons for parents? Do not be seduced by schools that are selective based solely on an entrance examination. Treat league tables with caution as sometimes all they reflect is how selective schools are. Avoid schools that refuse siblings for the sake of a few percentage points or who cull at the end of GCSEs. Ask how they differentiate their teaching (and setting and streaming could be part of this).

Good schools use interviews as a key part of their process. Be wary of schools that lack the staff to be able to differentiate (and especially those who employ staff based on the universities they attended rather than their ability to teach); ensure your children are comfortable in the schools that they are going to, for they need to be challenged, but not overwhelmed. Look for schools that measure their performance by value-added or by the breadth of what they offer. Whether schools stream and set their pupils is fine so long as classes and sets are not set in stone, but allow for development (and regression). Make sure their selection process, if they have one, is not based solely on a desire to move up the league tables for that is one way to ensure your child will not get the education that will sustain them throughout their lives. After all, the best measure of education is the skills, knowledge, attitudes and values that survive formal schooling, not by how much is learned, jettisoned and forgotten on the way. The happiest, most successful adults are those who have been challenged and enthused by their education, not downtrodden by it.

Why Is Selection by Wealth Better Than Selection by Ability?

Peter Hitchens

Enemies of the grammar schools have a favourite argument. What about those who fail to get into them, and are condemned to 'secondary moderns'? They treat us to tear-stained reminiscences of the sad day each year when the 11-plus divided brother from sister, neighbour from neighbour, friend from friend. The lucky winners skipped off in their blazers to a bright future. The miserable losers crept shamefacedly to a sink school, doomed to be hewers of wood and drawers of water. Actually, this day still takes place, all over England, every year at the start of March. It is called 'national offer day', and it is when parents find out if they have got their children into their 'first choice' secondary school. Officially, about one in five won't, but the truth is far worse than that. It is risky to aim too high, as failure to get into a top school will often rule you out of a place at a middling one, and send you sliding down the snake of misfortune. So many parents cautiously opt for a 'first choice' that is in fact nothing of the kind, settling for second or third best for fear of having their children exiled to the worst school in the town.

Most towns and cities in England have secondary schools that are known by the well-informed to be the best. Many are former grammar schools and quite a few are single-sex. The easiest way to get your children into them is to live close to them, and estate agents will tell you that such schools can add an average of £54,000 to the price of a house, in the capital.[1] In some cases it is more like £200,000. London left-wing parents are particularly good at this Game of Homes. It is also often a question of faith, real or alleged. Too bad if you don't have well-informed parents, who can navigate the complex entry procedures of the better schools. Take The Grey Coat Hospital (Church of England Comprehensive Academy for Girls), the elite secondary school favoured for their daughters by fellow-Blairites Harriet Harman and Michael Gove. Its admissions rules go on for pages, and give great privileges to those who show the outward signs of Christian faith. As there is no way to check the inner truth, points are awarded for observable levels of piety, work and commitment, such as turning up for services, contributing to the parish magazine and sitting on committees. (This is rather contrary to the spirit of Luke 18:10-14, in which Christ prefers the genuinely repentant to the ostentatious worshipper.) The Grey Coat Hospital also selects its sheep from its goats through the use of a catchment area so precise that it takes 134 words to explain. Here is a sample: 'Where it is necessary to differentiate between applicants living in flats using the same street entrance, priority will be given to the applicant(s) living closest to the ground floor and then by ascending flat number order.'[2] This sort of thing is not confined to church schools. One non-religious former girls' grammar school in London has a catchment area which currently extends 1,230 yards from the school gate, a measurement that does wonders for property prices in a few favoured streets nearby, and has caused at least one millionaire New Labour power couple to move house at great expense to secure good schooling for their daughters without committing the socialist sin of paying actual fees. If anyone can work out the true moral difference between these two forms of buying privilege, I should like to know what it is.

Thus can the whole course of a child's life be decided, by a parent's willingness, sincerely or not, to press their teeth on the Communion wafer, their readiness to warble in the church choir, their ability to afford to live sufficiently close to the school gate, or even their prescient cunning in choosing the ground-floor flat rather than one higher up the building. I could go on. These procedures, arbitrary, elaborate, labyrinthine and ever-changing, are well-known to the pushy and sharp-elbowed. They are baffling to almost everyone else. Forget jokes about putting children down for Eton at birth. To get into some of these alleged comprehensives it is necessary to start house-hunting before you are even pregnant. The bright child of a poor home, whose parents know little of schooling and perhaps care less, will seldom if ever penetrate through this thicket of trickery and self-aggrandisement to the best state secondary schools. And yet the enemies of grammar schools defend this system of secret knowledge, privilege and (often) false piety, as being fairer than open selection by ability. Perhaps that is because it is fairer to them, personally. Perhaps it is because it allows them to obtain all the advantages of the old grammar schools, while not in any way challenging the egalitarian comprehensive system or threatening their political or media careers. All parents are equal, but some are a lot more equal than others.

There's no doubt that the pre-1965 system had many faults. There were too few grammar schools in general, and especially in some parts of the country. There were far too few grammar school places for girls. An interesting result of this shortage was that by the mid-1960s, some secondary modern pupils were winning good A-levels and getting into university, both achievements rather more difficult than they are today. Few of the technical schools that had been planned and promised in the 1944 Education Act had ever been built. Many primary schools in poorer areas were not as good as they should have been at bringing on talent. No doubt the quality of grammar schools varied, and there was too little help for children from poor homes who wanted to stay in full-time education. Even so, the grammars themselves worked well in several important ways. None of their faults were fixed by their abolition, and all of them could have been addressed *without* their abolition.

The 1966 Franks Report into Oxford University, published at the very end of the pre-comprehensive era, recorded that in 1938-9, private school pupils had won 62 per cent of places at that university.[3] A further 13 per cent were won by direct grant schools, independent schools which took large numbers of bright state pupils in return for government or local authority payments. Just 19 per cent came from other state schools, presumably all grammar schools at that time. The rest were from abroad, or educated at home. By 1958-9 (14 years after the Butler Education Act created the national selective system and made grammar schools more widely available), the private school share was down to 53 per cent, direct grants up to 15 per cent and state grammars up to 30 per cent.[4] By 1964-5, private schools were down again to 45 per cent, direct grants up to 17 per cent and grammars up to 34 per cent.[5] How much further this revolution might have gone, we will never know. It was abruptly terminated by Anthony Crosland and Margaret Thatcher in their bipartisan dissolution of grammar schools, just as it was really gathering pace. The direct grant schools survived for a while longer, but were casually wiped out by Fred Mulley (more famous for falling asleep next to the Queen during an air show) in October 1975.

Was this burst of meritocracy just a feature of our post-war society, as some have suggested? I do not think so. Interesting figures suggest that the effect would have continued, if the schools had survived. In Northern Ireland, which still selects at 11 by ability, the university chances of a child from a poor home are now almost one-third greater than those of his or her equivalent in largely comprehensive England, and almost 50 per cent greater than in fully-comprehensive Scotland (according to figures supplied by the independent Higher Education Statistics Agency).[6] It is reasonable to suppose that the pre-1965 mainland grammar system (including Scotland's parallel system of academies) had a similar effect. More generally, a recent study of European schools has produced some very interesting results, worrying for those on the Left who believe selection is bad for the poor. Several continental countries still maintain selective state secondaries, and Germany has recently successfully restored them in the former German Democratic Republic (which, being Communist, was almost wholly comprehensive). This happened, in the states of the former East Germany, by popular demand. It is an interesting disproof of the repeated claim that 'you can't turn the clock back'. The survey, conducted across Europe by France's National Institute for Demographic Studies, actually set out to prove that selective education discriminated against children from poor backgrounds. But it found that, when children were taught according to ability, family wealth had almost no influence on their achievements. By contrast, in non-selective systems, a poor background did influence outcomes, with British pupils doing particularly badly on this scale.[7] The study, (published in the *European Sociological Review*) reached its conclusions by examining the reading performance of tens of thousands of 15-year-olds across 22 countries. So it is reasonable to say that, whatever was wrong with the pre-1965 secondary school system, destroying the grammar schools was not the cure. The policy of annihilating the grammars reminds me of Evelyn Waugh's response when news was brought to him that surgeons had removed a non-malignant tumour from some part of Randolph Churchill. 'How typical of the medical profession', he said, 'to have rummaged through the whole of Randolph, found the only part that was not malignant, and removed it.'[8]

Another much-used argument against grammars is the accurate contention that the few remaining academically selective secondaries are middle-class fortresses, with a low take-up of free school meals. This is perfectly true. But it is a consequence of the *abolition* of a national selective system, not an argument against such a system itself. The middle-class stronghold in selective secondaries proves nothing except that the middle-classes will fight very hard indeed to get an education worth at least £100,000 in taxed income. They will hire tutors, send their children to expensive preparatory schools and move into cramped houses in areas they can ill afford. None of this would be necessary if there were a national system of grammar schools. The remaining grammars are hopelessly oversubscribed because there are too few of them. The same is true of the secretly selective elite schools which exist where grammar schools don't, and it is not even mitigated by the continuing possibility that the child of a poor home might penetrate the screen of privilege. But the take-up of free meals in these schools tends not to be criticised by egalitarian leftists, because that would draw attention to the very large number of privileged middle-class families who have made cunning use of them. These objectors are also very reluctant to discuss the general destructive effect on state and private education which has followed the abolition of a national selective system. This may be the clearest sign that the comprehensive system has brought about a fall in all school standards. One of the saddest effects of this is that many private and state schools can call themselves 'excellent' because they regularly harvest sheaves of high grades in public examinations. But in fact there could well be huge differences between these schools, which modern examinations do not detect because they are hostile to or uninterested in excellence, and instead interested only in 'qualifications' for their own sake. They compress all reasonably high achievers into a single top grade, and allow children to pass who would until recently have failed. It is amazing how often defenders of the egalitarian system will defend it by saying that it has led to many more children possessing 'qualifications'. When challenged to show that these 'qualifications' are worth anything, or actually qualify their holders for anything, they fall silent or change the subject. As with all vast egalitarian projects, from collectivisation upwards, the statistics ultimately become more important than the truth, and end up concealing it.

There is little doubt that general levels of secondary education have fallen since selection on merit was abandoned. It is now 14 years since the Engineering Council revealed the results of a ten-year survey of undergraduates entering maths, science and engineering courses.[9] All were given an identical, unchanging test. This showed that, as these entrants' A-level grades had risen, their mathematical understanding had declined. Students who had narrowly failed their A-levels in 1991 had actually scored higher in the Council's tests than those who obtained 'C' grade passes seven years later.[10] Durham University mounted a similar exercise, giving a general ability test to its first-year students over a long period.[11] As Jenni Russell wrote in the *Guardian* 11 years ago, 'The results show that students of the same ability are now achieving two A-level grades higher in every subject than they were 15 years ago.'[12] The reality of grade inflation (shamefully denied by the education establishment for years, but now grudgingly admitted, even by them, to have taken place) was in fact quite evident very early on in the comprehensive experiment.

In October 1975 Raymond Baldwin, a member of Manchester's Education Committee, warned of a 'great comprehensive gamble' as GCE results in merged schools declined in that city.[13] Two months before, the *Daily Mail* had reported a severe fall in the GCE performances of schools in Liverpool, following comprehensive reorganisation in that city.[14] Sheffield's experience was similar. In a report in November 1974 the *Daily Telegraph* noted that Sheffield had experienced a 'gradual decline in the percentage of comprehensive school pupils succeeding in GCE examinations'.[15] Pupils at the about-to-be-abolished direct grant schools, meanwhile, showed 'a constant increase in GCE success rates'. But at about that time, the grading system of O-levels was altered, so that candidates who would previously have failed were now awarded pass certificates graded 'D' and 'E'. Even this did not manage to conceal the continuing fall in exam scores, which eventually led to a further dilution – the creation of the GCSE in 1987. This wholly different type of examination makes it impossible to compare today's secondary school performance directly with that of the old selective system. It is tempting to speculate that this was one of the aims of those who introduced it. But the Engineering Council and Durham University surveys both show that a measurable decline has taken place in the period following the abolition of selection by ability. Claims that the evidence for decline is based on nothing more than anecdote are simply false.

None of the facts above are particularly difficult to obtain, nor will they come as much of a surprise to anyone who has been either a school pupil or a parent of school-age children during the past 40 years. There is no doubt that English state and private education has experienced a revolution in that period. Not all of it resulted from the abolition of selection. Harold Wilson's expansion of teacher training in the late 1960s greatly changed the teaching profession. When I was an education reporter in the late 1970s, the (then) socially conservative *Daily Telegraph* was still crammed with advertisements for teaching posts. Now, most of this recruitment is done through the *Guardian,* and the *Daily*

Telegraph has adjusted smoothly to the age of drug decriminalisation and extra-marital sex. Even if the grammar schools had survived in large numbers, they would by now be very different places from the cane-haunted, mortar-board infested establishments of 1965. But then the same is true of the German gymnasiums. Even in conservative Bavaria, they have relaxed a little, but they still provide an excellent education, compared with our comprehensives.

All this is a rather cautious prelude to a sort of cry of pain. I have striven to rebut in detail the standard arguments of those who continue (against all facts and reason) to pretend that no harm was done by the closing of the grammar schools. As it happens, it is clear from Anthony Crosland's own book *The Future of Socialism* (recently re-published) that the man who wrecked state education had almost no idea what he was doing, and wholly misjudged the likely outcomes of his own policies. But the worst thing about this debate is that it is completely ignored in mainstream politics. The Left have their own egalitarian reasons for wishing to shut it off. They actually banned the creation of any new grammar schools in David Blunkett's School Standards and Framework Act.[16] Since then, they have been working hard to minimise selection by ability at the English and Welsh universities, putting pressure on them to make social as well as educational judgements and making public attacks on the ancient universities where selection by ability is still strong (such as Gordon Brown's ill-informed assault on Magdalen College, Oxford, over the non-admission of the state-school pupil Laura Spence).

The passion of the Left for comprehensive education is such that at least one former Labour MP (I will not name him because I find his behaviour almost admirable) claims to have attended a comprehensive school when he could not have done. The school involved, long ago merged, was at the time a secondary modern. But I feel quite differently about Frances O'Grady, now the General Secretary of the Trades Union Congress. O'Grady allowed the *Guardian* newspaper to say in 2012 that she had attended 'Milham Ford Comprehensive' in Oxford.[17] This is not exactly accurate. When she arrived there, in 1971, it was still a girls' grammar school. Like most of those who entered grammar schools during their transition into comprehensives, O'Grady is likely to have benefited from a selective education, in a 'grammar stream' until the end of her schooling. In fact (largely thanks to pressure from Muslim parents) Milham Ford survived as Oxford's last single-sex girls' state secondary until quite recently. I don't recollect it ever describing itself as a 'comprehensive' (few schools do, but see below). Had it really been a 'comprehensive' when she entered it, one has to wonder if O'Grady would now be in charge of the TUC. It is easy enough to see why a trade union official might fudge this matter. But far more significant is the behaviour of Theresa May, the current Home Secretary, now being spoken of as a possible future leader of the Conservative Party. May annually tells the MPs' reference book *Dod's Parliamentary Companion*, that she attended 'Wheatley Park Comprehensive'.[18] In fact, when she arrived there (from a convent school) it was still very much 'Holton Park Girls' Grammar School'.[19] Like O'Grady, she would have been kept in a grammar stream during the school's merger with the nearby Shotover secondary modern. Again had she not been treated so, one has to wonder if she would have gone on (as she did) to Oxford and to the Cabinet. Again, I don't think Wheatley Park has ever actually described itself as a 'comprehensive'.

The Tory surrender to the comprehensive revolution has been one of the most interesting political developments of the last 20 years. As late as the 1990s, John Major (who attended a selective school) talked of having a grammar school in every town.[20] Michael Howard used to boast of his grammar school past in parliamentary tussles with the privately educated Tony Blair.[21] Nothing happened as a result of these promises and flourishes. But since the advent of David Cameron, even the rhetoric has altered. In May 2007 the Tory leader had a damaging public quarrel with Graham Brady MP, and many other members of his own party, over his decision to abandon past promises to build any new grammar schools. Presumably Cameron thought the question important enough to alienate quite large numbers of supporters (which it duly did). It is interesting to wonder why a Tory leader might be ready to do this. In fact it is one of the most startling political facts of modern times – and so one of the least examined – that nominal Conservatives have adopted socialist attitudes towards education. They have done this most especially by speaking and writing as if it is a self-evident virtue to send one's children to a state, rather than an independent school. Yet this could only be a virtue for a dogmatic egalitarian, which nominal Conservatives have never openly said they are. After all, a rich person who can afford fees and sends a child to a scarce good state school is actually depriving a poor family of that place. For a non-egalitarian this must at least be morally dubious, if not actually greedy and bad. Yet in December 2005, soon after becoming leader of his party, Cameron was asked if he wanted his children to attend state schools and replied: 'Yes, absolutely. I've got my eye on a particular one. I'll make my decision for my daughter based on my views as a parent not as a politician. That's the right thing to do. But I would like them to go to a local state school.'[22] Nobody seems to have asked him why. Soon after this he (alongside then-Education Secretary Michael Gove) had succeeded in inserting his children into a wholly untypical, picturesque and hugely oversubscribed Church of England primary school in Kensington, far from his home. In November 2012, Cameron went further still. He said:

> I would like my children to go to state schools, that's my intention, and I think what's happening in the state school system is really exciting. What we're seeing is something we should have seen years ago which is the flowering of more choice, more competition, more diversity and crucially, higher standards. I want my children to be part of that and I'm very heartened by what is happening. [23]

The assumption in all these words and actions was that there was some sort of special virtue inherent in sending a child to a state school. What virtue is that? For left-wingers, it is obvious. In the state system the classes mix, religion is weak or absent, the purpose is egalitarian. But for conservatives, the classes mix on the wrong terms. In the grammar schools, everyone aspires to middle-classness. In the comprehensives, they do not. The difference is clearly encapsulated by the way that middle-class children now speak with fake estuary accents whereas grammar school pupils, such as Margaret Thatcher and Joan Bakewell, took elocution lessons to acquire BBC voices. Michael Gove's journalist wife, Sarah Vine, explained in the *Daily Mail* why she wanted her daughter to go to a state school:

> The private sector is built on very different principles. Its agenda is a fundamentally selective one, based not only on ability to pay, but also on pupil potential. And it is also, let's face it, about snobbery. Of course the parents of private school children are paying for the best teachers and facilities. But let's be honest: they're also paying for their child to mix with the right kind of kids.[24]

The school she has chosen for this act of anti-snobbish social mixing is The Grey Coat Hospital, miles from the Goves' modest west London home. Though it (very unusually) describes itself as a 'comprehensive' on its freshly-painted signboard, it is a former girls' grammar school which has somehow managed to stay single-sex, and whose entry requirements go on for pages, so much so it would take a combination of Einstein and Thomas Aquinas to grasp their full meaning. Its official uniform supplier is Peter Jones of Sloane Square. It may disappoint her if she wants her daughter to mix very much with 'the wrong kind of kids'. When the Labour politician Harriet Harman chose it for one of her children some years ago, the *Daily Mirror* accurately described it as an 'elite' school.[25] Just 14 per cent of its pupils are eligible for free school meals, hardly enough poor girls to go round for serious inter-class mixing.[26] Had the Goves been really keen on egalitarian rough and tumble, and the mixing of the classes, they would surely have been better off picking Burlington Danes Academy, which is also an Anglican school and is a couple of minutes' walk from their front door. What is more, it has the former Education Secretary's personal warm approval. In 2011 Gove wrote a newspaper article in which he listed Burlington Danes among schools in which 'excellence is becoming a universal expectation, academic study a driving purpose'.[27] Later he numbered it among 'some superb state schools in disadvantaged areas generating fantastic results'.[28] He said of these schools:

> They do much better in exams than many schools, including private schools, in leafy areas. Their students win places at Oxbridge on merit. All because their heads, from the moment any child arrives, refuse to accept excuses for under-performance.[29]

Why not then choose this paradise, and be spared the tedious shopping trips to Sloane Square for uniform? It can't be that it doesn't provide enough opportunities for social mixing. Tom Hodgkinson, a Burlington Danes parent, wrote in the *Independent* in March 2014 that nearly 70 per cent of its pupils were eligible for free meals, so sharply reducing the risk of snobbery.[30] He added 'Our daughter says some of her classmates were amazed she lived in a house with stairs.'

Somehow or other, the oddity of this decision by the Education Secretary at the time was not much explored by media who preferred to coo that he was the first Tory Education Secretary to send his child to a state secondary (actually even this is not true: Gillian Shephard did so 20 years before). But it does explain why the irresistible logic of selection by ability never seems to gain any supporters at the top of British politics or our great media empires. Left and right together have learned to use the state system to get their own children the advantages of grammar schools, without the need to face a difficult political battle. The recent movement for 'free schools' has created a similar escape route for the active and pushy middle-classes. It is hard to be sure whether these people actually imagine that their lives are normal. It would be much kinder to think that they do, for if they understand their own actions properly, they must know that they are actively abandoning the children of others to a fate they would not allow their own offspring to suffer.

Assessing the Damage: The Fracturing of Our Comprehensive System

Nic Dakin

Farewell Michael Gove, the most disliked Education Secretary of all time. There has been dancing in the corridors and classrooms of Britain. But that's just the teachers, classroom assistants and others who toil on the educational front line. The children have long since stopped dancing as creativity was squeezed from the curriculum by those who danced to his tune. After the Gove revolution what is the state of education today? What are the challenges for the future and how will success be judged? I ask this as our comprehensive system has been undermined, replaced with chaotic incoherence. In a landscape of ever more disparate provision, education today is increasingly selected and fragmented. Yet as this country moves further and further away from it, the case for comprehensive education becomes ever more apparent.

The best education systems are characterised by evolution not revolution. Look at the German system, bequeathed by Britain after the Second World War but built on with the same Teutonic efficiency that was on display at the World Cup in Brazil; a triumph of teamwork, grit and determination over egoism and individual self-importance. Sadly in this country, the incoming government in 2010 decided for its own narrow dogmatic reason to describe everything that had gone before as a failure and to assemble evidence to prove their argument. This led to a ground zero approach to policy where the received wisdom was that everything pre-2010 was wrong and a new architecture had to be built up from scratch to achieve future success. In contrast, a cross-party consensus around the nature and direction of education built the system in Finland that consistently tops the PISA league tables.[1] The UK reality was rather different. In 2010 secondary education had reached a reasonably sound place in terms of curriculum. Comprehensive education was delivering for youngsters and UK PLC. This was down to a government becoming less obsessed with targets, whilst school and college leaders together with innovative exam boards found ways to broaden the curriculum whilst strengthening rigour. BTEC Firsts and BTEC Nationals alongside GCSEs and A-/AS-levels helped drive up student achievement at the end of key stages 4 and 5. Importantly there were also improvements in maths and English as well as a greater vocational focus for those students that this benefited. However, there were still things that required improvement. Better connections were needed between the world of work and education, higher levels of youth employment needed to be achieved and there were issues in the primary curriculum. The Rose Review set a template for tackling these issues in partnership with schools and parents.[2] To then go down a prescriptive approach, as seen under the Coalition government, was naïve and flew in the face of letting schools choose what works for their communities, a strength of comprehensive primary and secondary education. The key thing is that, in choosing what works for their communities, schools have high expectations of the young people in their care. High expectations should be the order of the day, set by using data from schools with similar intakes that are succeeding in hitting new heights.

The ideological imposition of the English Baccalaureate (EBacc) on the key stage 4 curriculum and an equally ideological approach to giving some A-levels greater importance as 'facilitating subjects' has been flawed. Ironically there is a strong consensus on having a debate around which subjects should form an academic core and which A-levels, if any, should carry more value. A sensible approach would have been to ask the Qualifications and Curriculum Authority to carry out research involving parents, students, employers, higher education and those working at the educational frontline to recommend curriculum change based on a defined core. Instead of doing that the government rushed to an answer which is likely to have devastating consequences over time for the preparedness of young people for later life and the UK's competitiveness. Sadly the replacement Secretary of State for Education, Nicky Morgan, appears to be compounding this error by asking Ofsted to focus particularly on performance in 'traditional subjects' when reporting school performance.[3]

The renewed emphasis on numeracy and literacy in primary education is positive. I suspect there would be quite a strong consensus around a core of English, mathematics and science, with continuing development of IT skills also tackled though not necessarily as a discrete subject. I am uncertain that much is gained by insisting on studying history or geography, and the role of foreign languages needs to be more carefully considered. For the reality is that the bigger you make the core, the greater curriculum contraction you have in practice, and the more you move away from personalised learning. Timetables have their limitations as distributors of resource. The more you set in stone the less flexibility time-tablers have. At secondary level, an inevitable consequence of a large old-fashioned core through the EBacc, policed by Ofsted, is to reduce opportunities to study creative and vocational subjects. The Progress 8 measure, designed 'to encourage schools to offer a broad and balanced curriculum at [key stage 4] KS4' is a welcome attempt to ameliorate this.[4] However, the nature of the four 'buckets' that subjects have to be drawn from will mean that for some learners the curriculum that would get the best out of them will be sacrificed for the curriculum that will make the school look best. So, despite the rhetoric, the result is less vocational learning for those young people who would both welcome and benefit from it.

The de-coupling of AS levels from A-levels is another action in curriculum vandalism by the Conservative-led Department for Education. When pretty much all the stakeholder groups consulted came back strongly in favour of maintaining the link between the AS level qualification at the end of Year 12 and the A2 level at the end of Year 13 it was perverse to press ahead with an answer to a problem that wasn't there. Higher education was as vocal as schools and colleges on the value of keeping the AS nested within the A-level. The AS had become a useful part of the landscape after its awkward start as a lone one-year qualification where it got little traction. The AS now provides an interim qualification for students, as well as valuable information for universities giving out offers in the autumn of the student's second year of A-level. It also motivates students for their second year by giving a clear sense of where they are and allowing them to change their game plan if they need to, based on the information the results provide. Fortunately Labour, at least, has made it crystal clear that they have listened to the consultation on the scrapping of the AS level and will reverse them at the earliest opportunity.[5] In a time of hesitation around electoral promises for fear of the financial cost, here is a promise that costs the exchequer nothing but gives schools and colleges a clear sense of who Labour is listening to on education.

One of the biggest holes left in the education landscape is where the responsibility lies for local accountability of performance in an area. Historically this rested with local authorities. They were responsible for ensuring effective place planning, raising attainment and delivering those difficult services such as special needs support and transport. This has now become so dreadfully fragmented that it is unclear who is looking out for all the young people in an area, a key part of comprehensive delivery. Increasingly it appears that this responsibility lies with the Secretary of State. This is neither practical nor feasible. For example, when a parent in my parliamentary constituency contacts me unhappy about, say, the application of the uniform policy at a local academy school, where should she be directed to for a resolution of the problem once she has exhausted the academy chain's processes? Where is the independent arbitration of everyday concerns such as this that are better sorted locally before they become more serious issues? Essentially in the Brave New World of atomised education it no longer exists.

With the appointment of eight Schools Commissioners there is some understanding from the powers that be that a chasm has opened up between Whitehall and local areas. The solution is unlikely to cut the mustard but will take yet more resource that should be used for educating young people and place it into a new bureaucracy that has to 'do things' in order to justify its existence. In innovative areas, schools – be they academies, free schools or 'old-fashioned' community schools – have been getting together to work on school improvement, sharing of best practice and other such needs. This reinventing of the wheel has to be welcomed because it demonstrates the necessity for some sort of local structure around these matters. But are we happy that in some localities this isn't happening? Surely it would be better to make all the schools and colleges in an area collectively responsible for the performance of the whole area as well as the performance of their own institutions? A local authority or Local Schools Commissioner could be charged to lubricate and challenge the networks of local schools. I want to know that all local young people are getting the best possible outcome, not just those from the families most able to make school choices. I want to know that there is comprehensive reach for all young people. As someone who has led a college I know that the easiest way to impact on the performance of the institution is to control admissions. That's the temptation but it's wrong. It may end up benefiting one institution at the expense of the overall performance of the young people in the area. The very best academy chains have invested in collaboration and development as well as focused inspiringly on raising standards. Any future model needs to build on these strengths and spread that learning across the whole educational estate and workforce.

It has been interesting to observe how, even in times of austerity, politicians can find funding for their pet projects. In the world of education, this comes in the form of the plethora of new types of school that the Conservatives can find money to fund – free schools, university technical colleges, studio schools and the like. The shattering of comprehensive education has been replaced by a hotchpotch of provision that has little coherence to it at all. It appears that the philosophy driving this cavalier spending is that the inbuilt anarchy is deliberate; there is a confidence that competition will drive up standards and the market will sort out the wheat from the chaff. Despite this confidence there is no evidence that will be the case. But there *is* evidence that in tight times money will be splashed around on a few students whilst cuts have to be made in mainstream funding for the many. For example the 17.5 per cent cut in 18+ funding has been justified as something the government would rather not do but is forced to do as a result of scarce resources.[6] It therefore represents a 'tough choice'! But is it actually a tough choice to fund additional school and college places in, for example, my Scunthorpe constituency, by building a new university technical college whilst cutting funding to those students already in local institutions, or is it an ideologically driven indulgence funded by cutting the core funding for mainstream students?

The real worry is that not only are these new institutions funded at a cost to current students, but that they will result in further waste of public money. Marketing costs will potentially soar in all institutions as they compete for fewer students in an area which will have an overcapacity of school and college places. Although there will be a marginal increase in the choice of institutions for individual students and their parents, the likelihood is that the curriculum choices available will contract. The range of curriculum that can be offered in a variety of smaller institutions is likely to be less than what can be offered when there is a good match of student numbers to available places. The really infuriating thing about this government's ideological obsession with growing the school estate in an unplanned, deliberately chaotic way is that at the same time they have been presiding over the worst primary school places crisis in a generation. Better planning and better spending would have resulted in better provision for need and better value for money for the taxpayer.

In the old Further Education Funding Council inspection criteria there was a focus on 'responsiveness'. It was a focus that troubled some people at the time; but now more than ever it's a focus we need to get back to if we are to ensure that every young person gets the quality of education we would want for our own children. We need to be assured that those delivering education in a locality are responsive to the *needs* of that locality. We need to be confident that there is a good school place for every child in every community, and that the quality of leadership and collaboration exists universally to raise standards in every community. We need assurance that every young person has an entitlement to a basic but innovative curriculum, fair funding, fair access, support for special needs and a good school place within acceptable reach of the family home.

So how do we ensure that we have structures that help us rather than hinder us in achieving this goal for all students? Local authorities must have the responsibility to ensure that all children in their locality access a nationally agreed entitlement. They should ensure collaboration takes place to drive improvement but may use others to lead it. In my experience there are two things that are transformative – the quality of teaching and learning and the quality of leadership. Her Majesty's Chief Inspector, Michael Wilshaw, is right to highlight the shocking lack of accredited school leaders in parts of the country that consistently underperform.[7] He is right to challenge localities to do something about this. But we could go further. We could look to move some of that inspection resource closer to young people and make the local authority responsible for assuring the performance of all the educational institutions serving children up to 18-years-old. Ofsted would then regularly inspect local authorities and a number of institutions within their area to ensure that the local authority's judgements are accurate. Where local authorities failed in their duty to provide a good school place to every child via the levers at its disposal, including driving collaboration and sourcing best leadership practice, it would, quite properly, go into special measures. At which point appropriate interventions could take place that might include being run by another local authority, an academy chain or by central government.

A key element of comprehensive education is access to high-quality and impartial careers information advice and guidance. With the raising of the participation age this becomes more important not less. It is lazy thinking to imagine that with a change of the school leaving age young people will more effectively travel through the key stages on to a positive employment outcome. Added to that, we are currently blighted by unacceptably high levels of youth unemployment. This is one of the major challenges of our age and one that high-quality independent careers education can make a real contribution to; it needs to connect the world of work with the world of education. To their credit, in my experience employers are excited and eager to do this but there needs to be a framework for them to operate within if it is to be successful. In the welter of surveys of what is currently available in our schools and colleges – from the 2013 Education Committee report to the Humber Local Enterprise Partnership Skills Commission – there is universal concern about the parlous state of careers advice.[8] Getting this right is fundamental to both the future of our young people and the future economic wellbeing of the nation. The shared commitment of education and business to high-quality careers education will not produce results unless there is also some independent capacity to facilitate the necessary guidance, work experience and business link activity. To pretend otherwise, as successive governments have done, is unrealistic.

Local authorities, working alongside the local business community through Local Enterprise Partnerships and schools and colleges, can play a strategic role in providing the capacity and drive that will ensure that independent careers advice is delivered successfully and reflects regional needs. In Scunthorpe for example, with its proud engineering tradition, the age profile of those working in manufacturing means that a significant skills gap will open up in the next 20 years unless urgent action is taken.

We are worried about the widening gulf between the haves and the have nots in our society. *The Spirit Level* and the work of economist Thomas Piketty both show the dangers of growing inequality to future economic success and levels of personal wellbeing. When these are the concerns of our time it is a time for comprehensive education to step forward. The real strength of comprehensives is that people are educated alongside each other regardless of ability, class or background. They network with people during their formative years from all walks of life. The British obsession with private education, scooping off those from the most privileged backgrounds to only network with each other, must be contributing to an ever widening gulf in society that is potentially dangerous to us all. High-quality comprehensive education is the perfect antidote to this. To achieve this, comprehensive education needs a high-quality curriculum able to deliver a strong entitlement, alongside good independent careers guidance.

The Dilemma of Selection in Schools

Alan Smithers

The dilemma of selection in schools is that it is needed, but bitterly opposed. People differ greatly in their talents, interests and aspirations. Not everyone can do everything. Choice and selection are therefore inherent in society. One of the purposes of education is to prepare young people for the roles that are likely to be available to them. It would seem reasonable then for schools to be organised around choice and selection. But it is not something that most modern politicians are willing to contemplate. Any policy where it seems that there are going to be more losers than winners does not have much appeal for the vote-conscious. But since social justice, equality and social mobility took centre stage, identifying and developing potentially high attainers has been pushed even further to the periphery. Narrowing gaps has become the watchword.

One consequence is that England does not fare well when it comes to top performers in international comparisons.[1] In PISA 2009, for example, it came 26th out of 34 OECD countries in terms of the percentage of 15-year-olds reaching the highest level in maths. Only 1.7 per cent of English pupils made the top level, even with grammar and independent school pupils included, against the OECD average of 3.1 per cent of pupils. Korea, Switzerland, Japan and Belgium were the top performers in the OECD. But even their scores pale in comparison with those of Shanghai, Singapore and Hong Kong, where respectively, 26.6 per cent, 15.6 per cent, and 10.8 per cent were in the top category.[2] What these countries have in common, other than being Asian, is that they identify and develop talent from a young age. England used to do this. Children in their final year at primary school took tests of general reasoning, arithmetic and essay writing (the '11-plus') and those in the top quarter or so – it varied between local authorities – passed for grammar school. These were the engines of social mobility. The Sutton Trust's seminal 2005 research found that social mobility declined over the period in which grammar schools were being phased out, but it was reluctant to make the link.[3] During the heyday of grammar schools, independent schools, apart from the most prestigious, were struggling for survival, many having to rely on taking 11-plus failures.

As a beneficiary of the grammar school system myself I recall it very fondly. It opened up the world to me. My dad, a Billingsgate fish porter, and my mum, a sweet-packer, had both left school at the age of 14. Although ambitious for me they knew little about how the education system worked. But by dint of the 11-plus I was waved on from my working-class primary school to the best grammar school in the area. When I got there I was well off the pace, but by seeing what my fellow pupils were capable of, with the help of my teachers, I was able to lever myself up to their level and beyond. There are some who would like to see a return to the grammar school system, and I emphasise system here.

The surviving grammar schools have brilliant academic results, but they are a caricature of what once was. Without defined catchment areas, the few remaining have become Meccas for ambitious parents who jump for joy when a place saves them the tens of thousands of pounds that an independent school would cost. Today, even if there were a grammar school nearby, I probably would not get a look in against the tutored and practised rich kids.

But the argument against reintroducing grammar schools, even if it were electorally possible, is more fundamental than that the present ones are dominated by the higher socioeconomic groups. It is that while selection at age 11 and a grammar school education worked wonderfully well for most of those given the opportunity, it cast the rest aside. Most of the children I was with at primary school were consigned to a terrible secondary modern school where bullying was prevalent (there were some notorious future gangsters in the making), the teaching was poor, and there were no qualifications because it was thought that the minds of the children should not be troubled by external examinations.

There is no way back for grammar schools.[4] John Major fought the 1997 election on a manifesto that included a grammar school in every town.[5] But it was no help to him in his landslide defeat. 1960s Labour Education Secretary Anthony Crosland signalled the end of the grammar school system with his highly-charged line: 'If it's the last thing I do, I am going to destroy every f***ing grammar school in England. And Wales. And Northern Ireland.'[6] And there are people who still feel like that today. A Twitter love-in was not long ago sparked by an unremarkable *Guardian* piece by Fiona Millar reporting gleefully that a new supposedly tutor-proof entrance test in Buckinghamshire, which has retained its grammar schools, was not working particularly well.[7]

Given that the grammar school system rejected about three-quarters of 11-year-olds and left many feeling failures, the emotion generated is understandable. But what is seriously damaging is that it has generalised into a passionately held belief that any selection within school education is a bad thing. Governments of all colours have tied themselves in knots trying to avoid the taint. Harold Wilson promoted comprehensive schools as a grammar school education for everyone.[8] Tony Blair to his credit recognised their deficiencies, but his solutions – seemingly anything-but-selection – were contorted and short-lived. We had the empty rhetoric of 'personalised learning'.[9] There was a subject-specialist schools programme where the schools were barred from recruiting on ability.[10] As such, selection of a small percentage on aptitude was allowed for some subjects, for example, modern languages, which led to laboured attempts to distinguish 'aptitude' from 'ability'.[11]

The sophistry reached its peak in the attempts to introduce a 'gifted and talented' programme with no way of identifying 'the gifted and talented'.[12] There was first, in 1999, 'Excellence in Cities',[13] which was overtaken by a White Paper, 'Schools Achieving Success', which announced plans for a National Academy 'to support and challenge gifted and talented pupils'.[14] This was opened at the University of Warwick in 2002, but closed in 2007, because as the director explained, so much had been heaped upon it without extra funding that it had become undoable.[15] A new three-year national programme was then announced with the education services provider CfBT as the managing contractor. An interactive website was created for the programme, and significantly the emphasis switched from all 'gifted and talented' to just those eligible for free school meals.[16] The contract was not renewed and responsibility was passed on to the National Strategies Programme which itself was coming to an end. All the while schools were asked to say how many gifted and talented pupils they had and what provision they were making for them. The percentages returned ranged from zero to 100 per cent. The zeros came from schools where the teachers thought that it was intrinsically wrong to identify the more able, even had there been a sure-fire way of doing so.[17]

Not surprisingly, one of the first acts of the Coalition government was to sweep all of this away. It took the view that the gifted and talented (G&T) programme had ended on 31 March 2010. 'It was for the schools to decide what – if any – additional or more tailored support was appropriate for their G&T pupils.'[18] But the Coalition government, in turn, came out with confused messages on choice and selection. Through the English Baccalaureate (EBacc), league tables and inspections it signalled to schools that their pupils should be following the same core of study, to the same levels, to the age of 16.[19] This was underlined by stripping out, in response to the Wolf Report, many of the vocational qualifications that were in place from the age of 14.[20] Admittedly, many of these so-called vocational qualifications were very poor, but there was no attempt to replace them with something better. Contradicting this stance, the Coalition also indicated that it was open to new pathways from the age of 14. It paved the way for the university technical colleges, the brainchild of a former Secretary of State for Education, Lord Kenneth Baker, which would recruit from the age of 14.[21] It also enabled further education colleges to take in 14-year-olds.[22] Another ambiguity is that while the Coalition government is in favour of selection within schools through streaming and setting, with presumably the expectation that some pupils will progress faster and further than others, one of the intentions of its major examination reforms was to do away with tiering, so all pupils would be taking the same examination rather than being entered for different levels as in the past.[23] Perhaps ambiguity is the price of coalition.

While selection by ability in schools is one of the unmentionables, selection in the form of restricted choices does come into play at the previous school leaving age of 16. Post-16 there are different pathways available in A-levels, apprenticeships and vocational qualifications. Eligibility for entry to those pathways usually depends on specified minimum levels of performance in the GCSE and equivalent examinations. It is ultimately more choice than selection, however, because it is essentially about qualifying for pathways rather than competing for limited places. Full-blooded selection does not really kick in until higher education when some universities receive many more applications than they can accept. Entry is therefore highly competitive with applicants pitched against each other mainly in terms of A-level results. Ironically, the Sutton Trust spent a lot of effort and money trying to develop an intelligence test for 18-year-olds – when it strongly opposed the use of one at age 11 – to assess the potential of university applicants since it believes that A-level results are socially biased.[24] But the project foundered because the test that was devised was much less predictive of degree outcomes than were the A-levels themselves. How then to square the circle? Selection in schools is needed at some point because people are very different in their abilities, as well as in their willingness to work hard, and provision should reflect this.[25] But selection in education is emphatically a political no-no.

Under the radar a considerable amount of selection in school education already exists. There is not only selection within schools to form streams and sets, but also between schools. This involves not just the 163 surviving grammars, but in addition comprehensive schools, like the Watford Grammars (for boys and girls respectively), which are able to select a proportion of their intake on ability, and former specialist schools able to select up to 10 per cent on aptitude. Crucially, however, social selection is rife.[26]

In theory, parents are able to choose schools, although in fact, it amounts to no more than expressing a preference. Those who care about their children's education, naturally opt for what they perceive to be good schools. In large part a school's reputation depends on its examination results which, in turn, are mainly determined by the children who go there. Good schools become greatly over-subscribed and competition to get into them is intense. Parental preference thus turns into selection by schools. The criteria that can be used are closely regulated, but the one most often used is proximity. Parents with the means will do all they can to maximise their chances of a place, including living as close to a good school as possible. The areas around good schools tend to be, or to become, social enclaves, with house prices carrying a substantial premium. There is a very strong correlation between socioeconomic status and pupil performance, so some schools become progressively stronger as the social enclaves tighten their grip, while others increasingly struggle.[27] The top performing comprehensive schools are as different from the general run as are the grammar schools.[28] Is selection by house purchase really more just, fair and conducive to social mobility than selection on educational merit?

Peel away the surface and it is evident that a lot of selecting does go on between and within schools. Meanwhile, it is fiercely opposed at age 11, but accepted for university entry.[29] Choices restricted by prior attainment are an established part of the transition at age 16 to advanced studies or training for employment. New selective maths free schools operating from the age of 16 are being opened by both King's College London and Exeter University, and the government hopes that other Russell Group universities will follow suit, across the range of subjects.[30]

The real question about selection in education is therefore not whether it should take place at all, but rather what age and what type would be most appropriate. At present, restricted choice as a form of selection at age 16 is what is acceptable politically. But there is an educational problem with this arrangement: it leaves only two years for upper secondary education.[31] This worked reasonably well when the most talented young people were sped on their way to university through a narrow range of specialist A-levels, which in effect transferred the first year of higher education into schools. But the raising of the participation age to 18, demands that the final years of schooling be rethought.

Two years is not long enough to allow all pupils to go in the directions to which they aspire. That is certainly the experience of our European neighbours where upper secondary education lasts three or four years;

different pathways in upper secondary education build on three years of lower secondary education. In contrast, England has, in effect, five years of lower secondary education to just two at the upper level. In fact, such has been the apparent lack of activity surrounding the raising of the education participation age that one has to wonder whether the motivation was mainly educational or whether, as in some of the previous increases in compulsory education, the driver was to reduce youth unemployment.[33] One important consequence of the change is that the GCSE is no longer needed as a school leaving examination, so its existence has to be justified on other grounds. In the lengthened compulsory education the GCSE seems misplaced, five years on from the key stage 2 tests, but only two years ahead of A-levels and equivalent qualifications. There is a strong case for moving the national examination at 16 to one or two years earlier. At either 14 or 15 it would not be selection in a competitive sense; it would be a choice between options depending on the level achieved in that examination.

I have argued for adopting the OECD model of three years lower secondary education and four years of upper secondary education for nearly a quarter of a century. The first time was when I formed part of an Education Commission convened by Channel 4, which spanned the political spectrum from Sig Prais on the right, to 'Chelly' Halsey on the left.[34] We had a very convivial time looking at schools across Europe and we found it surprisingly easy to reach agreement. Much of what we recommended has become an accepted part of England's education landscape: a core national curriculum; putting English and maths at the centre of primary education; external tests at the end of primary school; examination standards to be regulated by a body set up for the purpose; and the need to sharpen up vocational qualifications. But the key proposal that there should be choice/selection at age 14, facilitating transition from a common national curriculum to an array of pathways leading variously on to university, further education and into work, has continued to fall on deaf ears. My latest and last attempt was in a chapter I contributed to Kenneth Baker's 2013 book, *14-18 A New Vision for Secondary Education*.[35] In spite of the clout of the former Education Secretary, differentiation at age 14 once again failed to spark enthusiasm.

All the arguments marshalled against the proposal in fact have straightforward answers. It is said that 14 is too young to be making potentially life shaping decisions, yet in the days when 14 was actually the school leaving age young people rapidly became adults, taking charge of their lives. It is argued that young people would be trapped into separate tracks by their decisions at 14, but the proposal is for routes with lots of interconnections and opportunities to change.[36] Alison Wolf in her influential report on the reform of vocational education suggested that in Europe the most common age of transfer is 16.[37] This is the case in Scandinavia, for example, where formal education starts at six or seven, and therefore three years lower secondary takes them through to age 16. In England children begin school earlier so they have completed six years of primary and three years of lower secondary school by the age of 14. Opposing choice between pathways at 14 for this reason thus boils down to an arcane argument as to whether three years lower secondary education ending at age 14 can be the same as three years ending at age 16. Another objection to transition at 14, especially by those who have to administer the system, is that it would involve too much upheaval in the use of school buildings. Again, there is a relatively easy answer: not far short of half of all secondary schools currently run through to age 14 or 16. These schools could therefore become the new intermediate schools, while the others could become the high schools.

A transfer age of 14 would bring considerable benefits. As well as a better balance between lower and upper secondary education, the new high schools would help to make sense of the now quiescent specialist schools programme, enable the university free schools to start at a more appropriate age, and it might even be a route by which some former direct grant (now private) schools could be reintegrated into the state sector.[38]

There are, however, the deep-seated objections and not being a politician I can cheerfully admit to changing my mind. I now propose – in the spirit of looking for practicable solutions – that the pivotal age for transition be 15. The shift takes a lot of the force out of the arguments that 14 is too young, too out-of-line with Europe, and involves too much upheaval to school organisation. It has the great merit that it enables three-year programmes to be devised to make full use of raising the participation age. A-levels have a lot to recommend them, but currently they create a narrow and very specialised curriculum. Studying them over a period of three years would enable more, and likely more contrasting, subjects to be studied. It would open the way for genuine breadth without the paraphernalia of the proposed Tomlinson diploma.[39] Three years would also allow very good practical qualifications to be devised in which an essential core of English, maths and science was blended with the practical skills and understanding that lead to a particular field of employment or advanced practical study. Organised in this way, education from 15-18 would have a much clearer shape than now. It would be much more easily understood by parents and pupils when making choices and by employers and educational institutions in using the qualifications.

In short, my answer to the central dilemma of selection in schools – needed, but strongly opposed – is to introduce it on a national scale at age 15. GCSEs should be scrapped or adapted to make way for a new qualification. Through to age 15 there would be a core national curriculum after which would follow an array of equivalent pathways lasting a minimum of three years ranging across the academic and occupational. Pathways would be chosen by parents and pupils on the recommendation of teachers and attainment in the new examinations at age 15.

Selection by Stealth

Chris Keates

The issue of academic selection has continued to play a dominant role in narratives about the aims, values and purposes of the state education system since its introduction in the latter part of the nineteenth century. For understandable reasons, much of the debate about the merits or otherwise of academic selection has tended to focus on the operation of formal, overt systems, in which some pupils gain access to dedicated schools as a result of their perceived abilities or aptitudes. The contested nature of the role of academic selection in the state education system in England, traditionally focused on selective grammar schools and their 'secondary modern' counterparts, is well-trodden ground. Advocates of academic selection continue to assert that grammar schools are a powerful driver of social mobility, providing a means by which working-class children can be given future life chances that would otherwise only be available to their privately-educated peers. Supporters of the alternative, 'comprehensive', model of school organisation counter that academic selection is divisive and that the potential of all young people can be best realised, to their benefit and that of wider society, in a school system that seeks to educate pupils of all backgrounds and abilities in common settings. Research into public opinion on such overtly selective systems of school organisation, and the enduring inclusion of themes related to academic selection in political discourses on educational policy, suggest that these debates will continue to consume attention for the foreseeable future.

In terms of official national policy in England, a settlement of a kind was reached through the 1998 School Standards and Framework Act. Through the Act, the last Labour government stipulated that no additional selective grammar schools could be opened, maintaining the size of the selective sector close to the 164 grammar schools open at the end of the 1997/8 academic year (there are now 163). However, it is worth noting that while the number of grammar schools remained constant, the proportion of the pupil population educated at these settings has gradually continued to increase.[1]

Covert selection

Notwithstanding the contested concept of selection on the basis of a child's 'aptitude', traditional formal academic selection has the defining characteristic that it is at least *overt*. The criteria for entry to selective schools, usually based on achievement of a particular standard in a written assessment, are made clear to pupils and parents alike. The validity and reliability of this assessment might be open to challenge, but it has been advocated by some, at least, as a readily understandable basis for determining entry to grammar schools. However, the issue of covert selection, in which schools seek to admit pupils on the basis of their 'ability' or 'potential' in a system where selection of this nature is prohibited, has tended to receive less emphasis in public debate.

In spite of the continued existence of overt academic selection in some parts of England, the Coalition government has maintained that its policy preference is for all other schools to operate on a genuinely comprehensive basis and for this to be supported by the legal frameworks within which schools operate.[2] It would, therefore, be particularly insidious for any government, having made such a public commitment to the maintenance of a comprehensive system, to fail to take effective steps to prevent the use of covert selection. Ostensibly, the education system in England seeks to implement a system of parental choice. Covert selection, however, inverts this position and leads to circumstances where schools seek to select pupils, and indeed parents, that they believe best suit their interests in ways that may be contrary to the wishes of parents and pupils. Evidence suggests that as a result of the policies of the Coalition government, not least the extensive autonomy given to schools and the obsessive pursuit of a deregulation agenda, the risks of increased covert selection have grown rapidly.

School admissions

On the face of it, the dangers of schools seeking to admit pupils through processes of covert, illicit selection in a system where they are responsible for their own admissions policies are recognised in the School Admissions Code, published by the Department for Education (DfE).[3] This code is underpinned by statute and maintained schools are required by law to have regard to provisions in determining their admissions arrangements. However, before considering the extent to which the current code and other admissions requirements on schools and local authorities represent an effective means of preventing covert selection by schools, it is useful to place the development of the current version of the code into its recent historical policy context.

In 2009, the former Department for Children, Schools and Families (DCSF) under the Labour government revised the version of the code in place at that time in order to ensure that it was sufficiently robust to tackle inequitable or discriminatory admissions practices. It also sought to address concerns that previous versions of the code had allowed a number of unacceptable admissions practices to become embedded within the system. The practices the Labour government's reforms to the code sought to outlaw included:

- schools asking parents to commit to making financial contributions as a condition of admission;
- not giving looked-after children the priority required by law;
- asking about the marital, occupational or financial status of parents;
- giving priority on the basis of family members who are not siblings attending the school;
- interviewing children and parents.

These reforms were an explicit response to investigations commissioned by the DCSF which had indicated that schools were seeking to apply these practices in order to 'screen out' those children they believed would be less academically able than others, thereby undermining the comprehensive basis of the non-selective system.[4] However, many of the reforms introduced by the last government and associated changes in regulations, including strengthening the role of local authorities in securing equitable admissions policies, enhancing the monitoring and enforcement power of the Office of the Schools Adjudicator (OSA) and extending the role of admissions forums, have been abolished by the Coalition government. In 2012, just over three years after these changes to the code were introduced, the Coalition government introduced a revised code, despite the fact that there had been insufficient time for the effectiveness of the version of the code it replaced to be evaluated. The implications of the changes brought in with the new admissions code in 2012 need to be considered carefully but in doing so it is necessary initially to consider issues related to the applicability and coverage of the code and other related regulations, to all state-funded schools.

The Coalition government's academies and free schools programme

The Coalition government took office in 2010 with a clear commitment to expand the proportion of schools with academy status and to allow for the creation of free schools. In many respects, both these forms of school operate beyond the legal frameworks that apply to all other state-funded schools on key matters. Critically, they are not required by statute to adhere to the admissions code and are not subject to the statutory oversight and monitoring of local authorities in respect of their admissions policies. In taking forward the expansion of the academies and free school programme, principally through the introduction of the Academies Act 2010, parliamentarians from all political parties raised concerns that significant expansion in the number of schools with academy and free school freedoms could lead to circumstances in which these schools could implement policies that would allow them to select their pupil intake.[5] These concerns, expressed particularly during the progress of the legislation through Parliament, were met by assurances from Coalition government ministers that the operation of the code in place at that time would ensure that the expansion of the academies programme and the introduction of free schools would not have adverse admissions consequences. Indeed, Nick Gibb, at the time the Minister for Schools, said:

> The admissions code will apply just as much to academies as to maintained schools, that the admissions appeals code will also apply just as much to academies as to maintained schools and that the co-ordination arrangements will apply too. So the local authorities will hold the ring on admissions in the same way as they do at the moment.[6]

In the summing up of the third reading of the Academies Bill, Nick Gibb also stated:

> Nor is it about scrapping the admissions code, another spurious claim about the Government's education policies by the Shadow Secretary of State. We are committed to fair admissions through the code, and all academies will be bound by it through the model funding agreement.[7]

The decision, therefore, of the Coalition government to change the code, following the passage of the Academies Act was highly disingenuous to say the least. Without question, it was entirely unacceptable for the Coalition government, subsequent to the introduction of the Academies Act, to seek to make significant changes to the content and application of the code that could lead to the increased use of the covert selection identified by Parliament as one of the most significant risks of the academies and free schools programme. These concerns were emphasised by the fact that academies and free schools are only required to comply with the code on the basis of their funding agreement with the Department for Education (DfE), whereas it is a statutory requirement for all other schools. Therefore, an academy or free school, acting in a way contrary to the provisions set out in the code, is not in breach of any statutory provisions but merely the contractual terms of its funding agreement with the DfE. Given the ongoing deep concerns about the arrangements established by the DfE to monitor and enforce the terms of funding agreements, these admission arrangements for academies and free schools must be regarded as being not only significantly less robust than those in place in maintained schools, but also increasing the risk of covert selection. There are further concerns in this regard relating to provisions which allow the Secretary of State for Education to vary the requirement of academies and free schools to comply with the terms of the code through their funding agreements, without making clear the basis upon which any such variation would be justified. There are no valid reasons for varying the terms upon which the code should apply to academies and free schools in comparison with maintained schools. If admissions are to be fair and transparent then the statutory basis must apply to all admissions authorities to ensure that covert selection can be tackled effectively.

As with so many of the changes introduced by the Coalition government, the changes it made to the code were premised on the basis of 'simplification'. However, it is clear that almost all of this 'simplification' was achieved by the removal of much of the important and useful non-statutory guidance in the code that supported the clarification and interpretation of its key provisions. The removal of this guidance represented a fundamental weakening of the code, making scrutiny and oversight of the admission policies and analysis of the equality and diversity dimensions of admissions practice far more difficult. As each school with the power to act as its own admissions authority, including all academies and free schools, now has an unacceptable degree of discretion within which it can develop its own definition of key terms used in the code, in the context of parental choice, far from making the system clearer for parents, their ability to compare the implications of schools' admissions policies has been hindered significantly.

The Coalition government's changes to the admissions system also resulted in a significant diminution of the roles of local authorities and the Office of the Schools Adjudicator (OSA). Previously, both the OSA and the local authority had represented an important means of securing fairness in the schools admissions system. Local authorities and the OSA were tasked with keeping the operation of the code under regular review and monitoring the cumulative impact of admissions policies on the fairness and transparency of local admissions arrangements. Through their activities, the OSA and local authorities sought to secure admissions equity at the local level, to support pupils and the families treated inappropriately by admissions authorities, and to promote the further development of effective policy and practice. The weakening of the code compounded the Coalition government's 2011 Education Act which had removed the duty of local authorities to establish an Admissions Forum for their area.[8] These forums had played an important role in ensuring consistency and fairness in admissions practice locally. The 2011 Act also undermined the role of the OSA even further, restricting it to considering specific complaints about admissions, rather than, as before, considering the consequences for admissions arrangements of schools' policy across a particular area.

All of these retrograde steps, together with savage cuts to local authority funding, undermined local authorities' ability to discharge their key role in ensuring the transparency, fairness and efficiency of local admissions processes. The abolition of the requirement for local authorities to report to the Schools' Adjudicator on local admissions arrangements, represented a serious weakening of the system and the scope for local authorities to pursue equity and fairness in the admissions system.

Having made all of these significant changes which were clearly not in the interests of parents or the public, the Coalition government went even further. For reasons that have yet to be adequately explained, it removed the requirement for schools to consult on their admission arrangements every three years, extending the period to seven years providing there have been no significant changes.[9] As the definition of 'significant' is left to the schools to determine, the extension plainly allows for incremental changes over a period of seven years, which could be deemed *in*significant and yet result in distinctly different arrangements being implemented over the course of this period without any consultation with parents or the community having ever taken place. It cannot be a coincidence that the length of funding agreements – the contract between the Secretary of State and academies and free schools that sets out the basis on which these schools are funded – is also seven years. It is reasonable to conclude that this extension to seven years in relation to admissions has been chosen to allow these schools to make gradual changes to their admissions arrangements by stealth over the course of the funding agreement period. Were there a requirement to consult more frequently, greater scrutiny of schools' compliance with provisions in their funding agreements relating to adherence to the code, would be permitted.

Additionally, the DfE's reforms to the code removed the previous requirement for schools to take into account the context of the local area when developing their admissions arrangements, thereby removing any route or mechanism for a local community to highlight the impact of admissions arrangements. It also weakened the appeals mechanism, through which pupils and their families are able to challenge decisions made by schools, by both removing training requirements for members of appeals panels and by effectively allowing members of panels to remain in post indefinitely, calling into question the transparency and fairness of the appeals process. A report from the respected and independent Academies Commission, published in January 2013, raised concerns about the risks in the academies sector of existing covert selection becoming more widespread.[10] In its conclusions, the Commission called for an increase in the powers of the OSA and local authorities to monitor and secure compliance with the code.

The impact of other Coalition government education reforms on selection

Opportunities for covert selection have been increased not only by the Coalition government's reforms to the code. Covert selection is also supported by the creation of a policy context which enables schools to make provisions which discourage some parents from either submitting an application for admission in the first place, or making it difficult for them to maintain a place at a particular school. The targets of such practices are often pupils from materially deprived backgrounds. To give some examples, schools are able to send out strong advance signals to prospective families that if their child obtains a place at the school they will be expected to make significant financial contributions to school funds, to purchase uniforms from expensive sole suppliers and to support expensive educational visits and other activities.[11] Such practices were enabled to flourish by the provisions of the Coalition government's Education Act 2011 which allowed schools to charge for educational activities which were previously free.[12] This provision was compounded by giving schools freedom over the curriculum and thus greater leeway to re-designate activities previously considered part of their core curricular offer, and therefore exempt from charging, as optional activities for which charges can be levied. Such practice can include educational visits and extra-curricular activities, many of which now place substantial costs on families. The Act also removed the cap on what academies and free schools were able to charge for school meals, enabling prices to be significantly increased as well as charges to be levied from parents for mealtime supervision.

Messages about the financial costs given by schools to prospective parents, for example in the school's prospectus and at events aimed at parents who are making choices about a school for their child, carry the risk that some parents will be deterred from seeking admission for their children on the grounds of affordability. Notably, this danger had been recognised in the reforms to admissions arrangements introduced by the last Labour government through specific provisions designed to prevent schools from adopting such practices, accompanied by clear arrangements for monitoring compliance.

Survey work undertaken by the NASUWT in 2013, polling over 2,500 parents' experiences on the costs of education highlight these concerns.[13] Over a fifth of parents responding to the survey reported that they were required to pay for field trips despite the fact that these activities are compulsory elements of examination courses, such as A-level geography and biology. The vast majority (93 per cent) of respondents also reported that they were required to pay for other educational visits such as trips to museums, theatres or nature reserves. Almost half of parents paid more than £50 over the previous year to ensure that each of their children could participate in educational visits required by the curriculum.[14] Parents responding to the survey described the impact of these charges. Here are two examples of parents' comments:[15]

> I have had four children go through the education system and it can be financially crippling at times as you don't want your child to miss out or be ostracised by their peers for not going.

> My children cannot go on trips. I simply cannot afford the costs.

School uniform costs were also identified as significant by parents. Out of those responding parents required to purchase a uniform, over half spent more than £100 per year on their eldest child alone. Following the Coalition government's dilution of the guidance in the code to schools which sought to deter them from practices which forced parents to purchase school uniforms from a limited number of stockists, it is concerning but perhaps not surprising that of those parents required to provide a uniform, two thirds (66 per cent) were required to purchase it from a particular supplier, a six per cent increase on the figure revealed by a 2012 NASUWT survey on the same issues.[16]

Returning to the 2013 survey, over a quarter of parents reported making regular contributions to a school fund, with some paying up to £1,000 per year.[17] This issue is of particular interest, as the strengthening of the admissions code in 2009 had deliberately sought to prevent parents making a financial contribution to a school a condition of admission. The disproportionate, adverse impact of these costs on low-income families is evident – but it does not end there. In the 2013 survey parents reported an increasing expectation to fund basic equipment, previously provided by schools, with four out of five parents required to purchase basic writing equipment, three quarters buying basic stationery, and nearly half spending at least £25 a year per child. A third of parents reported being required to purchase text books and reference books essential for the child's chosen programme of study.[18] The survey also revealed the expectation that families would provide IT equipment to support school and homework. Multiple respondents highlighted being required to pay for insurance for school iPads, book fees, locker hire and school proms. Concerns were also evident about the increasing cost of travel to and from school.

These charges are being levied in the context of 3.5 million children in the UK now living in poverty, with the figure set to rise by 600,000 by 2016.[19] Added to this is growing concern about the adverse impact of financial pressures on children and young people as a result of benefit cuts, public sector pay policies, loss of the Education Maintenance Allowance, unemployment and the wider effects of the recession.[20] It is now a reality that the access of children and young people to what should be their educational entitlement is increasingly based on parents' ability to pay.

A more effective way forward

It is clear that the regulatory and legislative changes which have increased 'freedoms' for schools, including those over curriculum provision, admissions, school finances and charging policies, have created the conditions in which selection by stealth – covert selection – can flourish. Given the Coalition government's stated opposition to covert selection, and its public commitment to ensuring a fair and transparent system of school admissions, it is unacceptable that ministers have driven forward changes that have placed this critical aim of education policy at risk. While the changes described in this article are relatively recent in nature, emerging evidence of the dangers they pose are becoming increasingly apparent. As a minimum step, the government must recognise that an urgent review must be undertaken of the risks of now increased covert selection. Increased risks brought in through the Coalition's changes to admissions arrangements, the granting of greater powers to schools to charge for activities which were previously free, the lack of scrutiny and oversight of academies and free schools, and the neutering of local authorities. Covert selection seriously compromises the values and ethos of a public education service which should operate in the public interest, securing and delivering the entitlement of all children and young people to access high-quality education.

Church of England Schools for the Common Good

Nigel Genders

The education of our children is one of the primary concerns of all parents and so it is no surprise that school admissions are always high on the agenda in any discussion about the nation's schools.

Two hundred years ago, when a formal education was not available to the vast majority of the population, the Church of England set out to ensure that there was a school for everyone and that it should be provided on the basis of need rather than whether an individual family could afford it. The resulting imperative to build schools for 'the poor', our original admissions code, led to a movement of mass education which, some fifty years later, the state recognised as being of significant value so joined in to help deliver it. In those early years, being able to access any education at all was the pressing concern, not the choice of school. The issue of admissions, as we define it today, was non-existent. It was only as universal provision was achieved that the question of which school a parent should choose for their children became such a significant matter. Schools operated with a catchment area, but the resulting rise in house prices around good schools meant that parental choice was more limited for those who could not afford to live there. However, the freeing up of the system and a greater expectation regarding parental choice of school has meant that the landscape has become increasingly difficult for many to navigate. Parents have become more discerning about the kind of education they want their children to experience, and so the clamour for places at what are considered to be the best schools has become more intense. It is not surprising that parents who want the best for their children will look at a system that offers the possibility of choice and seek to do what they can to select wisely.

But are parents really selecting schools, or is it the school that is selecting its parents and their children? The introduction of the 'Admissions Code', which prevents schools from having practices that are discriminatory or unfair, is to be welcomed. Asking parents to make financial contributions to the school or using very subjective criteria that are open to misinterpretation or abuse and lead to disadvantage being exacerbated should not be condoned. However, deciding whether an oversubscribed school has objective criteria that prioritise distance, wealth, family, faith, aptitude or academic ability is really a question about the level of social engineering we want for our society. A simple admission by distance from the school may seem desirable, but it will always lead to selection by house price as a school improves and becomes popular. Whereas a more random allocation by lottery in a given area may lead to disengagement and not provide the impetus that has come with parental choice to ensure that schools strive hard to improve and develop. Many demand 'fair admissions' but in this complex landscape one person's definition of fair is another's injustice. For example, we live in Kent and our children have grown up in a selective education system. It has the appearance of fairness as children are allocated their secondary school on the basis of their results in the 11-plus, but over the years I have observed a burgeoning market of private tuition that subjects increasingly younger children to intense pressure to achieve a place at the grammar school. But such opportunities are only available to those children whose parents can afford the tuition fees, and so the system is skewed against the poor or disadvantaged.

So what about religious criteria in schools with a religious character? Are they simply another means of discrimination, as some would argue? Is the prioritising of church attendance a criterion that is open to the same abuse as other systems for choice, and should therefore be prohibited, or is this freely available opportunity for an expression of commitment to a Christian worldview a means of avoiding some of the injustices inherent in other methodologies?

The Church of England's vision for education

In order to answer this question we begin by offering an understanding of the Church of England's vision for education. As described, the Church of England has been committed to freely available education for the whole population for over two hundred years. In 1811 the Church started an enormous school building programme as part of its responsibility as the Established Church to offer education for the common good. It was an education rooted in the principles and practices of the

Church of England but offered in an age when there were few alternative options available. Schools were opened in communities across the country, with a particular emphasis on serving the needs of the poor.

England today is very different to the England of the early nineteenth century, and a large estate of Victorian schools in rural villages that served farm labourers, the poor and disadvantaged, now find themselves serving an altogether different demographic.

Over the years the Church has continued to build and open new schools and has located them according to local need, sometimes based entirely on the lack of any school provision in a particular area of new development, and sometimes in partnership with other schools to offer a different approach to education that complements existing provision. Wherever these schools are located, the motivation is not to offer what has increasingly been termed a 'faith school' (by which is meant a school intended to educate people of the faith into the faith), but to provide a Christian school for all people. But why do today's parents choose such a school? Why do they go out of their way to access the education Church of England schools provide?

There is a wealth of information available to today's parents to help them chose a school. The academic record and the results students achieve is the primary focus of much of that data, but inspection report after inspection report tells the story of parents choosing a Church of England school for their children because of other factors. They want a school where their children will flourish; where they will be developed academically and achieve their very best, but where they will also be given a rounded education that enables them to grow as individuals who can play their part in wider society and make a genuine difference to the world. Of course, all schools would seek to offer those opportunities for their students, but Church of England schools are transparent about the values that underpin the life of the school and they offer that education within a framework that seeks to promote Christian character and a breadth of education that is about service and spirituality as well as being about academic achievement.

The prevailing view in education seems to be an instrumentalist one which sees education as being about producing economically viable units. The way worth is measured by salary or economic output is driving a view of education which values science and maths for the impact they make on the economy rather than the benefits they bring to the world. Banks complain of a lack of creativity in their recruits, doctors complain of a worrying absence of moral compass, whilst the education system seems to be set along a path that measures success by the future size of a student's pay packet, rather than by the difference that student can make to their community. The Church of England's vision for education has always sought to strive beyond this narrow instrumentalism; it is no surprise that our schools continue to be popular with parents because they trust us not to be swayed by the latest trends and political gimmicks, but to offer the lessons learnt from our hundreds of years of history in this sector to continue to provide a quality of education that has been benefitting people over generations.

How do Church of England schools provide the character and ethos that sustains this approach to education, which is not about being a school for Christians but rather a Christian school for all? They do it by providing excellent leadership, committed to a vision for education that is ingrained with Christian values and has the human flourishing of every child at its core. Such leadership, from staff and governors, drives a philosophy of education and a pedagogical approach that is underpinned by the rhythm and liturgical life of the community and offers the pastoral care of all students.

This combination of powerful elements has a proven track record of working in schools with a long history and leads to them being extremely popular and oversubscribed. It also works in new schools where there are no faith criteria for admission, but it will not be a surprise if, in time, those schools also become oversubscribed and governors will have to consider the nuances of their specific local context in order to set criteria that serve the needs of the children they seek to serve.

Schools on a journey

The education landscape has been through an unprecedented period of change in recent years. Like all schools, Church of England schools are on a journey. Many are well established and enjoy increasing levels of popularity because of the quality of education provision; others are struggling to get established in areas of significant poverty and disadvantage. Whether it be rural schools built for the local community but now adjusting to a dramatically changed demographic; long-established schools that were founded to provide a church school education across a much wider catchment area but are now facing the pressure on places from their local community who would prefer the Church school than the community school on the neighbouring site; or new Church of England schools which have been specifically opened in areas of disadvantage to serve that local community as part of the church's commitment to the common good, they are all at a particular phase in their journey.

Admissions criteria, which allow for a percentage of students to be prioritised on the basis that they are committed to the Christian principles underpinning the school, are not perceived to be a problem in a school that serves a large estate and is undersubscribed. But as that school's ethos and character produces the fruit of dramatic improvement and a new approach to education, other parents hear about it and seek to get their children a place, and suddenly the percentage of places which might be allocated on the basis of church attendance presents a problem. The problem is not just for those parents who would like their children to attend the school, but also for the school governors tasked with creating an oversubscription policy that is true to their vision for the school. So governors continually assess how best to use their criteria in a way that supports the ethos of the school and the vision for serving the locality. Many schools are presented with these challenges as demographics change and schools rise and fall in popularity. Sometimes it is a conundrum about siblings: in periods of low population of children in an area, the catchment broadens to a wider area and then prioritising those children's siblings in future years, if that coincides with a rise in performance and popularity of the school, brings added pressures on the oversubscription criteria. In such situations it is not simply a question of demanding 'fairness' because prioritising siblings is good for one family but may mean that a child who lives nearer to the school may not secure a place. Faith criteria are often used to provide a means for children outside a popular school's immediate expensive housing area to attend the school, but with the wholesale demise of denominational transport it is often only those who have the opportunities afforded by mobility that can access the education such schools provide, so this is not always as easy as it might seem.

Such issues demonstrate the complexity of admissions arrangements and these challenges require careful and skilful handling. Faith criteria can sometimes be used to ensure a mix of children that may not ever be achieved by a simple distance calculation from the school, but are more often used to provide a core of children who share the ethos of the school in a way that brings real benefit to the whole school community. Given the complex nature of such arrangements it is impossible to make generalisations that would work across the country.

The majority of Church of England schools do not prioritise their places on the basis of church attendance, and most of those that do still make places available for children in the school's immediate community. New Church of England schools, which are being established to meet the pressure on pupil places in a locality, are using distance from the school as the criterion for at least half of the intake, but in most cases for even more than that. But every context is different and schools use their criteria to best serve the interests of their community – wherever they are.

The following case studies give examples of two very different approaches:

St Luke's, a Church of England school in Kingston upon Thames is a long established and popular Church of England school. The mix of schools in the area means that for this school, serving the local community can now best be achieved by removing the church attendance oversubscription criterion from its admissions policy. Head Teacher Pat Allan wrote to parents about the consultation process for this change, explaining that this would not result in the Christian character of the school being diminished. She said:

> I am aware that several parents are concerned that removing the church criteria will change the Christian ethos of the school. The staff and governors want to assure all parents that the links with St Luke's Parish and the Christian ethos of the school will remain at the heart of school policies and practice. There is a trust deed which outlines our responsibilities as a church school to serve our local community and to uphold the Christian foundation of the school. St Luke's will still be a church school with Christian values at the heart of all we do. This is not because we are legally bound but because the governors and staff wish it to be so.[1]

The governors were able to reach this conclusion based on their detailed knowledge of the local context and understanding of how their school's admissions criteria will work in relation to the other schools in the locality.

A second example, Bury Church of England High School, has been engaged with education since 1748. Originally set up as the Charity School in Bury, it set out to serve the community. In those days, the Christian community was virtually the same as the geographical community. As time passed, the school became the Parish School, the Central Church School and finally Bury Church of England High School. This journey reflected the growing size of the school and the growing geographical area that it set out to serve. For many years now, the school has served both the Christian community and people across Greater Manchester and Lancashire. Society has also changed and it is no longer the case that the school's Christian ethos is understood by all sectors of society. Head Teacher Craig Watson explains the school's approach to admissions:

> Our admissions approach is to firstly comply with statutory categories for children with particular needs regardless of faith. We then have a category which gives priority to those who attend a place of public Christian worship. Clearly this will encompass families who are part of a Christian church, familiar with a Christian ethos and who want education rooted in that ethos for their children. We have, however chosen the wording carefully so that it does not discriminate against those who may not wish to follow the Christian faith but who may value the Christian ethos above the ethos available in other institutions. Such families are able to walk to their local Anglican church as there is a church in every parish in England. They can also walk to churches of other denominations if they so choose, increasing accessibility further. They can attend the worship without necessarily participating in it, in order to assess what a Christian ethos means in practice.

> The inclusive nature of the Church of England ensures that its churches are open to all, whatever their faith or background. This allows families, whether members of a church or not, to understand the ethos of the school and so make an informed choice regarding its suitability for their child if they wish to gain priority in the admission process.

We then have a final category which is based solely on distance from the school. This category allows any remaining places to be filled by families who are in the wider community and who regard a place at our school to be as appropriate as a place at any other High school, whatever the ethos.

The result of this admissions approach is to ensure that families across Greater Manchester and Lancashire can have access to a school with a Christian ethos, whether they live locally to it or not. This is important as not all areas have a Church of England High School available to them locally. We provide families with genuine choice when deciding upon the best school for their child. These families understand the Christian ethos of the school because of our admission process and are supportive of their children within it when they apply for, and gain a place at the school.[2]

In these examples we see two different approaches, but both are driven by the desire to serve the school's local and wider community effectively. They demonstrate that it is not possible to apply one set of criteria universally because the specific context is different in every case.

Admissions in the future

Although we may yearn for a much simpler system, unless we return to the time when children simply went to their local school, with no possibility of parents being involved in a choice about their children's education other than to move house, then the situation is likely to get ever more complicated, especially with the coming together of groups of schools in multi-academy trusts. Secondary schools that form a trust with a group of surrounding primary schools will have to decide whether attendance at one of the primary schools secures a place at the secondary school, or not. And there are further possibilities with the introduction of a new option in December 2014 which allows schools to prioritise children who attract the pupil premium. How schools use this freedom for the advantage of those children will be an important demonstration of a commitment to the disadvantaged, but some may feel that it is a step too far in the extent to which we see schools taking part in social engineering.

Conclusion

It has often been noted that the solution to the extremely complex arrangements caused by parental choice in school admissions and the oversubscription criteria that schools use, is to not focus on admissions but rather on quality of provision. Oversubscription criteria are only applicable when a school is oversubscribed. So the solution is not to focus all our energy on the admissions process but to invest more time building and running outstanding schools. The popularity of Church of England schools which serve children across religious, social and ethnic divides suggests that we need more schools committed to this approach, not fewer. Achieving the right balance of provision through careful use of oversubscription criteria allows governing bodies to work for the good of the communities and be responsive to the changing dynamics that are part of any vibrant community's life.

Divisive Faith Schools Urgently Need Reform

Jonathan Romain

Schools serve two purposes: to educate individuals, and to help create the society of tomorrow that they will inhabit and fashion. If we have schools that are tolerant and inclusive, there is every hope that society will develop in that way. Conversely, if we have schools that are restrictive and segregated, there is reason to fear that society will develop likewise.

This is the danger posed by faith schools – which not only are a third of all schools today, but are growing in number, especially among the minority faiths, with Jewish and Muslim ones increasing, while Sikh and Hindu ones have recently made their appearance. They reflect the fact that society has changed in the last century: from being predominantly Christian with a small Jewish minority, to consisting of a plethora of faiths. If you colour-coded Britain according to each religion in the 1930s and again in the 2000s, then the map of the UK will have changed from virtually monochrome to a kaleidoscope of colour. That can be seen as enormously enriching in many ways, but it begs the question of whether separating children of different faiths, which can also mean of different ethnic backgrounds, into separate schools encourages integration or inhibits it?

Ten years ago we saw the riots in Bradford; the ensuing 2001 Cantle Report referred to the 'parallel lives' between different religious and ethnic groups.[1] One of the three subsequent local reviews, the Ouseley Report, blamed part of the problem on the segregation in schools between different local communities.[2] Ted Cantle, leading the Independent Community Cohesion Review Team, concluded that it is vital for the future stability of the country that children mix with each other in harmony. That period also saw the terrible scenes of Catholic children trying to battle their way through screaming ranks of Protestants to the Holy Cross School in Belfast.[3] If, when they were children, those Protestant parents had mixed with Catholic children, they might have grown up knowing that Catholics are not demons, and they might not have been so hate-filled as to man the barricades against them.

In England, thankfully, we do not have such dire problems as Northern Ireland – but it seems astonishingly shortsighted to encourage the conditions that might lead to them. The Catholic-Protestant animosity was not caused by the education system, but dividing the children did help perpetuate the stereotypes and reinforce prejudice. It is all too easy for separation to degenerate into ignorance of each other, resulting in a downward spiral of suspicion, fear and hostility. Moreover, while many faith schools have laudable aims, others have been set up precisely because they wish to avoid any integration with wider society. Even if the better ones teach about other faiths, cardboard cut-outs from a school text book are no substitute for everyday interaction.

The key lesson, though, starts at the school gates: in terms of who is allowed in – those with the 'right faith'

– and who is not admitted – those with the 'wrong' or no faith. Consciously or not, we are giving a very powerful message to those children about others. The problem is that we are so used to it we fail to realise how offensive it is. In no other part of public life or state-funded institutions can you be selected or turned away because of your religion: not in hospitals, libraries, the police force, the civil service or anywhere else. It is illegal and morally unthinkable. Yet that is exactly what happens with state-funded faith schools, in the very institutions that we like to think are preparing young children for a better, fairer, more inclusive society. Separating children also means separating parents, who no longer meet one another outside the school gates, at parent-teachers meetings and sports days, thereby cutting huge swathes between the communities. Future historians may look back at this moment and blame us for increasing social fragmentation. We have spent over a century trying to rid ourselves of class divisions; surely it is madness to rush in and replace them with religious divisions. The good news in Northern Ireland, though, is the remarkable success story of the integrated schools. In 1981 a group of parents 'broke the mould' by coming together to open the first planned integrated school, Lagan College. Since the initial 28 pupils at Lagan College there are now 21,745 pupils at integrated schools throughout the province of Ulster, while the demand for places in integrated schools is continuing to grow despite a drop in the overall school aged population. Could that have any message for the rest of us?

An added problem is that if children from particular faith groups are largely in their own faith schools, it means depleting community schools of them and the chance to interact with each other. When I visited a school in Finchley in North London – an area of a high Jewish density – there was not a single Jewish pupil there. They were all in Jewish day schools, so the Christian, Muslim, Sikh, Hindu and non-religious children living locally saw Jews all around them but never actually met them. Schools should be used to build bridges, not erect barriers. Would it not be better for the health of British society to encourage schools that are cross-religious: that are open to all children, do not promote one particular faith, nor regard religion as a waste of time? Instead, they treat faith seriously, respect religious differences and acknowledge the richness of each tradition. Meanwhile, the children receive their own particular religious direction from the source that has the greatest impact: their home. Parents also have the option of taking them to church, synagogue, mosque and gurdwara, not to mention after-school classes, Sunday school or religious summer camps. Religious knowledge can come from the school, but religious belief from the home environment.

It is not good for children to be the religious equivalent of Rapunzel – locked away in her tower – because isolation is a poor teacher for later life, and it is certainly not helpful for Britain at large if the next generation grows up disconnected. It is important to note that these reservations do not stem from a secular attack on faith but are based on religious conviction. The Book of Leviticus (19.18) – which Jesus later echoed – urges us to 'Love your neighbour as yourself.' The only way we can achieve that is *knowing* our neighbour.

Would my own children, who are Jewish, do well in a Jewish day school? Undoubtedly, but there are higher values to be considered too: social cohesion, the national interest, the creation of well-rounded individuals. This is the reason I sent my children not to the local Jewish school but to a community school, because I considered it important for my Jewish children to sit next to a Christian in class, play football in the break with a Muslim, do homework with a Hindu and walk back with an atheist – for my children to know them, and them to know my children. Moreover, there has been a spate of independent evidence over how faith schools also divide children according to their socioeconomic backgrounds. Thus the Institute for Public Policy Research in 2007 showed that 'where faith schools are their own admissions authorities [i.e. voluntary aided schools] they are ten times more likely to be highly unrepresentative of their surrounding area'.[4] The following year appeared a report by the Runnymede Trust, entitled 'Right to Divide? Faith Schools and Community Cohesion'. It, too, detected a social discrimination problem posed by faith schools:

> Despite high level pronouncements that suggest a mission to serve the most disadvantaged in society, faith schools educate a disproportionately small number of young people at the lowest end of the socio-economic scale.[5]

The Runnymede Trust's evidence included research by Anne West of the London School of Economics, which found that some Catholic and Church of England schools are socially-selective 'elite' secondary schools which appear to select out low-income religious families.[6] This evidence was supported by comments by the then Department of Children, Schools and Families: 'Faith schools were found to be engaging in practices that were exclusive and favourable to those with greater social capital and higher socioeconomic status.'[7]

Returning to Ted Cantle's work in response to the Bradford riots, 2009 saw a further report by Cantle examining segregation in Blackburn. He found that the 'level of segregation in schools is high, growing and more extensive than the level of residential segregation would suggest', with a number of faith schools 'a particular issue'.[8] This selectivity is borne out by statistics about the most indisputable of objective measures, free school meals. A remarkable map of how schools in Britain select their pupils – published in 2013 by the Fair Admissions Campaign – confirms the previous findings: that many faith schools use their legal right to choose pupils by faith as a covert means of choosing them by ability or wealth. Whereas comprehensive secondary schools with no religious character admit 11 per cent more pupils eligible for free school meals than live in their local areas, comprehensive Church of England secondaries admit 10 per cent fewer, Roman Catholic schools admit 24 per cent fewer, Muslim schools 25 per cent fewer and Jewish schools 61 per cent fewer. This mapping shows that it is no surprise that some faith schools do well in league tables when they have edited their intake to such an extent.[9]

These are extraordinary figures in two other respects. First, there is the massive religious embarrassment that schools whose principles mean they should be supporting the poor and championing the vulnerable are failing to do so. This is reinforced by the fact that they also cater for fewer pupils with Special Educational Needs (SEN): 1.2 per cent of pupils at state faith schools had statemented SEN and 15.9 per cent unstatemented, compared to 1.7 per cent and 18.9 per cent at schools with no religious character.[10] Secondly, it begs the question of why a placement system allowing selection on religious grounds which was originally designed to protect faith has been so easily hijacked by those seeking to manipulate pupil admissions, be it by the parents or the schools themselves. A dramatic example of this was seen recently when The London Oratory School was criticised by the Schools Adjudicator for breaching the Schools Admissions Code and effectively discriminating against non-Catholics.[11] The school's criterion for entry included parents participating in church life for at least three years beforehand through activities such as singing in the choir, serving at the altar or arranging flowers. Such practices should not determine whether children qualify for a place in a state-funded school. The Fair Admissions Campaign's map illustrates that the issue is not limited to The London Oratory School, but is endemic to the way many other faith schools operate. Spending time in church to gain a school place has become the religious equivalent of paying cash for honours.

Further evidence of religious manipulation came in data released in 2014 by the Pastoral Research Centre Trust, on Catholic baptisms. While the number of baptisms for children in England and Wales under the age of one was in long-term decline, the number over one had risen dramatically in the previous decade. Rather than being an expression of piety, this new baptism trend suggested a level of deliberate strategy by parents keen to increase their child's chances of obtaining a place in a popular Church school.[12] These findings also mean that the traditional argument over equality in the education system – grammar schools versus comprehensives – is rendered barely relevant and completely misses the hidden unfairness that is secretly going on in the state sector. Whereas only five per cent of secondary age children attend grammar schools, over three times that number attend state schools that select according to faith, and it is in those schools that a high degree of socioeconomic jostling is taking place.[13]

Faith admission discriminations may not only be undesirable but illegal, for in August 2012 the Equality and Human Rights Commission published a report entitled 'Religion or Belief, Equality and Human Rights in England and Wales'. It warned that allowing publicly-funded schools to use faith-based admissions criteria may not be compatible with Article 2 of Protocol 1 of the European Convention on Human Rights (the right to education) and Article 14 (prohibition of discrimination).[14] The debate has been given an added impetus by the so-called 'Trojan Horse' debacle over certain schools in Birmingham last year. Attention was drawn not only to admissions policies, but also to the width of the curriculum that is taught and the competence of inspection regimes that are used. It has led to Ofsted cracking down on faith schools throughout the country and across religious boundaries, instigating no-notice inspections and being tougher in their verdicts. The irony is that the Birmingham schools at the centre of the original scandal were not faith schools, but the exposure of their failings raised major question marks about how faith schools operate. The alarming fact was that if the Birmingham schools had been designated faith schools, then many of the practices condemned – such as limiting the curriculum to exclude lessons about sex education and reinforcing a cultural identity to the exclusion of others – would have been permitted. How can that which we find offensive in what are designated 'community schools' suddenly be acceptable if they are labelled 'faith schools'? Blinkering the horizons of children must be wrong wherever they learn.

Part of the problem is systemic in that Religious Education (RE) is a statutory subject and so must be taught, but it is not part of the national curriculum, and so RE can be taught in any way. It means that while some schools follow a multi-faith syllabus, others limit their pupils to one faith only, especially faith schools. It would be much healthier to have a national curriculum for RE, with all schools having to teach about all belief systems (including humanism) and providing a balanced and inclusive education. This would be partly a matter of general knowledge – RE as an academic subject in its own right – and partly a way of promoting social harmony, so that those living in neighbouring streets understand each other and are equipped to emerge into a diverse society. Moreover, one cannot comprehend world events – from Sunni-Shia tensions in Iraq to Catholic-Protestant problems in Northern Ireland – without a grasp of the religious history behind them. This would not infringe on any religious rights, for it would focus on religious knowledge and not attempt to inculcate beliefs. Far from being an impossible ideal, such a syllabus already exists thanks to the work of the Religious Education Council of England and Wales. Moreover, it is supported by all the major faiths groups (and the British Humanist Association). At present it is voluntary and for guidance only; adopting it nationally should be an urgent priority.

Still, as some of the no-notice Ofsted inspections have demonstrated recently, it is not enough to propose a syllabus, the actual teaching has to be monitored. It has long been an extraordinary own goal that Ofsted has outsourced inspection of RE to teams from within the same faith as the particular school they are visiting. Some of those teams operate with the highest integrity, but others consider the purity of their faith as more important than wider social interests. As RE – much more than maths or geography – can be crucial in shaping the values and attitudes of children, it cannot be left to self-regulation, but should have the same independent assessment as do other subjects. The 'Trojan Horse' episode was a wake-up call for those who, until now, regarded benignly the ability of faiths to promote their traditions via the state education system without realising that it could mean allowing them to both indoctrinate children under their care and alienate them from others in society.

The growing sense of unease about faith admissions has permeated religious leaders too. In 2011 the then Bishop of Oxford, John Pritchard, who was also the Chair for the Church of England Education Board, suggested that Church of England schools should limit the proportion of pupils they select on religious grounds to 10 per cent of their intake.[15] In 2013 the Archbishop of Canterbury, Justin Welby, spoke approvingly of 'a steady move away from faith-based entry tests'.[16] Unease with the status quo also led to a new alliance of clergy across all denominations and faiths being formed in 2014. It brought together those from Anglican, Catholic and other churches (Methodist, United Reformed, Unitarian, Quaker), along with the Hindu, Muslim and Jewish faiths. They called for an end to discrimination in pupil admissions and teacher employment, as well as broadening the curriculum to make it obligatory for all children to study the major faiths in Britain. They speak from a position of deep faith, but feel the way faith schools currently operate is an affront to religious values of openness and equality. For example, they pointed out that schools can only select children according to their faith by having a specific exemption from the Equality Act – exemption from equality – and asked what that said about religious teachings?[17] In the run-up to the 2015 election, the alliance has called on the political parties to pledge in their manifestos to change the law in five ways:

1. To work towards ending the anomaly by which state-funded schools are legally able to distinguish between children on religious grounds in their admissions procedure;

2. In the meantime, to bring all state schools in line with the system under which free schools operate, limiting the number of children that can be selected on the grounds of their faith to 50 per cent of the annual intake;

3. To close the legal loophole which currently allows schools to refuse to employ teachers on the basis of their faith;

4. To recognise that removing the duty of Ofsted to inspect how schools promoted community cohesion was a mistake and should be re-instated;

5. To ensure that all children learn about the full range of faiths and belief systems in Britain by adding Religious Education to the national curriculum.[18]

The previous uncritical acceptance of faith schools is changing rapidly. A growing number of parents are resentful of children being denied entry to local schools because of faith restrictions, while an increasing number of clergy are realising that faith institutions should not be promoting division but encouraging harmony. It is becoming clear that it is possible to be in favour of faith, but against faith schools, both in principle and because of their effects. Discrimination and segregation are neither religious values nor good for social cohesion. The increasing number of faith schools means that there is a real danger of creating an educational apartheid, with not only a corrosive impact on children's outlooks, but a divisive effect on society at large. Britain today is a multi-faith society, but the division of children into faith schools risks turning it into a multi-fractious one unless steps are taken to modify the way they operate.

In Defence of Faith Schools and Religious Selection

Gillan Scott

Surveying the landscape

Try to imagine, for a moment, what sort of a country the United Kingdom would become if we could begin again from scratch. In this perfect nation, would there be need for a monarch? Would we create an unelected upper chamber in the palace of our democracy? What would our welfare system look like, or our health service? Would we make our tax system far less complicated? Would we choose to drive on the left? There are endless questions and few definitive answers to such a proposal, and a multitude of opportunities for disagreement over what sort of society we might create. One person's heaven may well be someone else's hell.

Such a scenario is an entirely hypothetical line of thinking, but is this not essentially what politics aims to achieve: a realisation of a better and more prosperous society? Party politics should be shaped by a vision of the future, but, unlike any utopian flight of fancy, it needs to start from the present – where we are now – and be grounded in the past. As individuals, and as a society, we cannot detach ourselves from the history that surrounds and shapes us. The decisions and actions of those who have gone before us have left their mark and, whether we like it or not, we are affected by the consequences. This is very much the state of play with our education system. The varieties of schools we have throughout our land carry the visible traces of our educational evolution. The schools that have centuries of history have undergone repeated transformations, which have reflected the demands placed upon them; and, with each new year, we see new schools that begin new chapters in that story. Would anyone choose to have a perplexing arrangement where, depending on their geographical location and personal circumstances, different children attend academies, free schools, two-tier and three-tier systems, faith schools, grammar schools, sixth-form colleges, and the array of independent schools? The answer may well be a resounding 'No', but that doesn't stop us having to deal with the situation we find ourselves in.

Faith schools are very much a case in point. According to 2014 government data of England's 20,117 schools, 6,844 (or 34 per cent) were faith schools. Out of the 3,329 secondary schools, the number of faith schools was 633 – which, at 19 per cent, was proportionally smaller than the 37 per cent of primary schools.[1] Yet, despite over 1.8 million children attending these schools, and their continued popularity, there is an ongoing debate – fuelled mostly by secular and humanist groups – as to whether they should exist at all in a country that is increasingly turning its back on religion. However, such arguments tend to disregard the reason why we have so many of these schools, as well as the considerable contribution that they have made over the centuries. Let us not forget that our education system was created by the churches, long before any government became involved. The Department for Children, Schools and Families emphasised this in its report, 'Faith in the System':

> Faith organisations have a long and noble tradition in education in this country – from medieval times, through the Reformation, to the present day. This involvement predates that of the state, catering for all children, especially the most disadvantaged. Between 1811 and 1860 the Church of England founded 17,000 schools through its National Society to offer education to the poor at a time when the Government was not prepared to take on the role. The first Jewish school for the poor was set up in 1732 and from 1852 the Catholic Bishops have worked to make available, wherever possible, schools for all Catholic children regardless of their parents' ability to pay. Church of England, Catholic and Jewish schools have existed in the maintained sector since the late nineteenth century, along with Methodist and Quaker schools.[2]

At this point, it is worth mentioning that, 'in law, there is no such thing as a faith school'.[3] Although the term has entered into common usage in the last few years, what 'faith school' essentially refers to is a school with a religious character. It is possible to have faith in many things that have nothing to do with religion. It is problematic because it implies that faith, in its broadest sense, has no place in non-faith schools, despite this being a natural part of understanding the world around us. The other issue is that it can give the impression that faith schools represent a wide spread of beliefs. Whilst this is true from a certain angle, 99 per cent of all faith schools in England are church schools. Of the 633 secondary faith schools in England, 324 are Roman Catholic, 207 are Church of England, and 77 are other Christian denominations. That leaves 12 Jewish, nine Muslim, 3 Sikh, and one 'other'.[4] So, when we are talking about faith schools in the secondary sector, which is this chapter's focus, in the vast majority of cases we are referring to church schools.

Returning to the nature of faith schools, by far the biggest grievance that has been aimed at them is the ability they have been given to select some or all pupils through their admissions criteria according to their religion – or, rather, that of their parents. Again, it is helpful to remember that not all faith schools' admissions policies work in the same way, and this largely depends on whether schools are voluntary controlled, voluntary aided, or have academy or free school status. Voluntary controlled schools (of which the vast majority are Church of England) have their admissions dictated by their local authority and, potentially, can select additional children on faith grounds when oversubscribed, although only about a quarter of local authorities allow this. Voluntary aided schools set their own admissions criteria and can select up to 100 per cent on religious grounds if oversubscribed. Academies that have converted from voluntary controlled or voluntary aided status operate their own admissions, but all new free schools can select only up to 50 per cent of students according to faith.[5] Amongst these different schools, the number of places allocated on religious grounds varies considerably, but approximately 16 per cent of all faith schools in England have no such places allocated.[6] Any pictures painted of our faith schools benefitting those solely of their own faith, or seeking to indoctrinate their pupils, are wildly unhelpful and misleading.

Although secular groups, such as the British Humanist Association, would quite happily see the back of faith schools altogether, they have been able to gather support from a wider range of groups on the particular issue of admissions, because of the perceived injustices associated with selecting by faith.[7] The two most high-profile campaigns against religious selection in state schools are the Accord Coalition, which was launched in 2008, and the British Humanist Association's Fair Admissions Campaign, which is less than two years old. There is a great deal of overlap between the two campaigns, including among those backing them. Both are supported by a limited number of groups and individuals, including a handful from a religious background. Despite lacking widespread backing and being recently established, they have been successful at getting their message out through the media, and their cause has received significant attention. The Fair Admissions Campaign has produced a list of ten reasons why religious selection by faith schools is objectionable.[8] Some of these concerns are superficial ('It is out of step with historic advances for the freedom of religion'), but others appear to have some legitimacy, and are worth considering carefully. Perhaps the two most substantial accusations against schools that select according to faith is that they increase the division between children along socioeconomic lines, and that they segregate children on religious and ethnic grounds, which is bad for community cohesion. These will both be considered further.

Charge 1: Faith school admissions increase the division between children along socioeconomic lines, which goes against what church schools say they stand for.

This assertion is backed up by the Fair Admissions Campaign's own research that has found that 39 out of the top 50 most 'socially exclusive' schools are faith schools.[9] Social exclusion, in this case, is measured by the proportion of pupils eligible for free school meals attending a faith school compared to that of those living in the local surrounding area. Those schools that have lower levels of free school meals have then been labelled socially exclusive. Their data suggests that comprehensive secondary schools with no religious character admit 11 per cent more pupils eligible for free school meals than live in their local areas. Comprehensive Church of England secondaries admit 10 per cent fewer; Roman Catholic secondaries, 24 per cent fewer; Jewish secondaries, 61 per cent fewer; and Muslim secondaries, 25 per cent fewer.[10] Other independent research has produced similar findings,[11] and this disparity is particularly pronounced where schools are in charge of their own admissions.[12]

Using eligibility for free school meals as a measure of social exclusion certainly has some value, but there is a limit to what conclusions can be drawn from the numbers, which can only be considered in the context of the methodology used. The Catholic Education Service has made the claim that their catchment areas are wider than the postcode or local authority area wherein their schools are situated. Neither does the free school meal research take into account the distribution of faith schools. The Catholic Education Service also has stated that figures from the Department for Education in 2012 revealed that some 17 per cent of pupils at Catholic schools lived in the 10 per cent most deprived areas, compared to 12 per cent of pupils nationally.[13]

It may be fair to assert that there is a different level of social exclusion that can be linked to faith schools, but that does not, in itself, provide any evidence that they are deliberately setting out to pick and choose along these lines. The government's School Admissions Code clearly prohibits faith schools from obtaining information from applicants that could allow them to discriminate against particular socioeconomic groups.[14] In a major poll by YouGov for the Westminster Faith Debates in 2014, the top two reasons for selecting a school given by respondents were its academic standards and location.[15] Faith schools, on average, produce significantly higher results than other state schools in league tables. It is inevitable that for schools that are performing well, demand for places will increase, leading to a variety of consequences, most outside the school's control, which will include a level of socioeconomic sorting. These are laid out in the publication, *More Than an Educated Guess*, by the Christian think tank, Theos:

> The numerous, sometimes conflicting theories which attempt to explain the perceived socioeconomic sorting at oversubscribed faith schools suggest there are complex and multiple causal factors. One commentator, for instance, argues that socio-economic sorting is inevitably bound to systemic issues like 'location disadvantage'. He argues that house price premiums in residential areas linked to the catchment areas of high performing state schools serve to exclude many middle- and low-income households. Unless the argument is made that all fee-paying independent schools should be abolished and access to high-demand housing made

more equitable, then a focus on faith schools as creating 'education apartheid' limits the state's role to preventing social separation on the basis of religion but not doing so on the basis of parents' economic (and indeed social and cultural) capital.

For academic Geoffrey Walford, diversity of school choice will always come at the cost of equity. He suggests freedom of choice advances an 'individualistic and inequitable education system'. Indeed, as many disillusioned parents have found, once popular schools are oversubscribed, it is the schools that select children rather than parents having a 'choice' of school. Within each area there is a likelihood that a hierarchy of schools will develop, and there is growing evidence that various privileged groups are better able than others to influence the selection of their children by those schools at the top of the hierarchy. Those with most concern about the education of their children are able to 'play the system' such that their children have a greater chance of being selected by the prestigious schools.

Rebecca Allen and Anne West conducted research which demonstrates that 'parents reporting a religious affiliation are more likely to be better educated, have a higher occupational class and a higher household income' and that 'higher-income religious families are more likely to have a child at a faith school than lower-income religious families'. Earlier research conducted by the IPPR supports this claim. The research found that families for which the mother had a degree or higher qualification are three times more likely to say that they knew how popular schools allocate places, and twice as likely to apply to a school outside the local authority. In contrast, parents from low socio-economic backgrounds 'are more likely to consider their child's friendship groups and proximity to the school as more important than its performance table position'.[16]

Schools that are oversubscribed and are perceived to be successful may have little incentive to change their admissions policies, but to think that, even if they did, all socioeconomic sorting would be eradicated demonstrates a lack of understanding. It is unfair to lay the blame for the choices of parents who want a decent education for their children at the feet of faith schools.

However, linked to many of these arguments is the ability of faith schools to set entry criteria, relating to church attendance, that will benefit parents who are willing to 'work the system'. The Fair Admissions Campaign claims that:

> By permitting faith selection, the best faith schools provide another way for sharp elbowed parents to get their children admitted. Anecdotal evidence suggests that some parents feign religious belief and practice to help their child into religiously selective schools...[17]

Such evidence is, indeed, anecdotal, but it is not difficult to find stories of families' church attendance drying up once their children have started attending the local church school. Some parents are undoubtedly playing the system, and it would appear that some schools are too, through complex admissions criteria. The case last year of The London Oratory School, a high performing Catholic state school, made the headlines when the Office of the Schools Adjudicator found that its policies had the effect of 'discriminating against pupils on their ethnicity and socioeconomic background'.[18]

Its report found that the school broke the School Admissions Code 105 times. These failures included:

- Asking for parents' baptism certificates;
- Favouring parents for giving support, such as flower-arranging, to the Catholic Church;
- Giving priority to those who had already attended 'any other Catholic school';
- Not allowing the admission of children of no faith.

It is this behaviour that can tarnish the reputation of all faith schools and give fuel to the fire of those who oppose their policies and existence. It is a completely unacceptable case, but, fortunately, also an unusual one. In 2011, Ian Craig, then head of the Office of the Schools Adjudicator, revealed that 45 of the 151 cases reported to them regarding admissions in 2010 were related to faith schools responsible for their own admissions. At that time, there were 6,753 faith schools in England.[19]

Charge 2: Faith school admissions segregate children on religious and ethnic grounds, which is bad for community cohesion.

It is not difficult to understand this viewpoint. Children who mix with others from a range of backgrounds, ethnicities and faiths should be expected to have a better understanding of the world and their society, and to develop a higher degree of respect towards others, irrespective of their differences. It might be expected that faith schools that select on religious grounds would be producing the exact opposite.

In 2001, following the riots in Burnley, Bradford and Oldham, the Cantle Report found that they had been caused in part by 'the depth of polarisation' and 'physical segregation', including separate educational arrangements, which led to communities operating on the basis of a series of parallel lives.[20] Over the following years, the accusation has often been made that faith schools, through their admissions, exacerbate existing tensions between different faith groups and ethnicities.[21] These fears and concerns relating to segregation and multiculturalism have continued to grow in recent years with the rise of Islamic extremism both in this country and abroad. Education was thrown into the spotlight in 2014 through the so-called Operation Trojan Horse, which led to the investigation of 21 Birmingham schools. Whilst the focus of attention was placed on religious groups imposing themselves on the life of the schools, it is important to note that none of these were faith schools. It is a clear example of the way that social, religious and ethnic segregation is an issue affecting all schools and not just those with a religious ethos. As a result of the government's reaction to the 'Trojan Horse' affair, we now find that the concept of 'British values' is at the top of Ofsted's agenda when visiting schools.[22] All schools must be found to be promoting these values and also to be ensuring that religious extremism is not allowed to take hold in any form. This recent refocusing by Ofsted has already caused several faith schools to have their ratings downgraded and, since the start of 2015, two free schools are facing closure.[23] How the concept of British values should be taught in schools is a controversial subject, amidst complaints from some schools that Ofsted has taken a heavy-handed and dogmatic approach to the new guidelines.[24] What is in little doubt is that, in the current climate, there is a good deal of pressure on faith schools to ensure that any segregation caused by faith selection will not be allowed to translate into pupils receiving a narrow and insular education, with no regard to others who hold different religious and cultural values.

Despite the perception that faith schools act as a cradle for social division, the Runnymede Trust, a race equality think tank and member of the Accord Coalition, found in their 'Right to Divide?' report that the intake of faith schools is ethnically diverse.[25] Though Catholic schools may have a low population of Asian pupils, they were found to have a much higher population of black Caribbean and black African young people than any other group of schools.[26] In addition, in some Church of England schools, up to 90 per cent of pupils are Muslim.[27]

Through their own research, church groups have argued that faith schools are able to play a key role in encouraging participation in mainstream society. The Church of England's analysis of Ofsted inspection findings on schools and social cohesion has demonstrated that faith schools at secondary level fared better, on average, than schools without a religious character.[28]

If there is a presumption that faith school admissions produce more segregated, intolerant children, then the other side of that same coin is that barriers will be broken down, and social harmony will increase if children attend more mixed non-selective schools. Anyone who has observed the way that children interact with each other will know that there is no guarantee that they will form friendly relationships with those from different backgrounds. Although there is extensive research that establishes that school diversity has a positive impact on community cohesion and mutual understanding,[29] intolerance is still a common problem. In 2008, the now-defunct charity,

BeatBullying, published findings on bullying due to religious belief. It found that one in four children were bullied because of their faith.[30] Those who had been bullied often began to question their faith, stopped talking about it, or even felt ashamed of it. It does not take a great leap of thinking to understand why some parents would want their children to attend schools where religious belief is encouraged, and is part of everyday conversation.

Pragmatic concerns versus principles

Much of the disquiet raised by campaigners fighting for the abolition of faith-based selection revolves around pragmatic aspects. Is it unfair? Does it discriminate? It is not difficult to find problems with faith-based admissions. There is good evidence that there is a level of socioeconomic sorting (which may indirectly privilege pupils from higher socioeconomic backgrounds), particularly at schools that act as their own admission authorities. Admissions criteria mean that those with an active religious faith will still be excluded because they attend a 'non-partner' church. There may, too, be some social segregation at some schools, though probably not as much as is generally perceived.

Pragmatic issues deserve discussion, and this chapter has covered some points, albeit in a limited way; but, really, when deciding whether faith schools should be allowed to operate as they do, the conversation should begin with principles and needs, rather than grievances and failings. Should we abolish our democracy because a handful of MPs fiddled their expenses? Are banks inherently evil because they brought our economy to its knees in 2008? Do universities stoke segregation because not everyone is able to attend them? Most systems that involve humans are not perfect. There are always some individuals or groups that will come out on top, one way or another. If faith schools were universally hated, few would be bothered about their selection criteria, because parents would be seeking to go elsewhere. It is the demand for places, due to their performance and ethos, that causes dismay and upset for those who fail to get their children accepted, and which creates the need for sorting in ways that will inevitably benefit certain proactive applicants.

It may come as a surprise, therefore, that in the previously mentioned 2014 poll for the Westminster Faith Debates, 62 per cent of those questioned did not object to faith schools discriminating on religious grounds in their admissions.[31] Perhaps this can be attributed to a widespread understanding that faith schools will retain their character better when a significant number of pupils share the school's religion; or, maybe, there is just a simple acceptance that those who have a religious faith should be able to have their children educated according to their beliefs. It is only secular humanists who are actively campaigning against both faith schools and their admissions in any great numbers. It is here that we see two worldviews collide. One sees religious belief as an important part of life for many people; and, even for those without an obvious faith, there is a recognition that its inherent principles and values can provide a strong foundation for life. The other is a belief that religion has no place in public, and that faith schools are increasingly detrimental in a secular liberal society, propping up antiquated belief systems. The abolition of religious selection is one step on the road to removing faith schools and their influence altogether.

Sitting in the middle of these two opposing views are the majority of parents who care more about their children receiving a decent education than ideological crusades – and that means being able to choose a good school. Selection by faith is only a problem if the only school they believe is of a sufficiently high standard in their area is a faith school and they will miss out because they will not meet the admissions criteria. This then becomes a failing of the other schools, rather than the faith school. Removing these criteria will not solve this problem, and will just leave a different set of parents dissatisfied. But, there is another large group of parents who want to see an extra dimension to their children's education. For the millions who hold on to their religious faith dearly, it is more than an interest or lifestyle choice – it sits at the core of their identity, and their desire is that it should flourish. Many would agree with the words of William Temple, as Archbishop of Canterbury in 1942:

> Education is only adequate and worthy when it is itself religious… There is no possibility of neutrality… To be neutral concerning God is the same thing as to ignore Him… If children are brought up to have an understanding of life in which, in fact, there is no reference to God, you cannot correct the effect of that by speaking about God for a certain period of the day. Therefore our ideal for the children of our country is the ideal for truly religious education.[32]

Most families with a religious faith want their children to grow up and be educated in their faith, not just in the confines of their home, but outside of it too. This is not an unreasonable expectation, given the prevalence of faith schools, and it is logical to see schools make space for those who subscribe to their beliefs. For the parents, choosing a school is not like having choice over which hospital one might pick for an operation. The decision will, potentially, allow a child to spend years in an environment where they will be able to share their beliefs with others, and be educated in them as a natural part of their upbringing and personal development. This is the reason that the principle of selection by faith has value and purpose. If we see our country as a place where religion is to be valued, and freedom of belief means being able to live it out in public, then it makes sense to have schools where religion is part of their inherent make-up. It is a sign of a mature and self-confident society, which seeks to serve all of its citizens well.

Banding: Selecting for a Comprehensive Intake

John Coldron

What is banding and how does it work?

Banding is an admission arrangement which uses pupil's scores in tests to ensure they admit children with a range of prior attainment.[1] Although primary schools are not prohibited, banding is currently only used for admission to secondary schools. A school's admission authority will, on the basis of the applicant's performance in a test, allocate the child to one of four or five ability bands. For purposes of illustration, call the highest attainment band 1 and the lowest 5. If an applicant's test score was in the fifth quintile (the 20 per cent with the highest test scores) they would be eligible for band 1, if in the third quintile band 3 and if in the first quintile band 5. Each of the five bands represents 20 per cent of the places available for that year. So if the planned intake to Year 7 is 100, only 20 applicants in each band will be offered a place. If there are more than 20 eligible applicants in any one band, the school will apply their other over-subscription criteria to offer a place to the 20 most eligible. These criteria vary widely between schools.[2] If the applicant is not eligible under these criteria they cannot be offered a place. If the school is undersubscribed overall, every applicant must be admitted and the banding arrangement is relaxed. The banding arrangement is in effect an oversubscription criterion.

Under current regulations banding can be used so that the school's intake either reflects the ability profile of those children applying to the school (proportionate banding),[3] those children applying to a group of schools banding jointly (group banding), the local authority ability profile (local or area-wide banding) or the national ability profile (national banding). If the school has decided to work alone and adopt proportionate banding, the intake will only reflect the ability profile of the applicants to that school. That profile could be very different from a group, the local authority (LA), or the national profile and, potentially, starkly different from neighbouring schools. If the school adopts group banding in collaboration with neighbouring schools, all applicants to the collaborating schools are banded according to their scores on a common test. The intake to each of the schools will reflect the prior attainment profile of applicants to all the schools. It ensures that the intake of one school in the banding arrangement varies little in terms of prior attainment from the intake of another. When all or most schools work together across a local area the balancing effect of local banding is likely to be even stronger.

Only four LAs currently have this arrangement across most of their secondary schools, all of them in London. They are Hackney, Greenwich, Tower Hamlets and Lewisham. Some individual schools have unilateral banding arrangements. The proportion is very small but increasing. In 2006 there were 35, with the great majority (27) in London. 31 out of these 35 used proportionate banding, three of the remaining four used area-wide banding and one was unknown.[4] In 2008, 98 schools used banding,[5] while a report for the Sutton Trust found that in 2012-2013, 121 (four per cent) out of more than 3,000 secondary schools were using banding; with 83 of these in London.[6] Overall 37 local authority areas (18 outside London) included at least one secondary school using banding. Academies and free schools are more likely to use banding.

Why do some admission authorities use banding?

There is little research into the specific motivations of these schools and local authorities using banding, although the detailed Sutton Trust report by Noden *et al* gives some indications.[7] We can however make some informed speculations on the basis of knowledge about the context in which schools now operate. There is ample evidence that schools, particularly in urban areas, compete not only for enough pupils to fill their places but also for pupils who will make it easier for them to achieve a good exam performance. While this is true not only in England but internationally, the longstanding policies of successive governments since 1988 to introduce market relations into education to drive system improvement, means such competition between English schools is particularly strong. Schools are largely, and still fairly crudely, held accountable by government and government agencies for the performance of their pupils in public examinations and being labelled as requiring improvement or in special measures has extremely serious implications for the school. But it is also the case that it is much harder for a school to perform to the necessary standards when the children it admits have low prior attainment and are from less affluent families. Despite policymakers minimising this fact it is well understood by schools and the connection between performance and intake is not disproved by examples of a few individual institutions that succeed against the odds. Schools are also well aware of how parents perceive the other children who would be their child's peers, and the residential areas from which they come.

If schools are competing for a finite pool of local children it follows that where one school has a higher proportion of the higher attaining and affluent, its neighbouring schools will get a higher proportion of lower attaining and poorer children. This social and ability segregation reinforces the different reputations of schools at the top and bottom of local school hierarchies. Hence, some schools have considerable difficulty in attracting easier-to-educate children while others do not. One plausible motivation for a school or group of schools to adopt banding is that it defends against these dangers and offers some mitigation of a dysfunctional polarisation of schooling in local areas. Banding, by better ensuring a range of attainment, offers schools a means of mitigating the impact of social selection on performance relative to other schools.

Highly polarised and segregated schooling has area-wide effects that might motivate stakeholders other than schools to advocate area-wide or local banding. Where schools differ markedly in prior attainment and social background, with some schools extremely popular and others heavily undersubscribed, management of school admissions is more difficult with more anxious parents, a greater likelihood of fraudulent applications, greater dissatisfaction with the outcomes and therefore more appeals with associated costs of time and money. In these contexts admissions to schools is seasonally fraught for local councillors, MPs, LA admissions officers and extremely popular schools. It is also likely to be accompanied by large differences in exam performance between schools, making it more likely that some will be regarded as outstanding while others are branded as failing which, as with schools, has serious implications for LAs. More generally, social segregation of schools, reinforced by residential segregation, may be potentially harmful to community cohesion and is unfair to children attending the lower-performing schools. In so far as banding reduces polarisation and segregation it contributes to reducing these wider problems. More positively, there is evidence of educational gain. Segregated schooling leads to lower attainment and lower educational opportunities for poorer children.[8] Furthermore, when children of all abilities are educated together, the attainment of the best-performing children does not suffer,[9] and that of the least-performing tends to improve.[10]

The need for fairer admissions

There is an enduring concern about the fairness of admissions. Because it selects an intake comprehensive in terms of prior attainment, and because prior attainment is highly correlated with socioeconomic status, banding might help significantly to improve the fairness of admissions, because it neutralises many of the determinants of segregated intakes. Why are there concerns about the fairness of admissions to schools?

Whatever one's views about comprehensives and grammars, or the role of the market in education, everyone can perhaps agree that, if we have parental choice, all parents should have an equal chance of getting their child into their preferred school. But it seems this may not be the case. Although parents from all social backgrounds consider the academic performance of a school as one among other important criteria of choice, higher-performing schools (whether selective or comprehensive) are attended more often by children from richer families while poorer children are more likely to attend a school that is performing less well.[11] In 2013, the Sutton Trust found that the overall proportion of pupils eligible for free school meals at the 500 highest-performing comprehensives was 7.6 per cent, compared to the average of 16.5 per cent for all other state schools.[12]

Schools vary in the proportion of children they have on free school meals as compared with the proportion in their neighbourhood. Community schools are least segregated on this measure whereas faith schools (voluntary aided) and converter academies tend to have more socially advantaged intakes.[13] Converter academies have an average free-school-meals proportion of 7.3 per cent, compared to an average of 16.5 per cent across all schools. The 163 remaining grammar schools are also populated disproportionately by children from more affluent families.[14] Cribb *et al* report that though 18 per cent of pupils in selective areas are eligible for free school meals, the grammar schools in those areas have only 3 per cent and poorer children with the same ability are less likely to attend a grammar school as their richer peers[15] – in selective LAs, 66 per cent of children who achieve level 5 in both English and maths at key stage 2 who are not eligible for free school meals go to a grammar school compared with 40 per cent of similarly high-achieving children who are eligible for free school meals.

Social segregation is greatest where there is structural and religious diversity between schools; where there are more schools that are their own admissions authority; and where the area is wholly selective.[16] There is no strong correlation between marketisation and the national level of social segregation,[17] and the determinants of the kind of segregation and polarisation between schools in an area are to be found in the local context.[18] Different kinds of segregation – ethnic, religious, English as second language, special educational needs – have different patterns and their determinants are likely to vary.[19] The reasons why richer parents have, or seem to have, privileged access is a complex mix of differences of financial and social resources, social solidarity, residential segregation, and criteria of choice as well as the legal admission criteria of schools.[20]

Such competition and the resulting differences in the fate of schools might be acceptable if popularity or unpopularity was a result mainly of a judgement on the part of parents as to the quality of education offered by the school, but there are good reasons why that is not likely to be the case. Added to strong suspicions (but little direct evidence) of covert illegal selection of children with higher prior attainment and from more affluent families by some schools, is the more significant fact of residential segregation leading to selection by mortgage. If poorer parents wanted to move into affluent neighbourhoods, which tend also to have higher-performing schools, they are less able to afford to do so. Because most schools use proximity as a criterion of admission,[21] and because attainment is highly correlated with socioeconomic status, richer parents have higher-performing schools as realistic choices while poorer parents have poorer-performing schools.[22] Another factor that confounds the operation of the market to drive system improvement, to give greater access for poorer parents to high-performing schools and reduce social segregation, is that a proportion of poorer parents actively choose lower-performing schools. If banding worked to reduce these market dysfunctions and led to parents choosing more on the basis of the educational quality of schools rather than their social characteristics, and reduced some schools' ability to admit more of their fair share of higher-attaining pupils, the policy of system improvement through competition might be more effective.

Effects, advantages, disadvantages and practical limitations

In the purely theoretical case that the intake of each school in an area perfectly reflected the social and ethnic composition and range of educational attainment of the population that they served we might expect the following effects:

- each school in an area would have the same composition in relation to prior attainment, social background and ethnicity;

- the incentive for parents to choose on the basis of the social or ethnic intake of a school would be removed;

- school performance would unequivocally be the result of the quality of teaching, management and facilities and not a result of the intake;

- there would be an opportunity for the foregrounding of genuine differences in educational approach and other kinds of diversity which might provide more choice for parents according to their views and beliefs;

- there would be a narrowing of the range of performance of schools; for example, a reduction in the number of failing schools and a proportionate reduction in the number of schools with outstanding results but not a reduction in the attainment of individual pupils;

- attainment overall would be likely to improve because the negative peer effect in schools with concentrations of disadvantaged children would be diluted and, because diluted, it would not have a proportionate negative effect on the performance of the balanced intakes;

- the denigration of certain schools would be reduced as a result of eradicating the division into highly desirable and highly undesirable schools on the basis of social composition.

Such perfectly balanced intakes across a local authority are of course practically unachievable. Social groups are not evenly distributed across a geographical area and many cities and towns are characterised by residential segregation both social and ethnic. In rural areas with relatively low population density, the distances between schools are much greater than in more densely populated areas, and even some metropolitan local authorities have geographical outlying sectors. In these cases banding across the whole area would probably reduce the proportion of parents getting their nearest school, exacerbate the problem of travel for some parents and/or add to costs for subsidised transport with negative environmental implications. In 2008, 25 per cent of parents already opted away from their nearest school and it is difficult to gauge whether and how far this might increase – religious and selective schools already draw from a much wider geographical area than their immediate neighbourhood – but it is unlikely to decrease with area-wide banding.[23]

The fact that children would travel away from their nearest schools also has implications for parental satisfaction. Having a school within easy travelling distance is important to parents especially at the primary stage, but also at secondary.[24] A policy of balancing intakes across a whole area might also cut across the preference of some parents and children to be with sufficient others of their own community.

But research suggests that even in densely populated urban areas the intended beneficial effects of banding can be muted. Noden *et al* studied in detail the effect of banding in three local authority areas where, in each, banding was adopted by several secondary schools. They looked at documentary evidence, interviewed local authority officers in the three areas and eleven head teachers from these and other areas using banding. This showed that schools being able to choose between proportionate, group and area-wide banding, together with different patterns of parental preferences, meant that the prior attainment of intakes of participating schools still varied quite considerably, although probably not as much as without banding. In addition, in all areas there were some (mostly voluntary aided faith) schools that did not collaborate in the banding arrangement. They also found that it can only have an effect on the intakes of both over- and undersubscribed schools if at least some participating schools are oversubscribed and have to reject some applicants. The effectiveness of banding is therefore constrained by the popularity of schools and the supply of school places.[25] Noden *et al* also identified issues with the testing. Although in all three areas a single banding test was carried out in the children's primary schools, some of the secondary schools required applicants to sit an additional banding test. Apart from the additional costs to the school, stress on children and inconvenience to parents this might, because of extra costs of time and money, inhibit some parents from applying to those schools. They conclude that: 'in striving to achieve balanced intakes, banding for the purposes of admission is not a panacea. It can however contribute to creating more balanced intakes than would otherwise be the case'.[26]

The aim of balancing intakes vies with other policy priorities and must overcome the practical difficulties of reducing segregation in different and highly complex local geographical and social contexts. Banding across a whole area is necessarily incompatible with the LA being wholly selective. But, the existence of any selective schools in the area would reduce the benefits. It is also possible, as noted above, for admission authorities, including those of voluntary aided and foundation schools, to remain outside any banding arrangements thus reducing the overall effect. The examples of the three local authorities currently using area-wide fair banding show that faith schools can be accommodated in fair banding arrangements. However, where the group of applicants to faith schools have notably different social characteristics (for example, if their families are on average more wealthy, or have more educational qualifications) than parents applying to non-faith schools in the area, then some differences of intake might still occur.

Ballots

The admission authorities of schools are allowed to use ballots (random allocation) as a main admission arrangement but it is explicitly prohibited for it to be used for all community schools in a local authority area.[27] Ballots (or random allocation) can, like banding, be used to counteract social selection by mortgage because, used as the only criterion for admission, it would give an equal chance to all applicants regardless of where they live. It would also guard against covert selection by schools or gaming by parents. Half of all secondary schools use ballots, most often as a tie breaker when other oversubscription criteria fail to distinguish between equally eligible applicants. Where this is the case it has no significant effect on intakes. No schools currently select children entirely at random – if they did it would likely be unpopular with parents because it would be more unpredictable, probably increase the number not getting into their nearest school and therefore increase travel to school. Balloting was used as a main ranking criterion, not just as a tie breaker, by only 42 schools in 2012 in combination with other criteria such as siblings, banding and catchments.[28] The early evidence from applications in England is equivocal as to effects on social and ability segregation because ballots were used in complex interplay with catchments.[29] Also, although ballots offer a theoretical guarantee of an equal chance of a place, this may not be the case when implemented in real contexts – there is some evidence from its use in the US that higher-attaining pupils are more likely to enter random ballots for school places than are lower-attaining children.

Concluding remarks

If one's concerns are primarily about improving local communities of schools by balancing intakes and reducing the harmful effects of social segregation, then banding is one of the best devices we have for achieving these aims. It is not however a panacea and presents some problems of implementation. Admission to school is becoming increasingly complex as a result of more schools becoming their own admission authority. This is illustrated by schools in the same banding arrangement using different kinds of banding (proportionate or local) in conjunction with different sets of other oversubscription criteria.[30] The effects of banding would be greatly enhanced if implemented uniformly across an area or across sub groups within the area tailored according to local contexts. This lends strength to the argument that greater fairness would result if admission arrangements, which affect all schools in a given area, were not decided by individual schools but by an area-wide body.

But what we ultimately hope to achieve through education and education policy determines what concerns us most when we look at schooling today. Rival visions about how best to achieve a prosperous, ordered and cohesive civil society drive debate about education. The history of education in England from 1870 on can largely be told as a struggle between those who advocate differentiated and separate educational pathways and those who argue for common schooling. Today, for example, the advocacy of an education market goes along with a concern to acknowledge differences of individual ability, parental preferences and educational approaches and we have considerable de facto separate schooling through segregated intakes. The adoption of banding, as well as offering some defence against the dysfunctions of this approach and its outcomes, expresses commitment to a rival vision of the role schools should play in society and the aim to achieve a system that delivers better outcomes for all. Given these widely diverging moral and political positions it is of interest that there are arguments arising from the perspective of both sides for policymakers to reduce social segregation. Banding – selecting for a balanced intake – can be an effective tool for doing so.

Selection and the Independent Sector

Neil Roskilly

On my shelves at home I've built up quite a collection of books ... *for Dummies.* Many of these hint at former interests, such as *Auto Repair for Dummies, Skiing for Dummies* and *Ukulele for Dummies*, though quite what I had in mind with the latter has been lost in the mists of time as I've never owned a ukulele. (I didn't get around to procuring *Sex for Dummies*, mainly as the title just boggled the imagination.) None of my purchases ever resulted in mastery and some even contributed to awkward and painful juxtapositions with leaking manifolds and snow drifts (which may *also* explain why I was never tempted to add *Sex for Dummies* to the library). Most of these 'helpful' guides now gather dust, though I was recently tempted to boost my collected works with *Catholic High School Entrance Exams for Dummies*. As well as containing six full-length admissions tests, it's full of helpful if rather obvious advice such as 'don't pay attention to other test takers', and 'don't waste your time on hard questions'. I think I know what it means. You will have guessed by now that *Catholic High School Entrance Examinations for Dummies* is targeted at the North American market, where I am sure it remains a bestseller. Yet given the number of revision guides and practice books available on Amazon's UK site, I suspect that we are not far from seeing, *Common Entrance for Dummies*. This wouldn't be surprising, given that parents crave all the help they can get when swamped in the mire of private school entrance procedures. In addition to this burgeoning sector of the publishing industry, parents are regularly bombarded by specialist tutors and agencies who promise to provide the necessary edge in return for hard-earned cash – a multi-million pound business in itself. As Gregory Ratoff put it, 'You're a parasite for sore eyes.'[1]

On the face of it the choice seems simple enough for parents. If you're happy with competitive selection and see it as a prerequisite for the future success of your progeny, you target a selective school and pitch your child into its formal admissions processes, most commonly at the age of 11 or 13. A child's current school may already be assisting of course, with a curriculum devoted to competitive entry, ultimately determined by the Independent Schools Examinations Board (ISEB) Common Entrance (CE) or other admissions examinations specific to senior schools. CE tests the core areas of English, maths, science and verbal reasoning with optional papers in French, geography, German, Greek, history, Latin, religious studies and Spanish. It's a traditional approach favoured by preparatory schools that may be tied to a single senior institution or, more commonly, furnish children on a best-fit basis to a range of senior schools with varying entry demands. Parents often select a feeder school on their preconceptions of its success in this capacity, even when resulting in a child 'over-reaching' and struggling later. In turn, junior or 'prep' schools commonly employ prescribed formal entrance examinations and interviews from the age of seven, with less-formal 'entrance screening' based on assessments of socialisation for the 0-5s.

Yet traditional entry routes are under pressure and examinations like Common Entrance are becoming Less Common Entrance. Some senior schools now accept results of a prep school Baccalaureate (PSB) aimed at assessing a wider array of knowledge, understanding and skills than features under CE. Others are employing new approaches collectively described as 'pre-testing', which may include bespoke or nationally benchmarked assessments in customary fields such as maths, English and verbal/non-verbal reasoning, perhaps even part of a taster or selection day (or longer) at a senior school. Success at such pre-testing may initiate the offer of a place, conditional or not on subsequent CE success. Also increasingly common is the chance to circumvent senior competitive selection entirely by signing up a term or even a year earlier than customary, an offer occasionally accompanied by the promise of fee remissions to cover any contractual 'in lieu' arrangements. As you can imagine, this annoys prep and junior schools considerably.

Many independent schools moved away from rigid entrance procedures as a result of having their selective fingers burnt on more than one occasion in the last twenty-five years. The 1991 UK recession brought high interest rates, falling house prices and an overvalued exchange rate. For all but the highly selective, adhering rigidly to an established entrance formula resulted in what many saw as falling standards, as schools tried to counteract diminishing demand by lowering their entrance thresholds. However, the effect was like buffalo drinking from a shrinking waterhole as the sun intensified; Independent Schools Council (ISC) schools lost pupils in aggregate for each year between 1992 and 1995. But that wasn't the end of it. Those schools combatting the recession by lowering their ticket price experienced a double-whammy when the impact of declining entry demands hit the league tables five or seven years later. These influential lists are important for pupil (and even teacher) recruitment in selective independents. Suddenly discovering that you have sunk to the lower divisions rather torpedoes a selective marketing strategy – i.e. reputation – carefully constructed over many years; unsurprisingly a few Heads rolled. Many private schools 're-evaluated' and converted to the benefits of a more flexible entry policy in areas such as mid-year transfers, early entry and (for boarding schools) weekly and flexi-arrangements. Now, keeping to a rigid selective approach was a luxury fewer could afford.

Following their chastening experiences of the 1990s, the UK's private schools were generally better prepared for the Great Recession that followed the banking crisis in 2008. Yet the timing of this could not have been more difficult. Pressures of increasing bursary provision to justify public benefit for charitable status combined with rising household debt, erosion of 'grey pound' pensions that often pay school fees, structural unemployment in key independent school constituencies and limited forward growth prospects. Some of the recent bursary expansions, now estimated to be worth £780 million annually within ISC schools, can be attributed to negotiated fee discounts.[2] If they hadn't done so before, schools rushed to reach out to 'new purchasers', many of whom assume that rigorous selection comes hand-in-hand with their purchase choice, which in turn proved to be an impediment to further market penetration. Some felt the need to advertise for the first time, even adding expensive marketing functions that created further tensions within the sector. As just one example, Sunderland High School was castigated by the Advertising Standards Authority for misrepresenting inspection outcomes.[3] Others looked overseas, only to be detained at the frontiers by a draconian UK Border Agency (now UK Visas and Immigration) that seemed to regard overseas pupils as the biggest threat to our shores since Hitler's Operation Sea Lion. The frenzy around the waterhole was intense.

Yet escalating competition wasn't the only issue schools have faced since 2008. Underlying the squeeze on numbers was the rising real cost of private education, with average termly fees soaring by 75 per cent in the ten years after 2003. Among other consequences, this created a relatively new phenomenon: a significant parental faction targeting specific key stages for independent education, with the chosen point of entry dependent upon the local variability of alternative high-quality state education. For these parents, it's the perception of what constitutes a good school in addition to affordability that matters, not whether it's private or maintained. Not being ideologically driven, these parents deliberate over all accessible schools in their area, almost a form of opportunity cost modelling with multiple 'what-if' scenarios e.g. school fees = no outside-Europe holidays for x years. And uppermost in their reasoning are the preconceptions of where private education may provide the necessary edge, perhaps in the junior years to gain a good start in basic learning, or in senior schools with advantages for higher education entrance in mind. The introduction of English university fees that averaged

£8,601 in 2013-14 effectively extended this calculation, with less available for private education.[4] Happily for private schools, such a pick-and-mix approach was partially balanced by the fillip of first-timers who experienced private provision as part of the Labour government's employment-based childcare vouchers scheme. Happy outcomes led many to re-evaluate and remain with the sector beyond the nursery years and the introduction of Tax-Free Childcare arrangements in late 2015 may lever similar benefits.

So schools have had to adapt their entrance procedures accordingly. Yet selection is further complicated by parents in catchments for one of the 163 state-funded fully selective schools in England, many of whom see independent schools as a form of insurance offer. They regard entrance tests, whether for local grammars or for private schools, as simply part of the same process, often engaging their children in both. Similar to pick-and-mix parents, it's a 'good' school that matters but the psychology underpinning this is equally important: highly competitive entry is a given, whether for the state or private systems, and there's social cachet to be gained through engagement in any selective system. Selective schools of all persuasions use such positive associations as effective marketing, albeit for the most part subliminal. This subtext allows a few independent schools to claim a highly selective process of admissions even when the authenticity of bums on every seat is somewhat shaky.

Of course, it would be wrong to imply that the experiences of private schools since the 1990s have destroyed all notions of selection. Highly-selective admissions mechanisms are still prevalent and the so-called traditional approach is perhaps typified by St

George's, Ascot. Registration for entry at eleven is submitted by the end of October prior to the year of entry. Prospective pupils attend an admissions day in the November of Year 6, and in the following January are invited to sit the St George's entrance exams in maths, English and verbal reasoning. Pupils are then interviewed by the Headmistress or a senior member of staff, with a short three-minute presentation on a subject of their choice – 'bugs, ballet or horses'. The school provides sample examination papers and takes into account a report from the previous school, and there's a language proficiency test for applicants for whom English is not the first language. Variations on this approach are commonplace and may or may not be combined with Independent Schools Examinations Board (ISEB) Common Entrance examinations. Once selection is thus engrained, these schools go on to apply streaming and setting rather than mixed ability approaches in the classroom. (Indeed, multiple-form entry non-selective schools often employ similar structures in core curriculum subjects.)

Private schools appreciate that highly-academic selection procedures are attractive to many parents. Tim Lello is the young Head who runs the enormously popular Babington House School in leafy Chislehurst. Outstanding in every category at its last Independent Schools Inspectorate (ISI) inspection, Babington is a typical all-through (3-18) girls' secondary with coeducational junior and senior sections. The school has recently initiated academic admissions after previously being marketed as non-selective. 'I wanted to raise the aspirations of the children in our Prep School,' Lello explains. 'I wanted the pupils to want to get into the senior school. I wanted to encourage them to work hard to secure this place and be proud if they were successful.' Yet practicalities also underpin this aspirant effect. Babington is now oversubscribed in most year groups and Lello 'needed to select on the basis of something. Effectively we have in the past had "first-come, first-served" selection which didn't seem to leave us with much control. For a school to claim it has an academic focus, it must be honest to parents whose children are unlikely to gain passes in English and maths at GCSE. To select on academic ability enables you to be more transparent and honest about the reasons for de-selection'. Not that turning pupils away sits easily with Tim Lello: 'The difficult conversations I have with parents of children I turn down – and I always do it face to face – is more constructive if I can explain it clearly in these terms. It also helps me advise them about other schools which might be more appropriate.'[5] And for every independent school that claims that rigorous selection through formal entrance examinations is a necessity, you'll find another that takes a sharp intake of breath whenever the subject is broached. Mention academic selection to some and it's as if you've suggested that Stalin was clearly misunderstood. To these schools, selection breeds a host of potential psychological problems, often evidenced by pupils that have been unsuccessful and perhaps even broken by less humane experiences than those employed by Tim Lello. To these schools, selection at 11 or 13 can only be a crude snapshot of prior achievement and holds little relation to future potential. Selection cannot measure the wide range of attributes that are truly important, including the soft skills and competencies that will govern success in an unpredictable and increasingly agile future. James

Wilding's view typifies this contention. The school he runs with his brother outside Maidenhead is one of the largest and most successful proprietary schools in the country. As Wilding passionately explains:

> The vast majority of the children who apply to Claires Court are suited for a broad ability, multi-skills education. With time, most will become highly successful in the areas of interest they develop, and be leaders of their age cohort on entry to university or employment. What amazes me is just how selection tests focus on narrow areas of ability, with no long-term correlation to life-time achievement.[6]

And Wilding is clear on the damage that academic selection can cause: 'This vanity of small differences perpetuates the myth that only the "most able" are capable of an academic education.' He designates this as, 'a major corrupting influence both on social mobility and the long-term development of all children, who are after all are our greatest asset for the future'.[7]

What enables academically non-selective schools such as Claires Court to compete is a holistic approach to their provision, specifically valuing pastoral care and a wider extra-curricular programme that isn't just a bolt-on. Narrow academic selection processes won't predict if a pupil will thrive within such an environment and league tables aren't a prime consideration for these schools. They frequently play the role of life coach and mentor for pupils who have tried their selective fortunes elsewhere. 'We often pick up the pieces of those who have got into the "hot house" schools and who have buckled under the pressure', clarifies Vicky Smit, the dynamic proprietor at Hurst Lodge, which occupies twenty acres of Berkshire parkland.[8] This 3-18 boarding and day school emphasises a supportive and wide curriculum that includes a forest school and strong parental links described by inspectors as 'outstanding'. Smit is as passionately opposed to academic selection as James Wilding:

> Our students, who have arrived having been discounted by schools who consider themselves elite, often leave us with between eight and 12 good GCSEs or with 4 A-levels.[9]

The head at Gosfield School outside Braintree takes a similar line. In the process of building a new prep and pre-prep building, this thriving 4-18 school's recent success lies in welcoming children of all abilities. Sarah Welch explains that: 'We conduct no entrance examinations, nor do we insist on specified levels of achievement for our applicants.'[10] Welch is clear on the reasoning behind this: 'At a school where children's individuality is encouraged and embraced, such selection is anathema. We invite applicants to spend one or more days with us, experiencing the normal routine of lessons and activities. If the children have been happy and engaged and we are confident we can help them achieve their social, creative and physical as well as academic potential, they are invited to join the school.' It's about a 'good fit' according to Welch.[11]

There are clearly recurrent themes here and they aren't limited to senior schools. Matthew Adshead is the ebullient head at the 3-13 Old Vicarage School in Derby and successfully feeds pupils to Cheltenham Ladies' College, Repton, Shrewsbury, Harrow and Uppingham. Adshead is a vociferous advocate of mixed-ability education. 'I have continually seen children develop academically at different rates. The brain is an amazing thing, so I am never prepared to write any child off as not able.'[12] While the Old Vicarage does not stream formally, academic selection is left for when a pupil has already joined the school. 'Streaming at our school takes place on a daily basis,' reveals Adshead intriguingly. 'Children may have certain aptitudes, but who is to say a child who is excellent at division of fractions will be excellent at working out angles? Therefore, we stream children via means of pre-testing before a topic begins and placing them in appropriate groups for learning.' Despite the recession, the school has grown by around forty per cent in the past five years, with fees akin to the average per-pupil funding received by state schools.

So, given the polarisation of views, who is right? However you measure it, the jury must still be out. The Independent Schools Council represents 1,257 private schools in the UK and a majority of its schools would be generally classed as non-selective, at least academically, acknowledging the selective effect of fees. However, it does not keep data on relative performance. Indeed, studies of comparative outcomes are sparse and conclusions from attainment regression analyses aren't conclusive. A 2004 study by Fernando Galindo-Rueda and Anna Vignoles concluded that the difference in outcomes for selective versus non-selective schools was relatively small. While the most able pupils in a selective school system did do better than those of similar ability in a mixed ability school system, the effect was minor and only applied to the brightest, with no evidence of significant negative effects of selection for low or middle ability pupils.[13] In 2000 York University's David Jesson concluded otherwise, finding no evidence for the superiority of either grammar schools or selective systems of provision in terms of GCSE value-added performance. Indeed, Jesson stated that: 'any advantages appear to lie with those schools and systems organised on non-selective lines'.[14] Claire Crawford at the University of Warwick, is similarly circumspect about any causal relationship between selection and results. In a well-publicised study looking at higher education participation and outcomes, Crawford concluded that those from non-selective school backgrounds may even do better.[15] However, being mainly driven by data from the maintained sector, it's clear that these studies cannot be easily applied to private school outcomes, where more research is required.

Yet the private school case studies above may perhaps give weight to the argument that they all exercise some form of selection, even where this might be relatively informal. When asked to unpick what she means by 'good fit', with the suggestion that this might be a form of 'unwritten selection', Sarah Welch at Gosfield elaborated on the process.

> Yes, we ask teachers to give us feedback on how our trialists got on. They compile a folder of work the pupils have undertaken in their classes which I review with them. Of course, we also look at school reports and interview the parents and children to get to know them as much as possible in advance. We also take into account, to an extent, how our own pupils reacted – they are good sounding boards![16]

Perhaps this is selection Jim, as Bones might have said in Star Trek, but not as we know it. Of course, die-hard critics of the private school system in the UK will argue that all independents exercise a form of social selection, though as pollsters Populus reported in 2011, only a quarter of parents say they would not send their child to an independent school if they could afford to, a proportion which has steadily decreased over time.[17]

Even if parents seem increasingly willing to educate their children privately, the vast majority of private schools in the UK must continually review their selection procedures if they are to flourish. The driving reason is the mounting burden of fees that once more dominates parents' decision-making. As the *Daily Telegraph's* then Education Editor Graeme Paton reported in September 2013, one in 10 parents have 'real doubts' that their children will be able to complete their studies at fee-paying schools due to concerns over costs.[18] Though private school day fees today average £12,700 per year, the variation is enormous both geographically and by range, from less than £3,000 per annum to over £24,000.[19] Parents are increasingly shopping around for best value, committing later and breeding more uncertainty in the sector. Elsewhere, a narrowing band of elite schools have become 'a luxury brand', as Nick Fraser's 2006 book, *The Importance of Being Eton,* described them.[20] Fees act in self-selection, just as with the purchase of a house, car or holiday. With a narrowing of the fees pyramid at its peak, high-charging schools tend to be more academically selective, with parents equating both to eventual success. Yet the educational outcomes of children, at least as measured by university entrance and academic results, aren't necessarily better. The sector has yet to fully embrace meaningful value-added measures in this area, a clear Key Performance Indicator if ever it was needed. You can have as much fun camping as you can in a luxury five-star retreat (I'm told). That doesn't stop many parents from choosing to shell out more on the promise of academic results, hoping their children will ride on the dual coattails of reputation and past attainment.

Of course, such discernment isn't limited to the private sector. Higher mortgage and house prices in catchments with strong schools provide yet another economic filter for selection, with premiums over average house prices of up to 42 per cent.[21] In 2012 the OECD reported that Britain's school system was one of the most socially segregated in the developed world as a result of such factors. The Sutton Trust's Peter Lampl described this as a form of social selection – perhaps no different from the selective effect of private school fees.[22] Interestingly, aggregated lifetime mortgage costs outstrip fees at many independent schools, though parents in an appreciating market argue that they will see a greater financial return from their bricks and mortar. That said, a 2010 Centre for the Economics of Education research paper concluded that the average lifetime net return to investment in a private school education in 1980 was 7 per cent for boarders and 13 per cent for day pupils, though recent above inflation fee rises, as highlighted above, may well have eroded those gains.[23]

There's no doubt that for many, competitive selection remains the only real choice, teaching children the most important lesson for an increasingly cut-throat and internationalised world. For others, selection at 11 or 13 (or anytime, for that matter) is badly timed and often poorly handled, destroying confidence and writing children off as unfit for learning. If anything, the economic and social pressures facing private schools since 1991 have served to further polarise opinion, with views bordering on zealotry on both sides. There's little middle-ground and if it does exist, it is marginalised and uncelebrated, fostered by the media's fascination with factionalism in the UK education sector.

Meanwhile, private school head teachers, whether leading highly selective schools or their non-selective counterparts, continue to do the best they can, with the most successful genuinely focusing on the needs of individual pupils, an act of moral imperative that rather transcends any notions of superiority.

Using the Comprehensive Ideal to Drive Education Standards and Equality

Geoff Barton

I'm writing this the day after we learnt that five sixth-form students in our proudly comprehensive school in Suffolk have received conditional offers to study next year at either Oxford or Cambridge University. This is in addition to more than a hundred other students who have so far received offers of places at other UK higher education institutions – more than half of them Russell Group universities. This makes me proud because for a good proportion of these students, they represent the first member of their family to go to university. It's what we do in schools like ours and, frankly, what we ought to be doing – helping with all our might to open doors for students, preparing them with the skills, knowledge and attitudes to step intrepidly via higher education into their respective futures.

I want to focus briefly on this Oxbridge success – not because I think that studying at Oxford or Cambridge makes anyone better than anyone else – but because it forms a handy starting-point for my reflection on the notion of selection in education. Oxbridge, after all, carries a significant social weight in our culture. It's a shorthand for academic excellence, of course, but also for something more. It carries a cachet that speaks of personal and social success beyond the narrowly academic. It's a sign that you've made it. Thus Oxbridge statistics are the kind of figures that get boasted about a lot at schools which aren't like mine but which, instead, select their students via an entry examination, or via a termly fee, or both.

Now rewind three days. I am eating lunch in the dining hall with a smattering of colleagues and around two hundred students. Music plays in the background; a biting East Anglian wind howls outside. Somewhere on the school field and around the corridors a team of staff is on duty keeping an eye on behaviour during our first wet lunchtime of the new year. Me – I'm eating lunch. The hall doors burst open and here's Jess, 17 years old, brandishing a letter at me and crying. 'I did it!' She shouts, 'I did it. I got in'. I ditch my salad, and Jess and I bolt excitedly around the school seeking out other teachers with whom to share the news that, all being well, she will head to Oxford in October, where she will study medicine for five years and then – unless her plans shift – train to become a surgeon. It's what she told us she wanted to do when she joined our school, what she wanted to become, and I have little doubt that this is her inevitable and wonderful career trajectory.

Jess is going to Oxford, one of the world's top ten universities. And she is heading there from our comprehensive school in a county, Suffolk, that is much maligned by Ofsted and which sometimes struggles to make students and parents see why university – any university – is an important next step in anyone's early life. Unlike Cambridgeshire, just along the A14 to the west, or Essex, just down the A12 to the south, ours isn't a county with a long-standing recognisable university. University, it seems, is to many families something that is done by other people in other places. As we hurtled round the school to find more teachers to tell of her good news, the door of the library was held open by a student in Year 11. His name is Harry. He wants to be a car mechanic. He hasn't got Jess's confidence, her social graces, her analytical mind, her understanding of how to manage adults, but in the past year – eleven years into his formal education, the end-product of dozens of teachers – we've seen him start to write in sentences, start to use capital letters through self-regulation rather than teacher reminders, and start in his writing to find a sense of voice. I know this because I teach Harry. Here he is holding the door, smiling, and saying, with heartfelt simplicity, 'That's great,' when Jess tells him her Oxford news. These two students are part of the same college within our school – a community of students of different ages who attend tutor time, assemblies, sporting and other events as part of our extra-curricular programme because it is in our ethos for students of different ages and different backgrounds to mix like this.

In some ways Jess and Harry inhabit different worlds. Certainly they have different interests, mix with different groups of friends, talk in different terms. Jess belongs to what we might call the 'word rich' – those who know and use the language of power, who relentlessly network, who speak, read and write like historians or scientists or literary critics. Harry doesn't. He is a member of the 'word poor'. He struggles to find much interest in reading, dislikes writing, and is counting down the time to leaving for his course at a neighbouring further education college later this year. Both students are members of a school that is deliberately, even brazenly, comprehensive. And both are 'pupil premium' students[1] – that is, they come from backgrounds without much money, and are part of a cohort who have too often in the past been let down by the English education system. On a day-to-day basis Jess and Harry sit in the same rooms, eat in the same dining halls, listen to the same assemblies, share many of the same teachers. They mix and interrelate just as people mix and interrelate in the world beyond schools. Outside their lessons they aren't segregated or categorised or told that one of them matters more than the other.

Thus the two of them attend a school which aims to model the best aspects of human society – a culture that aspires to be equally aspirational for all, but without creating enclaves and no-go-zones for the rich or the clever or the merely well connected.

I couldn't be prouder to be head teacher of a comprehensive school. I am, after all, the product of one. But ours today is far better, far more enlightened, far more ambitious and aspirational than the one I attended back in the mid-seventies. One of the things we have done – though this doesn't get much recognition – is to shake off some of the lazy caricatures of what comprehensives do and what they are like. The best state schools certainly don't treat all students as if they were the same. We aren't at all against grouping students according to talent, ability, interest, gender, expertise. We aren't afraid of rewarding the academic high-fliers, though nor will we deliberately marginalise those who struggle with academic work. We recognise that for some students in some contexts it is right to teach by ability, to use testing frequently to assess progress, to intervene robustly with students who aren't keeping up or working hard enough. We know all this. We aren't bringing any of our students up in a cotton wool world that tries to hide the fact that life has setbacks and difficult messages. It's just that we believe it is possible to do all of this in a school culture where students are there because it is the neighbourhood school – the place, as in most high-performing countries, where you would inevitably wish as a parent to send your child.

So there – colours dutifully nailed to the mast: I am attracted to the idea of good local schools, where we don't see from the corner of our early morning eye a huddle of young people clambering onto a minibus to be driven to the fee-paying school down the road. I like the idea very much that state schools – through quality and ambition and moral purpose and an egalitarian spirit – trump fee-paying and selective schools. I like localness and equality, and those two principles are part of my dislike of selection in education – whether it's via an 11-plus examination or via fees. Note that if I ran the world I wouldn't ban these things. I'd simply stack the priorities differently so that neighbourhood state schools which don't admit by selection or fee get the credibility, resources and – critically – the recognition they deserve. I'd want them to be the norm. This isn't pure self-interest either. I'm not arguing for stronger non-selective state schools just because it's where I happen to work and always have worked. It's because I believe it's what our society needs – an education culture that unites rather than divides, that exemplifies as well as teaches integration rather than segregation.

Most high-performing principalities appear to take a similar approach. They place emphasis on making their state schools as good as possible. Many of their politicians will, presumably, have themselves attended such state schools. That makes them different from the English. Here, our social mix continues to be riven by deep-rooted hierarchies, plus a sneering attitude that frequently depicts some types of school as of decidedly higher prestige than others. These, almost without exception, are independent schools or grammar schools.

If we had politicians on a real mission to create a more egalitarian society – again, remember that I am not arguing for everyone to be treated the same, just to be given similar opportunities – then we would begin deliberately to shift the emphasis from state schools being inevitably seen as second best. The discourse itself would begin to change.

Back in 1934, right at the epicentre of what W. H. Auden would later characterise as the 'low dishonest decade' of the twentieth century, the novelist Graham Greene edited a little-noticed anthology of essays about what are still sometimes called England's public schools. It was a mostly saccharine and mostly nostalgic retrospective by mostly male authors about their respective experiences at school. Most of them – it perhaps goes without saying – went to what we quaintly call public schools. It's a misnomer, of course: here in England these public schools were for anyone but the public. They were, and are, private schools. You went there, in the main, as the result of a financial transaction and possibly a selection test. You gained a place either because your parents paid for it or because you were deemed worthy of a scholarship of some sort. That was 1934. But it's pretty much the same today. And as a badge of their respectability these schools are granted – quite wrongly of course – the benefits of charitable status that give them tax advantages whilst reinforcing a sense that they matter a lot, which, if we had a genuinely meritocratic society, perhaps they wouldn't.

In a deeply old-fashioned way that still appears to have some resonance in the educational values of some of our most fearsome global competitors, I still subscribe to the notion that the state should aim to educate all of its citizens – richest and poorest – in a system of common values and shared resources. I'm attracted to the concept of good local schools educating the local populace, irrespective of parents' income. With that idealism comes an assumption that 'the best that has been thought and said' is the deserved lot of all our citizens – whatever their backgrounds and supposed abilities. That's why – again, exposing views which will be seen as woefully oldfangled – I cling to the notion of a national curriculum that applies across all schools, not just those which have proudly decided to stick it out as local authority establishments. I like the principle that wherever you go to school, whether you are from the wealthiest or most disadvantaged background, you have an entitlement to a curriculum devised by our best minds. It is your birthright and you should relish it.

So, yes, this is utopian, but it wasn't so much so when the great reformers of English education were in their prime. Matthew Arnold, T.S. Eliot, the National Society – all believed that the best that had been thought and said belonged to all of us, as part of a shared culture, a collective inheritance, and not to the moneyed or selected elite. That's why some of us – branded, we know, as social dinosaurs perched here on the precarious ideological promontory of the early twenty-first century – still have a distant glint in our eyes for an education system that is not predicated on wealth or early test results. We believe that independent and selective schools continue to carry a significant and, to many of us, disproportionate influence in our culture. They are spoken of in tones of hushed reverence, their names dropped in conversation as if some token of membership of a privileged club. But we think their time is running out. After all, only around seven per cent of the population actually attend private schools, and yet they are frequently presented as if anything else should be deemed vaguely dysfunctional or second-rate. Our global neighbours must think it bizarre that we rarify something so rooted in one-upmanship and unalloyed snobbery.

Graham Greene's collection was titled, inevitably, *The Old School*, a phrase that to any speaker of English familiar with its idioms will signify a meaning beyond the literal.[2] The old school isn't simply the old school – a historic institution of learning, or, more personally, the school that the speaker once attended. As we all know, the very phrase 'the old school' refers to a network, a shared culture of some kind, an insider's club. That's what Greene's anthology presents. His posse of the great and the good – a heftily male-dominated list which includes W.H. Auden, H.E. Bates, Walter Greenwood, Anthony Powell and others – reminisce about their life at their respective schools, often not very affectionately. It's from this collection, for example, that we get Auden's snarky witticism: 'The best reason I have for opposing fascism is that at school I lived in a fascist state.'[3] The 'honour' system at Gresham's School was a vicious and calculated regime to ensure that boys were conformist and compliant. It worked by weaving a culture of fear and youthful peer espionage. Greene himself, the unhappy child of the Headmaster of Berkhamsted School and the product of childhood depressive tendencies that drove him as a teenager to play Russian roulette with real bullets, writes a brief introduction before serving up a series of often illuminating essays by his contributors. In that opening essay he makes a massively misguided prediction: 'There can be small doubt that the system which this book mainly represents is doomed.'[4] He assumes, mistakenly as it happens, that state education will ultimately marginalise private education. He also, tellingly, ascribes the small-world values of the old school not to the children but to the adults: 'It was from the masters we learnt our snobbery and the means to express it.'[5] All of it speaks of an education world striven by class division, petty inward-looking obsessions with manners and rules, and academic concerns that are often defiantly mediocre.

That was education as it was before the war, not as it is now, surely. Yet I mention Greene's *The Old School* as a reminder that a world we might have thought had sloped off to social oblivion remains with us still, as do many of its values, and – with breathtaking unexpectedness – the awe in which some of the traditions are still held. Take our briefly influential former Education Secretary, Michael Gove, who, like so many politicians, flitted with moth-like ambition across the political stage before hitting the candle of governmental realpolitik to vanish again. Early in his tenure, as more Whitehall levers of structure and control were pulled with no forethought of how their impact may play out in schools, he made an odd and superficially interesting speech about his policies and his heroes. As so often, it wasn't short of hubristic breathlessness. Taking as its title the phrase the 'Progressive Betrayal', Gove said:

> We are clearing away the outdated and counterproductive assessment methods of the past. So that more time – much more time – is available for teaching, for reading around the subject, and for the cultivation of the habits of proper thought.[6]

We listened. The *Guardian* reported the speech, kindly, as 'a long, dense address'.[7] By this we assumed they meant that it was packed with learned references. Actually it appears to be a veritable smorgasbord of high and low cultural items, dutifully served up at a cocktail party for educational namedroppers. There are 'two particular individuals [who] have influenced me more than any others', said Gove.[8] We held our breath. His apparent heroes? Marxist economist Antonio Gramsci and TV reality star Jade Goody. Talk about a personification of C.P. Snow's *The Two Cultures*. Here it is on a platter. The argument seemed to be that Gramsci was the champion of muscular working-class intellectualism, eschewing the fashionable progressive tendencies that would dilute the hopes and dreams of Italian peasants. Goody, if I've followed Gove's gist, personified this ideal. Shortly before her death aged 28 from cervical cancer, she took the money made from her television appearances, put it in a trust and, as Gove puts it, bought 'the best education reality TV could buy'. The subtext was that this was a flight from the low expectations of the state sector and instead a chance to pay for what the rich have long been able to enjoy. Gove paints a picture of the values and methodologies of the private schools, as chosen by Goody for her children:

> You will find children learning to read using traditional phonic methods, times tables and poetry learnt by heart, grammar and spelling rigorously policed, the narrative of British history properly taught. And on that foundation those children then move to schools like Eton and Westminster – where the medieval cloisters connect seamlessly to the corridors of power.[9]

Many of us were surprised that an Education Secretary responsible for England's 24,000 schools would with such gusto want to caricature all state schools as riddled with corrosive low expectations and deliver a speech that serves up a paean to the independent sector, depicting it so universally as a shimmering upland of academic excellence. But that's what he did and that's what he said – an Education Secretary who, not for the first time, spoke about us but not for us, who generalised about state schools being second best.

The media narrative appears to be that if only we had more private and selective schools, then standards of education in England would be better. Michael Gove so often appeared to reinforce this view. I ought, I suppose, to declare my credentials at this point. I'm the product of a comprehensive school. In the scrubby nondescript environs of Stafford, my older brother and sister – respectively ten and fifteen years older than me – had attended the town's boys' and girls' grammar schools. Those schools institutions appear to have served them well. My sister went on – with some inevitability – to train as a teacher. My brother took his fascination with geology to Manchester University and is now a professor in the United States. But whilst ours was a generally bookish household, and as children we would be the first generation in the family to attend university, we weren't exactly the deserving poor. I certainly can't compete with Michael Gove's tales of adoption and then a small independent school which enabled him to claw his way up into thankful civilisation.

Ours wasn't an impoverished household. We had a caravan, for heaven's sake – that seventies touchstone of middle-class aspiration. My parents would drag us off to forlorn fields with no running water in which we would meet jaunty people, eat tinned corned beef, and salute the Caravan Club flag in a ceremony that even aged eleven struck me as kitsch. So with older brothers and sisters despatched to the safe waters of selective grammar schools, demarcated by gender, it left me as the lone guinea-pig of an early 1970s bit of social engineering. I was the comprehensive school boy. My mother never quite came to terms with this. It was in part the name of the school that riled her. Its name, Walton Comprehensive, wasn't distinguished. In her eyes, its initials – W.C. – reinforced a sense of scatological unworthiness. It would take a bold head teacher, steeped in the marketing culture of the mid-1980s, to reinvent the school as Walton High. That is what happened, after my time there.

I was an undistinguished student in a school which – like so many schools in its era – largely took in students from various social strata and delivered them results which could be predicted by their background. In the idiom of today's education system, I'm not sure how much it added value to our prior attainment. As in so many schools, the bright did well and the rest did less well. Thus my feckless lack of interest in education was bolstered by a modicum of parental pressure – nothing like the Tiger Mothers and Fathers I see in the system today – and I therefore drifted to a level of educational mediocrity that got me sufficient O-level grades to scrape into the sixth form and then sufficient A-level grades to get to a decent university. In hindsight there's much I might criticise about the school. But there's far more that I would criticise about myself. I am thankful to have gone there and grateful not to have sat some selection test which would have categorised me aged eleven and set me on a trajectory of someone else's making.

I listened to a teacher from another school the other day lamenting his 'bottom set Year 7 class'. They were, apparently, lazy and uninterested. I'm not averse to setting, but I do worry about the message – explicit or subliminal – that a student in a so-called bottom set must constantly receive and hear reinforced about her or his abilities which are apparently being written off in the language and underpinning attitude of the teacher. And I am concerned about it even more if what's at stake is not just the maths or science set you might end up in, but the very school you are sent to.

We are frequently presented with a shimmering vista of grammar school boys and girls who have now taken their rightful place in the most esteemed positions in our country. These schools, we are told, provided the leverage for the poorest to escape their grim backgrounds and clamber into social success. No wonder we hear cries from the political right craving a grammar school in every town. Me – I don't subscribe to it. I've been to Kent and Buckinghamshire and other counties still wedded to the selective system. I've heard about the conveyor-belt of 11-plus cramming sessions that gets inflicted on children, the destination stress for parents, the complacency of some grammar school teaching, the defensiveness of those teaching in schools not explicitly called secondary modern but, by definition because their top-end of students has been creamed off, exactly that. I've seen it and I understand that some people subscribe to its phony Darwinism – allowing students to thrive or fester. And I reject it. That's not like the world I inhabit where people of different backgrounds and different talents sit side-by-side on buses, eat in the same restaurants, drive on the same roads, watch the same television channels. That's why I cling to the notion of non-selective education or, as I prefer to call it, good neighbourhood state schools. And I think a couple of bits of research support my view. First, there's the work of educational assessment guru Dylan Wiliam. There are few in education more adept at using evidence to tell us what works in the classroom and in schools generally. In his paper 'Optimizing Talent: Closing Educational and Social Mobility Gaps Worldwide', Wiliam writes something significant:

> After controlling for social class, there was not a single country participating in PISA in which students attending private schools achieved higher scores than those attending government-funded schools. When one adds in the fact that class sizes in private schools are generally smaller than those in government-funded schools (average class sizes 19.4 and 21.4, respectively), then it is apparent that the quality of teaching in private schools is no better than in public schools.[10]

This, for many readers, may be counterintuitive. To people like me it is hugely reassuring: great state schools can perform as well as those that select – and we can do it not just in academic terms but in how we prepare students for the world as it is, in all its social messiness, rather than one that some might hope for as stratified, hierarchical, fixed. So if Wiliam has it right and the actual (rather than reported success of private education is limited, how come as a system it gets so much kudos? The answer is best provided by an extraordinary book from the US, Berliner and Glass's *50 Myths and Lies that Threaten America's Public Schools*. In it they say what suddenly strikes us as overwhelmingly obvious:

> Modern myths about schools (e.g. private schools offer superior teaching and learning compared with public schools) are likely to be articulated and communicated by organised private interests – by various think tanks and organisations that stand to gain from widespread belief in the myths… These conservative think tanks are sometimes richly endowed and dedicated to the promulgation of conservative ideology in multiple areas - education, environment, crime, to name only a few. They adopt a tone of scientific inquiry and publish policy briefs and appear in the media. Significant amounts of their budgets are spent on public and media relations. It is fair to say that many of the myths that most threaten our nations' system of public education, that seek to slash its funding and turn a formerly egalitarian institution into a bifurcated system of elite services for the rich and meagre services for the poor, have their origin and draw their staying power from the nation's conservative think tanks.[11]

The authors' point is that it is patently in the interests of some commentators, some lawmakers, some system leaders and some private companies to retread constantly the argument that state schools are failing and that selective schools – schools like those that perhaps they themselves attended – are better. It becomes the defining narrative, the reason that head teachers from tiny independent schools are wheeled out by the media to comment on education standards or character-building or social integration or whatever else the issue of the day might be. These schools carry prestige, as do their leaders and their alumni. Thus it sometimes feels as if not much has changed since Auden's low dishonest decade.

Except that I think a lot has. There's an increasing mood that social division through education is precisely what our society does not need more of, along with its accompanying attitudes of partisanship and condescension. There's an increasing desperation in the tone of those trying to cling on to selection as being in the interests of anyone but the well-connected few. That is why, after thirteen years as head teacher of a state comprehensive school, I feel more optimistic than I ever have that it's schools like ours that can make the real difference in our society.

So, from the midst of another university application season, well done to our students Jess and Harry: may both thrive in their respective paths through life. And well done to all the other proud neighbourhood state schools who, day in and day out, against a backdrop of constant sniping, continue to open doors for young people like these two – irrespective of background, parental income or ability in tests aged eleven.

It's schools like these that our society needs.

School Selection by Gender: Why It Works

Alice Phillips and Nicole Chapman

Selection in education is traditionally associated with ability or attainment. However, some schools select their pupils by gender. Single-sex schools play a significant role in UK education but what is it about them that continues to attract parents?

Whereas aspirational parents of the nineteenth-century sent their daughters to single-sex schools because there was simply no viable alternative, aspirational parents of the twenty-first century select single-sex schools for their daughters because they consider them to be the best. We know this because of a study undertaken to find out why today's parents choose single-sex schools for their daughters. This study looked at the aggregated results of the SchoolPulse parental satisfaction surveys carried out in 80 independent schools between 2011 and 2013.[1] It compared the responses of parents of more than 9,000 girls in 36 girls' schools and 34 co-educational schools, at both junior (up to Year 6) and senior (from Year 7) level and in both day and boarding schools. The responses – from parents with girls in both girls' schools and co-educational schools – were remarkably consistent. It was clear, from the information parents provided about the other schools they had considered before making their final choice that the vast majority looked at both single-sex and co-educational schools. This suggests that whether or not the school was single-sex was not necessarily the 'deal breaker'. Instead, the quality of teaching, pastoral care and extra-curricular provision was far more important in parents' minds and it just so happened that, for them, it was a single-sex girls' school that ticked more of those boxes. The big question – and the one that evokes so much discussion and argument – is a chicken and egg conundrum. Which impact comes first: the single-sex environment or the good teaching? To what extent is excellence in girls' schools down to the fact that teaching is done in single-sex environments and to what extent is it due to their simply being good schools?

Single-sex teaching is thriving

The current position of single-sex selective education is a fascinating one. For example, girls' schools today come in many different shapes and sizes. Some are exclusively all-girls; others have a predominantly girls-only environment with boys in the nursery and/or sixth-form. However, year after year the top of the A-level league tables is dominated by schools whose sixth-forms are exclusively single-sex. In 2013, for example, ten of the top 15 performing schools were single-sex and half of these were girls' schools.[2] Department for Education leaver destination figures, released for the first time in 2014, show that of the top 11 schools for sending students to Russell Group universities, 10 were single-sex, of which eight were girls' schools.[3] The same data shows that of the top 11 schools for sending students to Oxbridge, nine were single-sex, of which seven were girls' schools. In both cases, the other schools in the top 11 taught boys-only up to 16 with a co-educational sixth form.[4]

One thing is for certain: despite an undeniable decline in the number of UK schools which are exclusively single-sex over the last 20 years, teaching in single-sex groups – for girls *and* boys – is thriving. A number of UK co-educational schools are turning to single-sex teaching in an effort to improve results. One analyst on the subject, education journalist Nick Morrison, reports that:

> After looking at test and exam results from every state school in England, researchers at Bristol University suggested boys might do better in English if they were taught in single-sex classes, but maths and science were best taught in co-ed classes. [5]

Morrison goes on to cite how two co-educational academy schools are using single-sex classes to provide localised interventions for specific subjects. One example is David Young Community Academy in Leeds which is teaching pupils English, maths and sciences in single-sex classes in order to tackle a culture of low aspirations among girls. Executive Principal Ros McMullen explains: 'It is about the culture that the children come from. We needed to break that culture and allow girls to be clever.'[6] The result is that achievement has risen among both girls and boys, but among girls McMullen says it has 'rocketed'. Further south, Haywood Academy near Stoke-on-Trent has introduced single-sex classes in maths for middle-ability pupils, the impetus being the reluctance of girls to speak out in mixed classes. As Nick Morrison writes:

Assistant head teacher Mel Roberts says staff had identified that while boys were vocal in group work they were less enthusiastic about independent working. For girls, worried about looking stupid in front of the boys, it was the other way around. The project is still in its first year at the school but early signs are both genders are making better than expected progress.[7]

The Independent Schools Council's 2014 census shows that as many as 40 per cent of all the schools in its membership teach either all girls or all boys between Years 7 and 11; even at sixth-form level 36 per cent of member sixth-forms are single-sex, with all-girls' sixth-forms being more prevalent.[8] Cast further afield, and you will find that in the United States private single-sex schools thrive and, since the US Department of Education relaxed restrictions in 2006, the number of single-sex public schools has grown rapidly, although their proportion of total schools remains small.[9]

Gender segregation in the 'real world'

Those who are against single-sex education often claim that it is unnatural for girls and boys to be taught in separate schools or even separate classrooms. Critics say that in society and the 'real world' men and women must work together and that schools must reflect the reality of the adult world instead of artificially dividing the sexes. These are opinions which those of us who work in single sex-schools can counter with both opinion and fact.

First, the notion that children and younger teenagers should be treated as adults is wrong. Growing up is a tricky business and in the course of those all important, formative teenage years a child's self-awareness will go through many changes and the veneer of confidence will, on occasion, be alarmingly thin. During this sensitive time, both girls and boys can experience mild to severe anxiety when at the receiving end of over-enthusiastic or judgemental attention from the opposite sex. A recent YouGov poll found that one in three 16-18-year-old girls in the UK say they have experienced harassment at school.[10] If children are going to grow into confident young women and men they must first of all learn how to be comfortable in their own skins and to have a secure confidence in their opinions and abilities.

For girls in particular there is plenty of evidence that single-sex schools are an appropriate environment in which to develop this level of self-confidence. Some of the more robust examples follow.

Gender disparity

In January 2014 the OECD announced the results of analysis that found that across most developed countries, boys are better than girls at maths.[11] The difference in maths, according to the OECD's Andreas Schleicher, does not exemplify any innate differences but is driven by a lack of confidence amongst girls in their maths skills, alongside lower expectations that they will need maths in future careers.[12] There is, Schleicher says, a close correlation between expectation and achievement. The same study prompted then-education minister Elizabeth Truss to say that: 'In the past girls have been let down by outdated assumptions about what they are good at.'[13] Anyone may be forgiven for assuming that educating girls alongside boys would eradicate these 'outdated assumptions' and result in girls being every bit as likely as boys to study maths and boys every bit as likely as girls to study English. Unfortunately – at least in the UK – statistics trounce this hypothesis. Taking the opposite sex out of the equation for the few hours when young people are in the classroom can remove the obvious distractions and relieve significant pressure. It allows for focus, and experience shows that it gives pupils the space to study what they *want* to study – instead of what they and/or others believe they *should* study. For girls, it also provides time to develop the kind of grit and self-confidence that enables them to hold their own at university and in the workplace, when that time comes. This is a view that is shared by many colleagues who have worked in both co-educational and single-sex schools.

But ultimately these are opinions, albeit those of experienced educators, and, as strongly held as they may be, opinions come relatively cheap. What matters is hard evidence and there is plenty of that to exemplify the benefits of single-sex education. The latest substantial research on the subject undertaken by the Institute of Physics is titled 'Closing Doors' and looks at six subjects with big gender disparities. Three of these subjects have a male bias and three a female bias: English and mathematics, biology and physics and psychology and economics.[14] The findings showed that the majority of co-educational schools are failing to counter whatever external factors drive young people to make gender-weighted choices when picking A-level subjects. The study did find both state-funded and independent co-educational schools that were achieving, or at least approaching, gender parity among students taking these subjects at A-level. However, the proportions were relatively low, i.e. 3.9 per cent of state-funded and 22.5 per cent of independent schools co-educational schools.[15] What this does show is that it is possible to counteract gender stereotyping in subject choice but clearly it's not something that comes easily to the majority of co-educational schools. The Institute of Physics study observed that the fact that so many co-educational schools can be at or below average on 'gendered' subject choices indicates that single-sex schools are less likely to exacerbate gender imbalances. Furthermore, it concluded: 'Single-sex schools are significantly better than co-educational schools at countering the gender imbalances in progression to these six subjects.'[16]

Physics, STEM and languages

An earlier study by the Institute of Physics, 'It's Different for Girls', points to the greater propensity of girls in single-sex schools to continue studying physics to A-level.[17] The study explored data from the National Pupil Database to look at progression from key stage 4 to A-level physics in 2011 for girls from different types of school. Physicist Sir Peter Knight's foreword to the resulting report states that:

> In 2011, physics was the fourth most popular subject for A-level among boys in English schools but for girls the subject languished in 19th place. This... report from the Institute of Physics shows that many girls across the country are not receiving what they're entitled to – an inspiring education in physics. In turn this has led to the poor representation of girls in physics, denying them individual opportunities and contributing to the UK's shortage in STEM skills.[18]

The Institute acknowledges that other research has already shown that girls' perceptions of physics are formed outside, as well as within, the physics classroom. It references teachers' – often subconscious – attitudes towards girls who show an interest in physics as well as the lack of female physicists on television. It is interesting to note the distinct rise in female academics – such as space scientist Maggie Aderin-Pocock (on the BBC's *The Sky At Night*) – introducing science programmes on UK television screens since the report 'It's Different for Girls' was published.

When examining the influence of school type on girls' take up of A-level physics, 'It's Different for Girls' finds that girls who attend single-sex schools – in both the maintained and independent sectors – are more likely to continue studying physics. Specifically, in the independent sector, 4.9 per cent of girls in co-ed schools went on to take A-level physics in 2011 compared to 18.7 per cent of boys, but in independent single-sex schools, 7.2 per cent of girls took A-level physics compared to 19.1 per cent of boys.[19] In the maintained sector the pattern is broadly similar. In maintained co-ed schools 1.8 per cent of girls studied A-level physics compared to 10 per cent of boys, whereas in maintained single-sex schools 4.3 per cent of girls studied physics at A-level compared to 14.9 per cent of boys.[20] Put another way, in independent girls' schools four times more girls study A-level physics than is the case in maintained co-ed schools. Boys who attend independent boys' schools are almost twice as likely (1.9 times) to take A-level physics as boys in maintained co-ed schools. In the maintained sector, girls and boys in single-sex schools are 2.4 times and 1.5 times, respectively, more likely to study A-level physics than is the case in co-ed schools. In independent schools, the percentage of boys taking A-level physics is almost the same whether they are educated in a single-sex or co-ed setting but there is a marked difference with girls, who in independent single-sex schools are almost 1.5 (1.46) times more likely to take A-level physics than girls in independent co-ed schools.[21]

The Institute of Physics research reflects what the Independent Schools Council (ISC) found when comparing the propensity of girls in Girls' Schools Association (GSA) schools to study STEM subjects (science, technology, engineering and mathematics) and modern foreign languages. Looking at 2012 Department for Education (DfE) data for all girls in England who sat A-levels, the ISC found that girls at GSA schools achieve a disproportionately large share of the top grades in sciences, maths and languages and are effectively propping up these key subjects nationally. Girls at GSA schools are 75 per cent more likely to take maths A-level, 70 per cent more likely to take chemistry, two and a half times as likely to take physics and over twice as likely to take most languages.[22] GSA girls also achieve far greater A-level success than is the case among girls nationally. In 2012, for instance, over 21 per cent of GSA A-level entries were awarded an A*, as opposed to just 7.9 per cent of entries nationally.[23]

US research evidence

Across the Atlantic a similar picture presents itself. In the US in the 1990s, Cornelius Riordan, professor of Sociology at Providence College, wrote:

> Females especially do better academically in single-sex schools and colleges across a variety of cultures. Having conducted research on single-sex and

coeducational schools for the past two decades, I have concluded that single-sex schools help to improve student achievement.[24]

More recently, UCLA's Graduate School of Education and Information Studies conducted extensive research into the differences in characteristics and transition to college of women graduates of single-sex and co-educational high schools.[25] The study compares the backgrounds, behaviours, attitudes and aspirations of 6,552 women leavers from 225 private single-sex high schools with 14,684 women leavers from 1,169 private co-educational high schools. It concluded that there are several areas in which single-sex education appears to produce favourable outcomes for female students, especially in terms of their confidence, engagement and aspirations, most notably in areas related to maths and science.[26] Thus, this evidence suggests, the benefits of single-sex education are most significant in areas that have historically favoured men and therefore present a potentially effective vehicle for mitigating longstanding gender gaps.

Other key findings of the UCLA research were that women educated in single-sex schools are more academically engaged. They study more, are more likely to engage in group study and to help fellow students with their studies, and they spend more time talking to teachers outside classes. They have higher levels of academic confidence – particularly in their mathematical ability and computer skills – and a greater interest in pursuing a career in engineering. On this particular point, the research findings state that:

> Single-sex school alumnae are more likely than their co-educational school peers to state that they plan

to become engineers. The... gap is greatest in the independent schools, where single-sex alumnae are three times more likely than women graduates of co-educational schools to report that they intend to pursue a career in engineering (4.4 versus 1.4 per cent).[27]

All of this is powerful data that points to the success of single-sex schools in enabling children – and in particular girls – to counter stereotypical choices and expectations in their education. These studies are of particular note because their samples are of significant size making the findings difficult to ignore. A multitude of other studies, albeit with smaller sample sizes, come to similar conclusions. One example is research into gender differences in the engagement of risky behaviour, which tested the proposition that single-sex environments are likely to modify students' risk-taking preferences in economically significant ways.[28] The study was prompted by the under-representation of women in high-paying jobs and high-level occupations. It sought to determine whether attitudes to risk are innate or shaped by environment. If, for example, the majority of the remuneration in a high-level job is determined by a company's performance, those with a low risk threshold will tend to avoid such jobs. If attitudes to risk were found to be innate, under-representation of women in certain areas might be solved by changing the way in which remuneration is made, whereas if attitudes to risk were found to be influenced by environment, it may be possible to address under-representation through education and training. In a controlled experiment, subjects were given an opportunity to choose a risky outcome, a 'real-stakes gamble with a higher expected monetary value than the alternative outcome with a certain payoff'.[29] The results found that girls from single-sex schools are as likely to choose the real-stakes gamble as boys from either co-educational or single-sex schools, and more likely to do so than girls from co-educational schools. They also found that gender differences in preferences for risk-taking are sensitive to the gender mix of the experimental group in that girls were more likely to choose risky outcomes when working in all-girl groups. The researchers concluded that the findings suggested that 'gender differences in behaviour under uncertainty... might reflect social learning rather than inherent gender traits'.[30]

In Seoul in South Korea – where pupils are randomly assigned to either single gender or co-educational high schools – a study by the University of Pennsylvania found attending all-boys schools or all-girls school to be 'significantly' associated with higher average scores on Korean and English test scores.[31] The research paper states:

> Single-sex schools have a higher percentage [than co-educational schools] of graduates who attended four-year colleges and a lower percentage of graduates who attended two-year junior colleges... The positive effects of single-sex schools remain substantial, even after taking into account various school-level variables such as teacher quality, the student-teacher ratio, the proportion of students receiving lunch support, and whether the schools are public or private.[32]

Returning to the UK, in a report by Ofsted it was found that girls at single-sex schools are more likely to avoid preparing for 'stereotypically female' careers than their contemporaries in co-educational schools. 'Girls' Career Aspirations' was based on visits to 16 primary schools and 25 secondary schools, including 13 single-sex girls' schools. It found that girls were receiving poor careers education, making it difficult for them to take informed decisions about their future direction, and that the traditional stereotypes were alive and well.[33] However, the report also revealed that girls in single-sex schools, particularly those in selective schools, had 'The most positive attitudes… where most of the girls spoken to asserted that they would definitely consider jobs stereotypically done by men'.[34] In these schools Ofsted noted that girls did not view any career as being closed to them and felt that women should be encouraged into roles traditionally held by men.[35]

Wealth of choice

This impressive body of findings is gathered from research and analyses that have taken place in both the state and independent education sectors in the UK, as well as from studies in the USA and other countries. It provides irrefutable evidence of what those of us who teach in single-sex schools already know: teaching girls and boys separately has positive consequences for their academic performance, their ability to make non gender-weighted subject and career choices, and girls' academic engagement and confidence. Furthermore, when we put into a global context the educational opportunities for girls in the UK – with so many countries still failing to leave the starting blocks when it comes to girls' education – the mix of all-girls, predominantly girls, and diamond model schools (where girls and boys are taught together up to Year 6, separately to Year 11, and together again in sixth-form) as an alternative to the co-educational environment, selective or otherwise, provides a wealth of parental choice which is undoubtedly worthy of celebration. Whether parents are attracted to their single-sex environment or their good teaching, schools which select pupils by gender do so with impressive and noteworthy results and will undoubtedly continue to be an important feature of the UK's educational landscape.

What Does the Research Tell Us About Single-Sex Education?

Emer Smyth

There has been a good deal of debate internationally about whether single-sex education yields better educational outcomes for young people, especially girls. Differences between coeducational and single-sex schools have been attributed to the dominance of classroom interaction by boys, the 'distraction' of students by the presence of the opposite sex, and the emergence of greater gender stereotyping as boys and girls seek to construct their gender identities in a mixed setting. Countries differ significantly in the prevalence of single-sex schools; in Ireland, Australia and New Zealand, for example, a relatively large single-sex sector represents the historical legacy of the role of the Catholic Church in the establishment of secondary schools in the nineteenth century. In contrast, in countries like England or the United States, there are relatively small proportions of single-sex schools, many of which are located in the fee-paying sector. Regardless of the national context, there is some degree of selectivity in the profile of those attending single-sex schools; that is, they differ from those in other schools in important respects, such as social class background, income, etc., respects which are likely to influence achievement and other educational outcomes. There may also be differences which are difficult to measure, principally, parental motivations in sending their child to a single-sex school which may reflect a nexus of reasons including their views on gender. This poses challenges in assessing the impact of single-sex schools, since it is important to compare 'like with like' if we are to understand the *net* effect of the gender mix of the school. This chapter outlines some of the main research evidence relating to the impact of single-sex schools on the educational and other outcomes of girls and boys across a number of countries. The evidence mainly relates to the secondary sector which has been the focus of most existing research.

Academic achievement

The majority of research on single-sex schools focuses on academic achievement rather than other educational or social-psychological outcomes. Achievement is measured in different ways, often as a summary or overall measure of achievement in state examinations, and sometimes as grades in particular subject areas, such as maths and science. Systematic research on single-sex education in Britain dates back to the late 1960s, with a major study pointing to no overall advantage in academic achievement for girls attending single-sex schools, but some evidence of a performance advantage in relation to typically male subjects such as maths and science.[1] Research in the 1970s and 1980s on gender and schooling suggested that girls tended to have higher academic achievement levels in single-sex classes and/or schools.[2] However, many of these studies were small-scale in nature and did not take account of important social background and prior achievement differences between students attending single-sex and coeducational schools. The availability of multilevel modelling techniques led to increased attention to school-level effects in British research from the 1980s onwards as it became easier to disentangle the influence of school context and composition. Using National Child Development Study data on the cohort of young people born in 1958, one study found that 'very little in their examination results is explained by whether schools are mixed or single-sex once allowance is made for differences in intake'.[3] This lack of a significant difference when we compare 'like with like' was echoed by other British studies conducted in the 1990s.[4]

Some more recent studies point to somewhat different conclusions on the effects of single-sex schooling in the British context. One study found an advantage for girls, and for lower-achieving boys, attending single-sex schools across a range of achievement outcomes, especially in the field of science.[5] Similarly, a reanalysis of National Child Development Study data found that the impact of single-sex schooling differed by subject area, with students achieving higher grades in gender-atypical subjects (science and maths for girls; languages for boys) when they attended single-sex schools.[6] As indicated in the introduction to this chapter, many single-sex schools are located within the selective fee-paying sector. One research study suggests that the effects of single-sex education may vary by the selectivity of the school.[7] This study found that both boys and girls in more selective single-sex schools had a performance advantage over those in selective but coeducational schools; however, within non-selective schools, only lower ability boys and girls achieved higher grades in a single-sex setting.

A number of research studies have been carried out in the United States, where (until very recently) single-sex education was confined to the private school sector, especially to Catholic schools. Several studies of the Catholic school sector have indicated small but significant negative effects of coeducation on girls' achievement as well as other outcomes such as social and personal development.[8] However, these findings have been contested by other researchers who have found no significant differences between single-sex and coeducational schools.[9] Other American studies have further explored the extent to which any advantage of single-sex education is confined to certain groups of students, with some research suggesting that any positive effect of single-sex schooling is limited to socially disadvantaged and ethnic minority students.[10]

It may be easier to determine the impact of single-sex schooling in systems where it is more common and there is therefore a greater overlap in student profile between single-sex and coeducational schools. The Republic of Ireland is one of the countries with a historical tradition of single-sex schooling, with single-sex schools still making up over a third of all secondary schools. Even though single-sex schools are numerous in Ireland, they do tend to attract more middle-class and higher ability students than coeducational schools. Controlling for these differences in social background and prior academic ability, a large-scale study conducted in the 1990s indicated no significant differences in overall academic achievement or in

English grades between single-sex and coeducational schools for both girls and boys at lower and upper secondary levels.[11] However, there was evidence that girls achieved somewhat lower maths grades in coeducational than in single-sex schools. There are also relatively large single-sex sectors in Australia and New Zealand. Studies there have generally found that, when the differing profiles of students in the two school types are taken into account, there are relatively few differences in overall achievement levels.[12]

One way of assessing the evidence on single-sex schooling and achievement is by drawing together findings from a large number of studies through a meta-analysis. In a meta-analysis of 184 studies in 21 countries, a modest difference was found in favour of single-sex schools in studies that did not take account of prior differences between students in the different school types. In contrast, when differences in background were taken into account, any differences in achievement were found to be 'trivial'.[13]

Subject take-up

Although the main focus of existing research has been on academic achievement, a number of studies have investigated the extent to which girls and boys in coeducational settings may seek to construct their gender identities by choosing traditionally male or female subjects. In England, one study found higher rates of enrolment in higher level maths and science among both girls and boys in single-sex schools.[14] Single-sex educated girls were somewhat less likely to take gender-typed subjects (such as languages and food technology) than their peers in coeducational schools.

However, contrary to expectations, single-sex boys were even less likely than coeducational boys to take non-traditional subjects. Similar findings were found in Catholic schools in the US, where single-sex educated girls showed a greater interest in maths and were more likely to enrol in maths courses.[15] The findings have been somewhat different in systems where single-sex education is less selective. One Australian study found that, all else being equal, there were no significant differences between single-sex and coeducational schools in the take-up of physics, chemistry or biology.[16] In the Irish context too, the take-up of science subjects has been found to reflect school-level characteristics rather than the gender mix of the school.[17]

Personal and social development

A number of studies have assessed the extent to which single-sex education influences young people's personal and social development. Both male and female students in coeducational settings are more positive about their schools and about the developmental aspects of their schooling, with these schools being seen as a more 'natural' environment which reflects the real world.[18] Results have been mixed when other outcomes, such as self-concept, are considered. In a systematic review of studies concerning a wide range of measures, including locus of control and attitudes to school and homework engagement, the results are almost evenly divided between those favouring single-sex education and those finding non-significant differences.[19] Some studies have shown that girls are more confident about their own abilities, and consequently hold higher aspirations for the future, when they are not exposed to competition from boys within the classroom.[20] An English study investigated the extent to which both male and female students felt they were good at different kinds of subjects.[21] This study found that students were more positive about their abilities in gender-atypical subject areas – boys in English, girls in maths and science – when taught in single-sex settings. These findings are not consistent across all studies, however. Indeed, a small number of studies indicate that single-sex schools may actually be more academically competitive and thus may have negative effects on how young people rate their own abilities.[22]

Adult outcomes

Fewer research studies have looked at the longer-term consequences of having attended a single-sex school. An English study of outcomes up to the age of 42 found no differences in overall attainment levels, but some differences in the type of post-school education pursued, with women who attended a single-sex school being more likely to study 'male' subjects and less likely to study 'female' subjects at their highest post-school qualification.[23] Similar findings are evident in the United States, with no significant differences in college entry rates but an increased likelihood of entering the least gender segregated fields of study among those who had attended single-sex schools.[24]

Single-sex by design?

The chapter so far has looked at the impact of single-sex schools on educational and wider outcomes. Because of the perceived benefits of single-sex classes, there has been a trend in a number of countries, including Britain, the US and Australia, to introduce single-sex classes within otherwise coeducational schools or to establish separate single-sex schools.[25] The rationale for this policy response has differed; in some instances, it is aimed at addressing male under-achievement, in others it seeks to promote achievement in science and maths among girls. In Britain, the Raising Boys' Achievement initiative was introduced in 2000 to combat male under-achievement; one of the measures introduced was the use of single-sex classrooms. Research on this initiative indicated mixed results in relation to actual achievement levels, and varying perceptions across the schools studied of the value of single-sex schooling, related in part to differing levels of teacher commitment to the initiative.[26] The effectiveness of single-sex classes in raising the achievement of boys and girls was seen as predicated on the extent to which practices within the classroom challenged gender stereotypes. Other studies of single-sex classes across a number of countries have shown very mixed results. Perhaps one reason for this inconsistency is the difficulty in disentangling the impact of single-sex classes from other elements of school reform. Furthermore, the success of such interventions is likely to be based on the extent to which they transform gender relations within the classroom so that merely having a single-sex class may not be enough to challenge existing stereotypes.

Conclusions

This chapter has summarised the main research findings on the potential impact of single-sex education on student outcomes. It is clear that there is very little consensus on whether single-sex education is advantageous to the overall academic achievement of girls or boys. Even though there is little evidence of overall differences in achievement, there does appear to be, at least tentative, evidence that attitudes to certain subject areas such as maths and science may be more gender-stereotyped in a coeducational setting. Reaching a consensus is hampered by the difficulty in accurately comparing 'like with like' given the different profile of students attending single-sex and coeducational schools. Indeed, researchers have argued about which variables to take into account in 'controlling for' prior differences – is social background sufficient, or do we also need a measure of prior ability/achievement? There has been debate, too, about how to separate out the effect of being in a single-sex school from the impact of other school characteristics – are we just interested in measuring the effect of gender composition, or are we concerned with other features of school organisation and process that may emerge in single-sex schools?

The debate about the merits of single-sex schooling is all the more pertinent in a policy context where the (re)introduction of single-sex classes and schools is seen as a solution to a range of problems. Overall, existing research indicates that the introduction of single-sex classes or schools does not represent a 'quick fix' to address the numbers of girls taking science subjects or to tackle male underachievement. Rather, studies point to the fact that gender differences in educational processes and outcomes are constructed and reconstructed in both single-sex and coeducational settings. Indeed, the way in which schools 'manage' gender may ultimately be much more important than the gender mix of students in the class or school.

Selection by Choice

Gabriel Heller Sahlgren

Few issues generate so much disagreement in the education debate as the one regarding pupil allocation to schools. Since the introduction of comprehensive schooling, which abolished the tripartite system, proximity to residence has been a guiding principle throughout the English primary and lower-secondary stages. Broadly speaking, this is also the approach favoured by the political left. The idea is to produce 'good local schools' in which pupils from all socioeconomic backgrounds can meet and learn together without the divisions produced by selection.

At the same time, many on the political right favour a return to a situation in which pupils are divided into different schools based on ability. An important reason behind the support for such differentiation is the difficulty of ensuring appropriate levels of teaching for pupils of all aptitude in the same setting. A more homogenous pupil population, it is argued, makes it easier to generate higher performance among all children. In general, selection by ability also allows for more specialisation, which may in turn have a positive impact on achievement.

While there are arguments in favour of both approaches, this chapter supports a third way. It holds that the most promising mechanism to efficiently and equitably allocate pupils is by maximising consumer choice. Allowing the postcode to decide which schools pupils attend is misguided as it leads to strong residential sorting, and in fact allows parents of means to buy their children a better state-funded education via their houses – in sharp contrast to the egalitarian aims of the proponents of proximity-based schooling. Meanwhile, while selection by aptitude has a place in education to some extent, it should not be the principal allocation device at primary and lower-secondary level. Little rigorous evidence suggests that school-level ability selection has strong direct effects on achievement. Moreover, to a certain extent, selection within schools could in fact fulfil a function similar to the one that proponents of between-school selection envisage, without the potential negative side effects on competitive incentives.

Overall, the maximisation of school choice offers a more compelling alternative since it allows for a combination of (1) better matching between pupils and schools, (2) migration from poorly performing to good schools, and (3) competition, which in turn may generate further improvements across the board. Yet to ensure that choice is maximised in reality rather than merely in theory, it is crucial to pay close attention to market design, which policymakers to a large extent have ignored thus far.[1]

The potential advantages and problems with choice as a mechanism for raising achievement

Why would we expect choice to generate better outcomes? Here, it is useful to distinguish between three main mechanisms. First, explicitly allowing parents to choose schools may generate a better pupil-school match than is the case when residence decides. This may in turn generate a 'choice effect', which leads to improved performance.[2]

Secondly, if choice generates a reallocation of pupils from low-performing schools to high-performing ones, it is expected that achievement would increase overall. For example, privately-operated schools may be better than state-owned ones and, if so, reallocating pupils to the former would increase achievement. This effect may arise because such schools are more autonomous, thus being able to respond to pupils' needs better.[3] Of course, the same impact could arise if pupils are allocated to better state schools as a result of an expansion of choice that is not tied to their residence. In general, therefore, this mechanism may be called a 'school effect'.

Furthermore, consumer choice forces schools to compete for pupils. According to microeconomic theory, one would generally expect markets to be more efficient than monopolies in allocating resources, leading to competitive pressures, emulation of best practices, and innovation. The result would be that failing schools improve or that they go out of business. If the latter occurs, one would again expect a reallocation of pupils from poor to good schools, in which case the school effects kick in. In this way, choice may be a 'tide that raises all boats' via a 'competition effect'.[4]

It is important to note that education and other public services are of course quite different to goods and services that are sold in the marketplace. A key issue is the potential for principal-agent problems: it might be difficult for parents to hold schools accountable because of information asymmetries that favour the latter. Education quality, especially academic, is not easily measured. Indeed, it is difficult for parents to judge whether a school contributes to their children's learning, especially since they most often have no access to a counterfactual situation. Even if a child obtains all A*s in their GCSEs, for example, this may have nothing to do with the school itself, but more with the child's innate ability. If so, the pupil would have achieved the same or very similar results regardless of which school they attended, a counterfactual situation parents do not observe. In essence, therefore, judging the quality of schools is quite different and much more difficult than judging the quality of, say, a sandwich.

This, in turn, means that the long-term incentives for schools to build a reputation of quality may then instead translate into incentives to cream off the best pupils. It is easy to see why this would be an attractive strategy. For example, staff may in this way be able to work less but still generate higher results than would otherwise be possible. In fact, if it is difficult to understand, identify, and contract quality, economic theory does not necessarily predict that competition will generate improvements. As economists W. Bentley MacLeod and Miguel Urquiola have argued: 'A reputation is nothing more than a belief regarding the quality of the good that a school is producing.'[5] And such beliefs may be instilled in other ways than being earned by bona fide success in improving academic outcomes.

The reality is that choice in education should probably not be treated as a 'self-playing piano' that conforms entirely to the ideal of microeconomic theory. The most obvious evidence of this is that there is an economic case to at least partly fund education via taxes – unlike the case for most goods and services – due to, for example, the risk of underinvestment in education that might be detrimental to society at large.[6] Estimates suggest that the government should cover about 50 per cent of educational costs.[7] There is a role for the government in education, but this does not mean that it should attempt to suppress choice; instead, it means that the government should facilitate it. One way to do so is to ensure good information regarding schools' academic quality. This does not mean absolute outcomes, but rather the added value schools provide to the learning process. While it has been difficult to develop reliable value-added metrics, recent American research clearly displays that it is possible. The requirement is quite straightforward: in order to capture schools' true contribution to learning, two separate measures of previous attainment are necessary.[8] With more data, it is possible to get around many of the problems that have plagued value-added metrics in England.[9] And studies suggest that parents do care about such value-added, if they have access to it.[10] Furthermore, randomised research shows that parents react quickly to new, less complicated information by choosing different schools – which in turn has large positive effects on their children's academic outcomes.[11] It is far from impossible, therefore, to overcome information asymmetries in education markets.

At this point, it is also important to note that all parents do not have to be well-informed and able to make good choices for the education market to function successfully. Indeed, few markets would work well if that were the case. Not all of us compare quality and price of all different types of coffee in the supermarket in a meticulous fashion, but it is enough that some consumers do. This informed minority – the marginal consumers – actively choose and generate gains also for those who do not search and utilise information to the same extent. And one would expect this to apply also to schooling. Marginal parents affect other parents with their revealed preferences, and they also are more likely to push schools to improve – meaning that only a portion of parents have to be well-informed for choice and competition to work.[12]

Furthermore, education is about so much more than just producing higher academic performance. Indeed, one of the key arguments in favour of selection by choice is that parents are better suited than bureaucrats to make trade-offs between 'hard' (academic) schooling quality and 'soft' aspects of it, such as emotional satisfaction and the production of social capital, which parents can more easily observe among their children. As economist Derek Neal has argued: 'Expansions of parental choice in whatever guise could allow governments to acquire an army of educational performance monitors.'[13] Since there is little way of knowing exactly what combination of different types of knowledge and skills will be most important in the future labour market, there is also no way to compute these trade-offs centrally.[14] Maximising consumer choice as a way to allocate pupils to schools allows for the application of local knowledge among those who know children best and are therefore more likely to make accurate trade-offs in this respect. As it happens, parents appear to first and foremost care about academic quality, and only after a minimum level has been fulfilled do they turn their attention to other important goals.[15]

But what does the empirical research show? Overall, the evidence has tended to find small-to-moderate positive choice effects on academic outcomes in different education systems worldwide. There is very little evidence of *negative* effects. In addition, there is also evidence that choice generates better non-cognitive outcomes, including social and political capital as well as entrepreneurship.[16] Nevertheless, it is important to highlight that most programmes suffer from significant design flaws, which theoretically decrease their impact. While some countries have better systems than others, none has been good enough. For example, despite the positive effects found in recent Swedish research, indicating that academy/free school choice has cushioned the country's fall in international league tables, the system is plagued by a mishmash of centralisation and decentralisation that has failed to target quality deficiencies. Indeed, given the lack of joined-up thinking regarding the overall incentive structure, it is quite remarkable that there have been any positive effects at all.[17]

In general, it is clear that policymakers have rarely attempted to seriously support the introduction of choice with a scaffolding structure to fundamentally change the provision of schooling. With this in mind, the generally small-to-medium positive impact that is found in most studies appears more noteworthy – and hints that the gains would be considerably larger with complementary reforms that aim to maximise choice in the system. Indeed, research analysing programmes that have unambiguously and significantly increased choice, compared to the baseline situation, does indeed find fairly large positive effects.[18] In other words, all choice is not equal, which makes it difficult to make sweeping statements regarding its efficacy or inefficacy without taking into account the overall structure in which it operates.

What about equity?

Whether or not equity would suffer with a system of choice is another central question. Of course, it is certainly possible to think of theoretical mechanisms that link an expansion of choice to higher school segregation. For example, more motivated parents from higher socioeconomic backgrounds may use their choices to separate their children from pupils of lower socioeconomic background or ability.[19] Such parents may also understand the system better, enabling them to place their children in the most attractive schools, to the detriment of other children who are then more likely to end up in less attractive schools. In addition, supply-side factors may increase segregation pressures, for example if schools have incentives to focus primarily on high-performing pupils since these are cheaper to educate than low-performing ones.[20] If this is the case, choice may generate higher segregation because schools effectively discriminate against certain types of pupils, leaving them no other alternatives but schools that remain after parents of higher-ability children have made their choices.

Yet it is crucial to understand that proximity-based selection, which is often upheld as a more egalitarian alternative, does not in fact ban choice at all, but merely ties it to residence. For example, recent research suggests that at least 20-30 per cent of parents in North Carolina exercise choice by moving residence.[21] Since better-performing and more desirable schools raise house prices in their vicinity – as the houses act as entrance tickets for children to attend them – parents who can afford to buy a house near such schools can in fact effectively also buy a better state education than parents who cannot afford it.[22] This hardly conforms to the egalitarian ideal. Moreover, it is essentially impossible even for the most draconian government to remove this type of choice since it requires it to control residential patterns, which is neither feasible nor desirable in liberal democracies.

The question, therefore, is whether choice increases school segregation overall, after counterfactual opportunities to choose schools, and changes in parental preferences for specific residential areas once choice is expanded, are taken into account. It may well be the case that publicly-funded school choice, decoupled from residence, reduces school segregation compared to a situation of proximity-based selection.[23] This is of course not the case if we allow schools to select pupils by aptitude, which almost by definition leads to social segregation since ability and background are highly correlated.

Even if choice does increase school segregation, the effect it has on the impact of parental background on achievement – a key measure of equity – is far from clear and depends on the structure of peer effects. The idea that mixed schools generate better outcomes among lower-ability pupils hinges on the assumption that such pupils benefit disproportionally from being surrounded by high-performing peers. In fact, a forthcoming literature review displays that there is little rigorous evidence suggesting that peer effects are meaningful or that they operate specifically in this way. Strikingly, there appears to also exist a 'big-fish-small-pond' or 'ranking' effect in which pupils benefit from being more able than their peers. A hypothesised mechanism is that relatively high-achieving pupils, who are surrounded by less able peers, are more likely to keep their motivation high. Overall, the literature therefore suggests that some form of school segregation that creates a certain degree of homogeneity is not necessarily harmful for equity, and that it in fact may benefit both high- and low-ability pupils to some extent.[24]

But what does the empirical evidence on the direct impact of choice on equity suggest? The international evidence on school segregation is mixed, although researchers often do find that larger choice opportunities lead to higher levels of school segregation.[25] The problem is that they cannot take into account that choice itself affects housing patterns. Indeed, research also indicates that choice that is decoupled from residence decreases residential sorting. Cross-national research, which attenuates the problem, since it is unlikely that parents move countries to put their children in a particular school, does not find that larger choice opportunities impact school segregation. Overall, given the complications discussed, it is hard to judge the overall effect of school choice on segregation, when decoupled from residence, based on existing evidence.[26] At the same time, there is essentially no evidence to suggest that selection by residence is preferable to selection by choice in relation to how it affects the impact of social background on achievement. If anything, choice appears to decrease the effect of background on achievement and often produces the best outcomes among less advantaged pupils.[27] Overall, concerns that choice would harm the least well off, either in an absolute or relative terms, do not receive much supporting evidence in the literature.

Taking system design seriously

However, as noted earlier, the design of school choice is key for its outcomes. This becomes obvious when considering the fact that parents technically have been allowed to apply to any school they want since the Education Reform Act of 1988. Yet, due to poor design, this has not materialised into more than a theoretical right in most cases. Key reasons behind this are (1) the low supply-side dynamic in the schools market and (2) that proximity to residence has remained the main selection device when schools are oversubscribed.

The lack of a supply-side dynamic has meant that good schools do not 'scale up', which in turn means that many children are stuck in the poorly performing ones simply because there is nowhere else to go. The goal should be to replicate the dynamic in the Texas Charter School sector, which has seen significant improvements in the past decade as a result of market forces that have pushed good schools to expand and bad ones to contract and eventually close down.[28] In England, the main way to improve the supply-side dynamic is by liberalising the free schools approval process. All providers meeting stipulated minimum requirements should be approved. If ownership requirements were also liberalised simultaneously, specifically by allowing for-profit providers to run schools, the incentive and ability to set up new schools and expand existing ones would increase considerably. This is because profit-making organisations have stronger incentives to start new schools and scale up as a result of increased demand, while also being able to attract investors in return for future potential profits to obtain the funding necessary.

This move would require the government to stop funding upfront capital costs, which is desirable anyway. Being able to find funding in the market, as a profit-making or non-profit-making provider, is part of the market test – if owners are not willing to invest their own money or persuade investors or philanthropists to back their ideas, they should probably not start or expand in the first place.[29]

Because of the poor supply-side dynamic, the selection device used for deciding who gets accepted to oversubscribed schools has become crucial. And since the main device is proximity to residence, the incentive for parents of means to move closer to the most sought-after schools and thereby crowd out less affluent parents has remained strong. Indeed, the most important reason why children of less affluent parents attend worse schools is because they have less access to good schools due to their less favourable housing situation.[30] Selection devices will always have a role in the allocation of pupils – although it can be considerably reduced if the supply-side dynamic is improved since fewer schools would be oversubscribed – and proximity to residence clearly favours parents from higher socioeconomic background. It also decreases the size of *de facto* market areas and therefore dampens competitive incentives to raise achievement for all pupils, since popular schools can rest on their laurels of having an advantaged intake as a result of residential sorting.[31]

But what should replace proximity to residence as the main selection device when schools are oversubscribed? Here, there is a potential marriage between choice and the application of school-level selection by ability. For example, parents could apply to any school, but schools would then be allowed to select those they want and turn away those they do not want. In this way, it would perhaps be possible to maximise the benefits of both choice and selection by aptitude. Yet this is not necessarily the case because of the high likelihood for simple cream skimming – which in turn may reduce both choice opportunities for the poor and competitive pressures on schools to improve. Theory indicates that allowing selection is likely to encourage schools to compete by selecting better pupils rather than by raising quality in order to boost their reputation.[32] While better information supply that reduces asymmetries between schools and parents is likely to ameliorate this problem – to the extent that parents care about academic quality – it is not necessarily sufficient to reduce it entirely.

An interesting real world comparison here is between Chile, where primary and lower-secondary schools have historically been allowed to select pupils, and Sweden, where they have not been able to so. The evidence on the impact of choice and competition is in general more positive in Sweden.[33] Indeed, a recent reform in Chile that among other things abolished selection in primary schools and parental interviews in secondary school had a positive impact on achievement.[34] Such selection practices have also been shown to decrease *de facto* choice opportunities among Chilean pupils attending poorly performing schools.[35] School selection of pupils in Chile appears to have effectively decreased choice opportunities for many children and therefore also undermined competitive pressures on schools to improve.[36] In addition, the research directly analysing the impact of selective schooling worldwide is in general mixed and uncertain.[37]

As such, the best default selection device for oversubscribed primary and lower-secondary schools in a choice-based education system is likely to be lotteries. This ensures that all pupils who apply to a specific school have the same opportunity to get in. Since this system is likely to increase the need for school transportation, some of the phased-out capital funding for free schools could simultaneously be spent on paying for transportation costs for poor children. Intriguingly, some research finds that doing so in combination with using lotteries as the selection device could halt school sorting by income.[38]

It is also important to note that entrance selection by ability is not always necessary to achieve some specialisation and an appropriate level of teaching in the classroom. Instead, one could advance selection by aptitude *within* schools as a compromise, which recent randomised research from Kenya suggests raises achievement for all pupils in comparison to using lotteries to allocate pupils to classrooms.[39] Interestingly, this type of selection is in fact used in Finland, a country often acclaimed for its comprehensive schooling system: while the variation in international test score achievement between Finnish schools is very small, the variation between classrooms is considerable.[40] As Sirkku Kupiainen of the University of Helsinki puts it: 'We have selection between classes rather than schools.'[41] In primary school, this selection mostly occurs indirectly via special music and language classes – which create ability grouping in other subjects as well because of high inter-subject achievement correlation – but in lower-secondary school there is more direct selection and differentiation of pupils into classes based on ability.[42] In other words, focusing more on in-school selection allows for a combination of maximisation of parental choice with the benefits of specialisation.

But if school-level selection by aptitude in primary or lower-secondary education is discarded, does this mean that it should be abolished in upper-secondary (16 plus) education? The answer is probably not. At this stage, the room and need for specialisation is higher since pupils have more choice in regard to which subjects they study. Pupils also become more active choosers themselves, and have to rely less on their parents' indirect knowledge about their specific situations, which means that information asymmetries are also likely to be reduced. Furthermore, since pupils are older, the likelihood that they are wrongly classified in different streams is lower than at the earlier stages in their educational career. Retaining school-level selection by aptitude at the upper-secondary level also ensures that the positive incentive effects that raise pupil achievement prior to the point of differentiation, as pupils work harder to get into more desirable schools, would also not be entirely lost.[43] Nevertheless, it would be valuable to experiment with lotteries among upper-secondary schools to evaluate whether these would allow choice to generate better performance and equity at this level too.

Conclusion

Deciding the principal method of pupil allocation in the state-funded education system is far from easy. Historically, comprehensive, proximity-based schooling and selective education have been the two key competing principles in this respect. Yet this chapter has argued that the maximisation of real consumer choice offers a preferable third way. This is because such choice is most likely to raise efficiency and equity via a combination of better pupil-school matching, migration from poor schools to good ones, and beneficial competition.

Of course, elements of proximity-based and selective schooling will always be relevant in any education system. For example, living close to the school attended by one's children may be preferable in the sense that it makes life easier. Some trade-off between preferences for quality and proximity is therefore expected to remain, which would in that case act as a natural check on ensuring that children do not have to attend schools that are too far away. Similarly, as noted, it is possible to utilise in-school selection to achieve the benefits associated with selective systems, while maintaining the benefits of the maximisation of choice at the school level. The principle of selection by choice is therefore malleable and can certainly accommodate for elements of both proximity and ability selection.

Overall, the question is therefore not whether we should advance choice as a method of pupil allocation, but rather how the details should be crafted. While consecutive governments have paid lip service to the expansion of choice, the lack of complementary reforms has unfortunately ensured that it has not materialised as more than a theoretical right among many parents. System design is crucial for how choice-based arrangements work, and this chapter has proposed reforms that could help us improve the current situation. Producing a well-functioning education system based on choice requires politicians to implement a coherent reform package that transforms the overall incentive structure in a positive direction.

Unlimited Potential

Eddie Playfair

In this chapter I try to make a moral, philosophical, political and pragmatic case against educational selection. I first outline the scale of selective practices in education and summarise the egalitarian position I am adopting in contrast to notions of fixed 'potential'. I then examine three key arguments made in favour of selection, the curriculum and structural implications of selection and the way that selection and marketisation reinforce each others' divisive impact. I touch on the issue of selection at 16 which is widespread and increasing, the politics of selection and some of the most recent research evidence available about the performance of selective systems in England and internationally. I conclude by making the case for a revitalised and modernised comprehensive national education system as the best way to promote excellence for all.

The context

Education in England is riddled with selective assumptions and practices from top to bottom. Learners are routinely selected and segregated into different provision, particularly at secondary and tertiary level: by prior academic achievement, by faith group, by gender, by wealth, by class and by ability. We have never had a national education system, let alone a fully comprehensive one. What we have is the result of a tension between comprehensive and selective tendencies operating in a context of market competition between unequal schools in an unequal society.

In this context, I want to question our acceptance of selective practices and ask: why support institutional segregation? If we take the perspective of the rejected, the question becomes why support education practices which exclude them? From this standpoint, advocates of grammar schools also become advocates of secondary moderns. They are not championing opportunity but shutting it down. This perspective can be applied elsewhere in education and I will argue that academic selection at 11 is not the only type of selection which needs to be challenged.

If we agree that the state should shape the kind of education system we have, then we can also probably agree that such a system should broadly value the things we value and reflect the type of society we want. Do our current arrangements reflect this? Do they serve all young people well? If we want a cohesive and open society where everyone can develop and flourish as citizens, workers and community members and an education system that works well for everyone then I think we need to start by consigning academic selection to the dustbin of history.

The case against selection is based on an egalitarian outlook

If you had the choice of the type of society to be born into but didn't know your status in advance, what type of society would you choose? No doubt most of us would choose a more egalitarian society if only to minimise the risk that we might face insurmountable odds against living a good life. The American philosopher John Rawls in his *A Theory of Justice* invites us to adopt this 'original position' and imagine ourselves behind a 'veil of ignorance' about the personal, social and historical circumstances we might find ourselves in.[1] He argues that the most rational choice of society for anyone in the original position includes the basic rights and liberties needed to secure our interests as free and equal citizens: equality of educational and employment opportunities and a guaranteed minimum income to pursue our interests and maintain our self-respect.

To many of us already born, the moral and political case for a more equal society is very strong. A large and enduring majority of people, 73 per cent in 2004, agree that the gap between rich and poor is too large.[2] If we need convincing evidence that more equal societies are better for everyone, this can be found in Richard Wilkinson and Kate Pickett's *The Spirit Level*. Amongst many other benefits of more egalitarian societies, they argue that 'it looks as if the achievement of higher national standards of educational performance may depend on reducing the social gradient in educational achievement'.[3]

The case for selection is based on notions of fixed, measurable potential

The idea that 'intelligence' is a single attribute which is fixed and measurable has been widely discredited despite its regular revival, most recently in genetic or neuropsychological forms. However, even when advocates of academic selection don't rely on IQ tests or fixed measures of ability, they replace the idea of measurable and fixed 'ability' with something equally fixed called 'potential'. Both these concepts start from a deterministic approach to learning which implies that an individual's ability to learn and to achieve academically is substantially pre-determined and unchanging. This view leads to practices which gradually close the doors to certain opportunities for human flourishing to certain people rather than keeping all doors open.

'Selection plays to people's strengths'

One argument is that selection plays to people's strengths, that academic selection simply supports the institutional specialisation needed to help everyone flourish. Being academically selective is just like being the Royal Ballet School or a football academy – we need to identify those who have demonstrated the potential to benefit from a specialist education. This is the flip side of the 'one size fits all' charge which implies that advocates of comprehensive education seek forced uniformity rather than universalism, and collective standardisation rather than individual flourishing. It ignores the opportunity for specialisation, diversity and pluralism which can be available in comprehensive schools and colleges. Young people can and do develop as expert dancers and footballers within a comprehensive system and without being segregated from their peers.

When Richard Cairns, Headmaster of fee-charging and selective Brighton College, said 'we must get away from the idea that we can successfully deliver both vocational and academic courses in the same school', he offered no evidence for this assertion.[4] The achievements of thousands of students every year in the many successful colleges which offer both types of course make the eloquent case to the contrary. The desire to segregate is strong but once we start to draw such arbitrary lines why stop there? What about the idea that we can successfully deliver science and art courses in the same school? Or history and engineering in the same university?

Selection becomes more acceptable as students get older

The case for specialist and differentiated offers becomes stronger the further along the educational journey one travels. Different students clearly need a range of different experiences based on the educational and career journey they've chosen. Clearly everyone is not the same and increasing differentiation is needed. Crucially, however, we need to distinguish between differentiation and selection. The range of needs is wide and overlapping and therefore the range of educational offers to meet these needs should be made available within a common system rather than requiring us to invent a new type of provider for every need. The arbitrary divisions in a binary or tripartite system are simply too crude to reflect the diversity of student needs. The fact that in England academic selection is permitted and resurgent post-16 makes it more likely that advocates of selection at 14 or 11 will reason in reverse, making the case that if it's fine to select at 16, why not do so at an earlier age. If there's no principle at stake, what difference does a few years make?

'Selection is meritocratic, allowing poor bright students to be rescued from mediocrity and become upwardly mobile'

A second common claim in favour of selection is that it is meritocratic, allowing poor bright students to be rescued from mediocrity and become upwardly mobile. The promise of greater social mobility within a meritocracy is a distortion of the egalitarian impulse. This essentially offers equality of opportunity to get on within a stratified and unequal society while failing to question existing profound inequalities. While 'getting on' is a valid aspiration, such approaches can actually function as palliatives; justifying inequalities by providing high achievers with the sense that they deserve their place at the top of what remains a grotesquely unequal society.

When a new selective sixth form college was created in our area, it was described by its founders as a 'lifeboat', presumably because it was going to save poor bright students from drowning in mediocrity. Sticking with this analogy, by setting high entry requirements and offering a narrow curriculum the lifeboat in question was cherry-picking the 'saved' very carefully, leaving most to 'drown' and subsequently pushing quite a few of the chosen back into the water if their grades were not high enough half way through their courses. Surely, a genuine lifeboat would aim to save everyone by providing appropriate routes for all students, including those who have achieved less well at school. The reality is that such selective practices depend on the existence of more inclusive, comprehensive providers to act as the real lifeboats, picking up the rejected.

The comprehensive school or college improves social mobility by keeping students' options open, allowing movement between different pathways and at different rates while also promoting social cohesion by creating a single community where everyone's aspiration can be nurtured and everyone's contribution valued.

Separate but equal: a divided curriculum for a divided society

The existence of selection by performance implies the need for a different curriculum for different 'types' of student. These different curricula reflect fixed assumptions about the different aspirations and trajectories of different groups of students as sorted by ability. This division generally boils down to some variant of the academic/vocational divide which sees young people belonging to one of two basic types; those with academic 'potential' and who can cope with abstract and theoretical concepts, and those who can't and need more applied, practical learning. This gross simplification of knowledge, skills, learning and motivation does everyone a great disservice. We need an egalitarian vision of the content of education as well as its organisation. In the same way as the Nuffield 14-19 Review set out to define the educated 19-year-old we need to ask as a society what should we wish for in an educated young member of this society.[5] Our egalitarianism should not restrict choices or promote uniformity of ambition or talent but should aim to offer the best to everyone. We might even take a tip from what the elite choose to pay for in the fee-charging private sector. If a broad and enriched liberal education is good enough for those privileged young people whose parents pay for their education then surely it's good enough for everyone. A popular version of that curriculum could be a good starting point for what we could offer all young people. Shorn of the trappings of snobbery and exclusivity it could be described as elite culture without the elitism. Our version of egalitarian education should not be based on 'dumbing down' for some, but on 'wising up' for all.

A new tripartism?

In December 2010, Wellington College Headmaster Anthony Seldon in his Sir John Cass's Foundation Lecture advocated a return to selection and the tripartite system.[6] In this attempt to reignite the debate on selection Seldon told his audience: 'Let me tell you straight – our schools and universities no longer know what they are doing.' Ignoring all the success, good practice and innovation taking place across the system, he went on:

> Government should divide schools into three streams at 14, an academic, technical and vocational stream, each roughly a third in size. The academic stream would ensure that all pupils who have genuine academic ability and interest could be again stretched at school...[7]

The technical stream in the middle would offer a blend of an academic and vocational curriculum. The third element, the vocational stream, would consist predominantly of practical-based learning.

Seldon also proposed an equivalent tripartite split for universities. He wanted the state to withdraw from the running of education, but he also wanted it to impose new rigid and hierarchical institutional divisions, a very contradictory position for a libertarian! Seldon was proposing the recreation of a discredited mid-twentieth century model as a solution to twenty-first century challenges. It is difficult to see how a return to selection would achieve his aim that schools should 'open minds and hearts' and 'educate for twenty-first century life in all its unknowable dimensions'.[8] The system he proposed makes unfounded assumptions about the innate ability and aptitudes of young people, the roles they might play in society and the proportions of various strata. How did he conclude that only a third of young people have 'genuine academic ability and interest'? This closing of options is the very opposite of the liberating and stretching experience which he claims to want for all.

When Seldon came to outline who would oversee the content of the education offered by each stream, the stratification became clearer. Universities (presumably not the technical or vocational ones) would look after the academic stream, the professions the technical stream and the employers the vocational stream: a classic vision of social reproduction where every 14-year-old is clear about where they are heading. Seldon made no comment about the means for selecting young people for these streams but claimed that this would not lead to the recreation of secondary modern schools as a 'dumping zone for children of low ability'.[9] Would the academic stream engage with any practical learning beyond playing sport or music? How would he ensure that the vocational stream is seen as a 'flourishing option'? The plan was riddled with contradictions and elitist assumptions but would nevertheless appeal to the independent sector, the grammar school lobby and those promoting separate vocational studio schools or university technical colleges from age 14.

While he claimed not to be attacking the state sector, Seldon was clearly attacking the comprehensive principle upon which much of the sector is based. In parts of the speech he was inclusive: 'all children should have the chance to learn musical instruments' and 'students in all three streams would have to pass a diploma in which they showed proficiency in physical activity, the arts, volunteering and personal skills'.[10] However, the core proposals were highly exclusive and Seldon was adamant that 'nothing less than the tripartite division beginning at 14 will provide the solutions that Britain needs'.[11] Confronted with the challenges of twenty-first century education, Seldon has provided some good diagnosis but offered us a highly toxic prescription.

This embracing of selection goes well beyond anything that Michael Gove said in his time at the Department for Education. In fact, the former Secretary of State was at pains to say that introducing selection where it does not already exist was not on his agenda and he framed his market reforms in a non-selective context. Neither academies nor free schools are allowed to overtly select on ability pre-16. Nevertheless, bi- or tri-partism and selection still have a strong following. Anthony Seldon's speech was just one salvo in a fresh attempt to reintroduce it into public education, and the ideology of selection is alive and well in more recent proposals from bodies such as the Sutton Trust.

Selection operates within a market system

Selection and marketisation go hand in hand. Selection is a way of rationing choice within a system which worships choice. It encourages hierarchies, reproduces inequalities and creates scarcity and elitism where they are not needed. In a market, schools and colleges feel obliged to say 'we're better because we have something others don't' and the selective ones need to add 'apply to us because we might not let you in'. Market selection puts greater power in the hands of the institution doing the choosing rather than the individual 'consumer' who thinks they're doing the choosing. Decisions about the basis of selection are taken by people in power; a highly conservative process where judgements about what skills or knowledge are valued and what are good measures of 'potential' reproduce those already valued by the current system. In effect, the decision about where and what you can study is taken by others and the existing power structures remain unchallenged. Even if selection operated without a market system, it would still be reproducing inequalities. If the basis for selection was regarded as fair and legitimate and people were given second chances to get into selective providers (for example at 11, 14 and 16), there might be fewer 'errors' or 'wastage' but the overall effect would be the same.

Some Conservative politicians, including former Education Secretary Michael Gove, claim to want a more equal society. In discussion with Richard Wilkinson on Radio 4's *Today* programme he praised *The Spirit Level* saying its analysis was 'fantastic'. He qualified this by saying that 'more equal societies do do better... we need to make opportunities more equal in this country and... [take] action to deal with inequality throughout life'.[12] He was convinced that more market choice and diversity of educational providers would promote this policy aim. All the evidence, however, shows that markets have a poor record of promoting equality. Unless purchasing power is heavily weighted towards the poorest, the better off will always have a head start in any market system. Does the government have the courage to regulate the market they have created to prevent it from widening the educational opportunity gap between rich and poor? Or will they continue to tolerate a divided system with unequal outcomes?

We need to reverse the marketisation and commodification of social goods such as educational opportunities. Public service values are undermined when public services are treated more and more as commodities with a commercial value and in some cases subject to outright market forces and privatisation. For instance, young people are encouraged to value educational qualifications in terms of the alleged additional earning power they attract and to equate higher level skills to labour market advantage. The individual student is increasingly regarded both as a consumer and a commodity; making individual choices based on calculations of personal advantage and competing against fellow students for the limited opportunities the education and labour markets have to offer.

Selection at 16 and beyond

There is a strong case for extending the comprehensive ideal beyond 16, even to university. At Newham Sixth Form College where I am Principal, we persist in describing our college as comprehensive even though the term has been unfashionable for some time and there is no requirement to have inclusive admissions policies. We are proud to be comprehensive and, for us, using the 'c word' is the clearest way of defining one of our core values; the fact that we aim to provide for the educational needs of all young people in the age group we cater for, i.e. 16- to 19-year-olds. However, this is not the norm. The case for a comprehensive post-16 college still needs to be made given that there is such a wide range of potential courses available at different levels for this age group and also that 16-year-olds have complete freedom of choice about where they study. Sixth form education has become the new front-line of selection with a plethora of new providers, whether 11-18 academies or 16-18 free schools trying to outdo each other in setting ever more exclusive entry requirements. Post-16 performance table measures and cheerleading from the media and politicians encourage this selective bubble.

Those schools and colleges which aren't aiming to be comprehensive should be asked: Why segregate? What is the case for exclusion? After all, a comprehensive intake is the norm for primary schools, why should things change after 11 or 16? Faced with a proliferation of selective post-16 providers, we should be asking: Why is it OK for a school to be comprehensive from 11-16 and become selective in the sixth form, thereby excluding most of its former students? Why don't you provide the 'non-facilitating' A-level subjects many students want? Why don't you offer the vocational courses which help so many students progress to university? Why don't you offer the foundation and intermediate courses which provide vital stepping stones to advanced study for so many students who did less well at 16? The range of courses and specialisation available post-16 do require a larger system or network of providers to provide them cost-effectively but there is no reason why all these courses can't be offered within a single institution or even under one roof. Because they operate in a market where students choose where to study, this doesn't mean that the post-16 providers have to be either 'niche' or selective.

Beyond this, the case for the comprehensive university has yet to be fully articulated. Why set a 50 per cent ceiling on the proportion of the population who can benefit from a university education and tell some young people that university is not for them? Why shouldn't publicly funded universities be tasked with leading a renaissance in lifelong learning with the aim of engaging all adults in some form of tertiary education, whether at postgraduate, degree or pre-degree level?

The politics of selection

The modern Conservative Party has moved away from a full political endorsement of selection at age 11 while nevertheless tolerating selective systems and practices where they exist. The right-wing populists of UKIP seem to have taken on the mantle of champions of selection, advocating 'a grammar school in every town' and therefore three or four secondary moderns in every town.[13]

If academic selection and the 11-plus are back on the political agenda then they should certainly be vigorously challenged. Many of us will want to defend the comprehensive principle because we believe that the common school, college and university, like the NHS, are part of the foundations of the good society.

New Labour was squeamish about 'equality' preferring to substitute 'fairness' or 'equity', perfectly good concepts in themselves but the change of language appeared to signal a dilution of Labour's commitment to actually challenging inequalities even of the grossest kind. Perhaps it is time for the party to give English education its 'NHS moment' and apply an egalitarian litmus test to its thinking about publicly funded schools and colleges. Labour might even find that this plays well with an electorate fed up with the 57 varieties of segregation we are currently experiencing.

The comprehensive school is a successful and popular expression of solidarity which transcends all social differences. The idea that children and young people should be educated with their neighbours and their peers in a learning community which reflects the composition of the geographical community they live in is still valid, even if some have abandoned it. A comprehensive system discourages competition for positional advantage by school, and seeks to ensure that every school and every student can flourish.

The evidence

There is a considerable body of research into the performance of selective systems compared to comprehensive ones. A 2011 *Financial Times* analysis of GCSE achievement for 2011 in selective and non-selective areas in England demonstrated that students from poorer backgrounds and the bottom 50 per cent did significantly worse in selective areas while the wealthiest five per cent did better.[14] The Sutton Trust report 'Degrees of Success' suggested that given their intake 'grammar schools would appear to be under-represented among the most successful schools for Oxbridge entry'.[15] An OECD report has shown that the top five education systems as measured by the Programme for International Student Assessment

(PISA) are non-selective and comments that 'early differentiation of students by school is associated with wider than average socio-economic disparities and not with better results overall'.[16] Recent research by Matt Dickson, Lindsey Macmillan and Simon Burgess also demonstrates that selective systems increase inequality; lowering incomes at the bottom as well as raising them at the top.[17] Students can and do achieve outstanding results in comprehensive settings and there is no evidence that selection increases most students' chances of success. Quite the opposite, selection restricts opportunities for achievement and increases social segregation.

Conclusion: making the case for universal comprehensive public education

We still live in a class-ridden society and this is reflected in the classification, hierarchy and competition between providers in education as in so many other areas of our life. Our understandable desire for an education which helps us or our children 'get on' is translated into striving to find the 'best' school or college, often with diminishing returns. We are obsessed with the pecking order rather than being obsessed with education and flourishing.

So what does a genuinely egalitarian approach look like in relation to education? It means rediscovering and proudly championing the virtues and achievements of universal public services. The comprehensive school or college is a place where citizens experience equality. People are treated with equal respect, meet and work with others on equal terms and have their individual needs met regardless of their starting point or ability to pay. It's time we saw our successful comprehensive schools and colleges as the benchmark even if they don't top the performance tables for raw exam scores. By doing a great job for all students, they pose a daily challenge to more selective providers to justify segregation. It is the advocates of more selection who need to explain what their proposals are for the education of all those students they keep out. Surely they should be raising their game rather than simply picking the low-hanging fruit?

Like other public services at their best, state-funded education providers model the social relationships of a more equal society. As Basil Bernstein rather depressingly reminded us, 'education cannot compensate for society',[18] nevertheless the fact that people's experience of equality in one sphere is not mirrored in every other aspect of their day-to-day experience should be a source of anger and action rather than a reason for giving up. People clearly do not all engage with education from the same starting point and many face enormous barriers. However, the right kind of public education can challenge injustice and give people a lived experience of more equal social relations and practices, so it is worth trying to 'compensate for society'.

I absolutely agree with Anthony Seldon that 'schools should be places of delight, challenge and deep stimulation where all the faculties that a student possesses can be identified, nurtured and developed' and this is precisely why I oppose selection.[19] We need a broad liberal and practical curriculum for all young people, one which offers challenge, choice, depth, breadth, stretch and progression for all, which values both knowledge and skill and provides something to build on throughout life. This is not a theoretical argument. When parents and potential students experience what being comprehensive means, in all its diversity and ambition, they respond very positively and continue to support the practice.

English education has yet to have its NHS moment but the founding principles of a single universal health service which meets the full range of people's needs can be applied just as well to a national education system. Schools, colleges and universities for everyone are better placed to promote excellence for everyone. The challenge is to re-found the comprehensive system rather than to abandon it.

Endnotes

Foreword *Fiona Millar*

1 Department for Education, 'Schools, Pupils and Their Characteristics: January 2014', Statistical First Release, 12 June 2014; J. Simons and N. Porter, ' 5 Reasons Why a Return to Grammar Schools Is a Bad Idea', 5 December 2014.

2 D. Boffey, 'Ofsted Chief Declares War on Grammar Schools', *Observer*, 15 December 2013.

3 Comprehensive Future, 'Fair Enough? School Admissions - The Next Steps', 2007.

4 British Humanist Association, 'Ground-breaking New Research Maps the Segregating Impact of Faith School Admissions', 3 December 2013.

Introduction

1 K. Spours quoted in 'Issues Paper 10: General Education in the 14-19 Phase', Nuffield Review of 14-19 Education and Training, England and Wales, June 2008, p.1.

Selective, Comprehensive and Diversified Secondary Schooling in England: A Brief History

1 We are grateful to David Crook and Emma Wisby for their help in developing this chapter. We would like to thank IOE Press for permission to adapt material first published in D. Crook, S. Power, and G. Whitty, *The Grammar School Question: A Review of Research on Comprehensive and Selective Education*, London, Institute of Education, 2000.

2 F. Ringer, *Education and Society in Modern Europe*, Bloomington and London, Indiana University Press, 1979.

3 H. Silver and P. Silver, *An Educational War on Poverty: American and British Policy-Making, 1960-1980*, Cambridge, Cambridge University Press, 1991, p.167.

4 P. Thane, *The Foundations of the Welfare State*, London, Longman, 1982, p.204.

5 A.C. Kerckhoff, K. Fogelman, D. Crook, and D. Reeder, *Going Comprehensive in England and Wales: A Study of Uneven Change*, London, Woburn Press, 1996, p.136.

6 D. Lawton, *Class, Culture and the Curriculum*, London, Routledge and Kegan Paul, 1975, p.3.

7 I. Fenwick, *The Comprehensive School, 1944-70*, London, Methuen, 1976, p.58; H. Judge, *A Generation of Schooling: English Secondary Schools Since 1944*, Oxford, Oxford University Press, 1984, p.68.

8   Quoted in D. Rubinstein, and B. Simon, *The Evolution of the Comprehensive School, 1926-1966*, London, Routledge and Kegan Paul, 1969, p.37.

9   M. Barber, *The Making of the 1944 Education Act*, London, Cassell, 1994.

10 A. Kerckhoff and J.M. Trott, 'Educational Attainment in a Changing Educational System: The Case of England and Wales', p.149, in Y. Shavit and H.P. Blossfeld (eds.) *Persistent Inequality: Changing Educational Attainment in Thirteen Countries*, Boulder, Westview Press, 1993, pp.133-153.

11 H. Silver, *Good Schools, Effective Schools: Judgements and their Histories*, London, Cassell, 1994, p.77.

12 B. Jackson and D. Marsden, *Education and the Working Class,* London, Routledge and Kegan Paul, 1962; J.W.B. Douglas, *The Home and the School*, London, Macgibbon and Kee, 1964; R.R. Dale and S. Griffith, *Down Stream: Failure in the Grammar School*, London, Routledge and Kegan Paul, 1965.

13 P.E. Vernon (ed.) *Secondary School Selection*, London, Methuen, 1957, pp.43-44, quoted in B. Simon, *Education and the Social Order, 1940-1990*, London, Lawrence and Wishart, 1991, p.209.

14 A. Yates and D.A. Pidgeon, *Admission to Grammar Schools*, Oxford, Newnes, 1957, pp.191-93.

15 Ibid.

16 J. Ford, *Social Class and the Comprehensive School*, London, Routledge and Kegan Paul, 1969.

17 D. Crook, S. Power, and G. Whitty, *The Grammar School Question: A Review of Research on Comprehensive and Selective Education*, London, Institute of Education, 1999.

18 A.H. Halsey, 'Education and equality', *New Society*, 17 June 1965, p.13.

19 Department of Education and Science, 'The Organisation of Secondary Education', (Circular 10/65), London, Her Majesty's Stationery Office, 1965.

20 See, for example, London County Council, 1961.

21 A.C. Kerckhoff, K. Fogelman, D. Crook, and D. Reeder, *Going Comprehensive in England and Wales: A Study of Uneven Change,* London, Woburn Press, 1996, p.201.

22 Ibid.

23 B. Simon, *Education and the Social Order, 1940-1990*, London, Lawrence and Wishart, 1991, p.439.

24 C. Chitty, *Towards a New Education System: The Victory of the New Right?* London, RoutledgeFalmer, 1989, p.69.

25 Department of Education and Science, 'Comprehensive Education: Report of a DES Conference', London, Her Majesty's Stationery Office, 1978.

26 B. Simon, *Education and the Social Order, 1940-1990*, London, Lawrence and Wishart, 1991, pp.482-83.

27 T. Edwards, J. Fitz, and G. Whitty, *The State and Private Education: An Evaluation of the Assisted Places Scheme*, Lewes, Falmer Press, 1989.

28 J. Fitz, D. Halpin, and S. Power, *Grant Maintained Schools: Education in the Market Place*, London, Kogan Page, 1993.

29 Department for Education, 'Choice and Diversity: A New Framework for Schools (White Paper Cmnd. 2021)', London, Her Majesty's Stationery Office, 1992.

30 S. Castle and J. Judd, 'How Could Labour Fail This One?', *The Independent on Sunday*, 28 January 1996.

31 Department for Education and Employment, 'Self-Government for Schools', 1996.

32 See, for example, *The Independent*, 26 February 1992.

33 T. Blair, speech at the Barber Institute, University of Birmingham, 14 April 1997.

34 Department for Education, 'School Standards and Framework Act 1998', 24 July 1998.

35 Department for Education and Employment, 'Excellence in Schools', 1997.

36 The distinction between aptitude, ability and attainment was somewhat blurred, and aptitude was sometimes seen by critics of such policies as a proxy for selection by academic ability (see T. Edwards and G. Whitty, 'Specialisation and Selection in Secondary Education', *Oxford Review of Education*, 23(1), 1997, pp.5-15; J. Coldron, B. Willis, and C. Wolstenholme, 'Selection by Attainment and Aptitude in English Secondary Schools', *British Journal of Educational Studies*, 57(3), 2009, pp. 245-264: stated that, although the great majority of specialist schools did not use selection, the potential was there to do so).

37 Cited in C. Chitty, 'Thirty Years On', *Forum*, 36, 3, 1994, p.89.

38 A. Adonis and S. Pollard, *A Class Act: The Myth of Britain's Classless Society*, London, Hamish Hamilton, 1997, p.61.

39 National Audit Office, 'The Academies Programme', TSO, 2007.

40 Although most such schools were technically non-selective, over 80 per cent of the remaining 163 grammar schools had adopted academy status by 1 January 2013.

41 T. Blair, Speech at the Barber Institute, University of Birmingham, 14 April 1997.

42 Department for Education and Skills, 'Higher Standards, Better Schools for All', 2005.

43 E. Morris, 'We Need Your Help to Make a Difference', *Education Review* 15, 1, 2001, p.4.

44 A. Campbell, *The Blair Years: Extracts from the Alastair Campbell Diaries*, London, Hutchinson, 2007.

45 D. Jesson and D. Crossley, *Educational Outcomes and Value Added by Specialist Schools – 2005*, London, SSAT/iNet, 2006.

46 The Sutton Trust, 'The Social Composition of Top Comprehensive Schools: Rates of Eligibility for Free School Meals at the 200 Highest Performing Comprehensive Schools', 2006.

47 S. Gewirtz, S. Ball, and R. Bowe, *Markets, Choice and Equity in Education*, Buckingham, Open University Press, 1995; P. Newsam, 'Diversity and Admissions to English Secondary Schools', *Forum*, 45, 1, 2003, pp.17-18.

48 J. Coldron, B. Willis, and C. Wolstenholme, 'Selection by Attainment and Aptitude in English Secondary Schools', *British Journal of Educational Studies*, 57, 3, 2009, p.261 argues that 'selection to grammar schools by prior attainment is currently also largely selection by social background'.

49 S. Tough and R. Brooks, *School Admissions: Fair Choice for Parents and Pupils*, London, IPPR, 2007.

50 The Sutton Trust, 'The Social Composition of Top Comprehensive Schools: Rates of Eligibility for Free School Meals at the 200 Highest Performing

Comprehensive Schools', 2006. A more recent study, the Sutton Trust, 'Selective Comprehensives: The Social Composition of Top Comprehensive School', 2013, found that the overall rate of free school meal uptake at the top 500 comprehensives measured on the five good GCSE scale was just below half the national average. They further found that schools controlling their own admissions policies were overrepresented in this top 500.

51   Selection by faith schools was also an issue raised at this time, but it is not directly addressed in this chapter (see G. Penlington, 'Why New Labour Found Itself Converted to Church Schools', *Parliamentary Brief*, 2, 2001, pp.42–3).

52   Department for Education and Skills, 'The Government's Response to the House of Commons Education and Skills Committee Report: The Schools White Paper: Higher Standards, Better Schools for All', 2006; Education and Skills Committee, 'The Schools White Paper: Higher Standards, Better Schools for All', 2006.

53   Department for Education and Skills, 'Higher Standards, Better Schools for All', 2005.

54   R. Allen, J. Coldron, and A. West, 'The Effect of Changes in Published Secondary Schools Admissions on Pupil Composition', *Journal of Education Policy*, 27, 3, 2012, pp.349-366.

55   For example Education Alliance, 'A Good Local School for Every Child: Will the Education Bill Deliver?', Conference report, Institute of Education, University of London, 25 March 2006.

56   S. Laville and R. Smithers, 'War Over School Boundaries Divides Brighton', *Guardian*, 2007, p.4.

57   The Sutton Trust, 'The Sutton Trust Mobility Manifesto', 2014.

58   F. Green, R. Allen, and A. Jenkins, *The Social Composition of Free Schools after Three Years*, London, Institute of Education, 2014.

59   D. Boffey, 'Ofsted Chief Declares War on Grammar Schools', *Observer*, 15 December 2013.

60   H. Eysenck, 'Equality and Education: Fifteen Years On', *Oxford Review of Education*, 17, 1991, p.164.

61   BBC News, 'Saying "No" to Selection', 24 October 1998.

62   D. Willetts, speech to the CBI Conference on Public Service Reform, 16 May 2007.

63   D. Crook, S. Power, and G. Whitty, *The Grammar School Question: A Review of Research on Comprehensive and Selective Education*, London, Institute of Education, 1999.

64   At that time we reviewed studies by Benn and Simon (1970), Steedman (1980), Marks *et al* (1983), Steedman (1983), Gray *et al* (1983), Gray *et al* (1984), Department of Education and Science (1983 and 1984), Marks and Pomian-Szrednicki (1985), Marks *et al* (1986), McPherson and Willms (1987), Reynolds *et al* (1987), Marks (1991), Benn and Chitty (1996), Kerckhoff *et al* (1996) and Marks (1998). Subsequently, the wider political emphasis on social mobility and 'closing the gap' under New Labour (and, to an even greater extent, the Coalition government) has been reflected in the emphasis of more recent studies, such as Jesson (2007), Harris and Rose (2013) and Burgess *et al* (2014). These studies do not seem to have found that existing grammar schools contributed significantly to this wider political agenda, even where they identified some limited advantages for individual pupils. Research on the

diversified school system by Machin and colleagues (Machin and Vernoit, 2011; Machin and Silva, 2013), particularly on the performance of New Labour's academies compared with other schools, concluded that even where they performed better overall, they did not necessarily succeed in closing the achievement gap.

65   R. Coe, K. Jones, J. Searle, D. Kokotsaki, A. Kosnin, and P. Skinner, Evidence on the Effects of Selective Educational Systems: A Report for The Sutton Trust by CEM Centre, University of Durham, 2008.

66   D. Jesson, 'The Creation, Development and Present State of Grammar Schools in England, A Report for The Sutton Trust by the Centre for Performance Evaluation and Resource Management', University of York, 2013.

67   G. Whitty, 'Developing Comprehensive Education in a New Climate', in M. Benn and C. Chitty (eds), *A Tribute to Caroline Benn: Education and Democracy*, London, Continuum, 2004.

68   J. Cribb, D. Jesson, L. Sibieta, A. Skipp, and A. Vignoles, 'Poor Grammar: Entry Into Grammar Schools for Disadvantaged Pupils in England', London, The Sutton Trust, 2013.

69   D. Jesson, 'The Creation, Development and Present State of Grammar Schools in England, A Report for The Sutton Trust by the Centre for Performance Evaluation and Resource Management', University of York, 2013; The Sutton Trust, 'The Sutton Trust Mobility Manifesto', 2014.

70   Ibid.

The Twenty-First Century Case for Selection

1   J. Parker, 'Education Bill', Hansard, Vol 396, CC207-322, 19 January 1944.

2   A. Sampson, *The New Anatomy of Britain*, London, Hodder & Stoughton, 1971.

3   The Sutton Trust, 'The Educational Background of the Nation's Leading People', November 2012.

4   F. Musgrove, 'School and the Social Order', New York, John Wiley and Sons, 1979, in A. Adonis and S. Pollard, *A Class Act: the Myth of Britain's Classless Society*, London, Penguin Books, 1998, p.196.

5   A. Adonis and S. Pollard, *A Class Act: The Myth of Britain's Classless Society*, London, Penguin Books, 1998, p.55.

6   A. Sampson, *The New Anatomy of Britain*, London, Hodder & Stoughton, 1971.

7   M. Bentham, 'Parents "Cheated" to Win Assisted Places', *Daily Telegraph*, 2 July 2000.

8   G. Brady, Commons Debate, Column 52, 2 June 1997.

9   The Sutton Trust, 'Open Access: A Practical Way Forward', June 2004.

10   R. Garner, 'Private School Children Will Earn £200,000 More on Average Than State-Educated Kids by 42', *The Independent*, 3 July 2014.

11   R. Harris, 'Tony Blair is the Greatest Ally of Private Schools', *Daily Telegraph*, 9 July 2002.

12   C. Woodhead, *A Desolation of Learning*, Petersfield, Pencil-Sharp Publishing, 2009, p.143.

13   C. Woodhead, *A Desolation of Learning*, Petersfield, Pencil-Sharp Publishing, 2009.

14   Department of Education for Northern Ireland, 'Statistical Bulletin: Year 12 and Year 14 Examination Performance at Post-Primary Schools in Northern Ireland 2013-14', 2014.

15   J. Marks, 'The Betrayed Generations', Centre for Policy Studies, 2000.

16   Department for Education, 'School Performance Tables: Trafford', 2014.

17   Department for Education, 'A-Level and Other Level 3 Results: 2013 to 2014 (Revised)', SFR03/2015, sub-table 12a, 2015.

18   A. Burns, 'Conservatives Must Have the Confidence to Bring Back Grammar Schools', *Daily Telegraph*, 6 August 2013.

19   BBC News, 'Blunkett Pushes Learning for Work', 24 January 2001.

20   Speech by Lord Andrew Adonis, as Parliamentary Under-Secretary of State for Schools, 'Sir John Cass's Foundation Inaugural Lecture', 2007.

21   P. Wintour and N. Watt, 'Schools Told to Raise the Bar on GCSE Exam Results', *Guardian*, 14 June 2011.

22   Department for Education, 'GCSE and Equivalent Results in England, 2012 to 2013 (Revised), Subject and LA Tables', SFR01/2014, 2014.

23   Department for Education, 'GCSE and Equivalent Attainment by Pupil Characteristics: 2014', SFR06/2015, Sub-Tables 4 and 5, 2015.

24   The Sutton Trust, 'Degrees of Success: University Chances by Individual School', July 2011.

25   University of Cambridge, 'Undergraduate Admissions Statistics, 2012 Cycle', May 2013; University of Oxford, 'Undergraduate Admissions Statistics: School Type, 2012', November 2013; K. Parel and R. Adams, 'Oxford University Data Shows Private School A-Level Pupils' Advantage', *Guardian*, 15 August 2013.

26   J. Sherman, 'Academic Apartheid Against North Must End, Leading Universities Told', *The Times*, 17 January 2015.

27   Department for Education, 'A-Level and Other Level 3 Results: 2013 to 2014 (Provisional)', Sub-Table 1C, 2014.

28   C. McDonald, 'Classics in Schools: The Research Report', Friends of Classics, March 2010.

29   Department for Education, 'A-Level and Other Level 3 Results: 2013 to 2014 (Provisional)', Sub-Table 9, 2014.

30   Calculated from: Department for Education, 'Schools, Pupils, and their Characteristics: January 2014 (Local Authority and Regional Tables) SFR15/2014', Sub-Table 7b, 2014.

31   The Sutton Trust, 'Rates of Eligibility for Free School Meals at the Top State Schools', 2005.

32   Department for Education, 'National Curriculum Assessments at Key Stage 2, 2014 (Revised)', Sub-Table 9a. 2014

33   Calculations made by the House of Commons Library. Source data available from: Department for Education, 'GCSE and Equivalent Attainment by Pupil Characteristics in England, 2010/11', 2012.

34   Hansard (House of Lords), 'Grammar Schools: Written Question – HL2914', 2014.

35   A. Smithers and P. Robinson, 'Worlds Apart: Social Variation among Schools', The Sutton Trust, April 2010.

36   B. Francis and M. Hutchins, 'Parent Power?', The Sutton Trust, December 2013.

37 Department of Education for Northern Ireland, 'Statistical Bulletin: Year 12 and Year 14 Examination Performance and Post-Primary Schools in Northern Ireland 2013-14', 2014.

38 Baker Dearing Educational Trust, University Technical Colleges.

39 T. Blair, 'Higher Standards, Better Schools for All: More Choice for Parents and Pupils, Foreword, Department for Education and Skills, October 2005.

40 M. Portillo, 'Why Won't Any Political Party Dare Champion Grammar Schools? I Owe Mine Everything', *Daily Mail*, 5 January 2012.

41 National Grammar Schools Association, 'Support for Grammar Schools is High and Growing', March 2010.

42 Ibid.

The Case for Comprehensive Schools

1   R. Alleyne, '11-Plus Failure That Still Hurts 50 Years Later', *Daily Telegraph*, 20 December 2005.

2   G. Paton, 'Adults "Put off Education for Life" After Failing 11-Plus', *Daily Telegraph*, 18 December 2012.

3   A. Asthana, 'Early Starts for the Children Desperate to Pass Their 11-Plus', *Observer*, 11 October 2009.

4   P. Bolton, 'Education: Historical Statistics, Standard Note: SN/SG/4252', House of Commons Library, November 2012.

5   Ibid.

6   Ofsted, 'The Annual Report of Her Majesty's Chief Inspector of Education, Children's Services and Skills 2010/11', November 2011.

7   C. Baker, D. Dawson, T. Thair, and R. Youngs, 'Longitudinal Study of Young People in England: Cohort 2, Wave 1', Department of Education, November 2014, p.70.

8   P. Bolton, 'Education: Historical Statistics, Standard Note: SN/SG/4252', House of Commons Library, November 2012.

9   I.G.K. Fenwick, *The Comprehensive School, 1944-1970*, London, Routledge, 2007, p.67.

10 Her Majesty's Stationery Office, 'Education in a Changing World', Crowther Report, London, 1959, p.5.

11 S. Jenkins, 'Cameron's Historic Victory Over the Gilded Myth of Grammars', *Sunday Times*, 27 May 2007.

12 P. Wilby, 'Margaret Thatcher's Education Legacy is Still With Us – Driven by Gove', *Guardian*, 15 April 2013.

13 D. Randall *et al.*, '10 Things You Thought You Knew About Margaret Thatcher's Downing Street Years', *The Independent*, 14 April 2013.

14 K. Baker, 'Legacy of a Woman Who "Liked a Fight"', *Evening Standard*, 12 April 2013.

15 Conservative Home, 'David Willetts Answers Your Questions', 26 May 2007.

16 M. Gove, 'Michael Gove: My Revolution for Culture in Classroom', *Daily Telegraph*, 28 December 2010.

17 M. Taggart, 'Majority Favour Academic Selection', BBC, 26 January 2004.

18 R. Pedley, 'The Comprehensive School, 1963', in M. Benn and F. Millar, *A Comprehensive Future*, London, Compass, 2005.

19   J. Rae-Dupree, 'If You're Open to Growth, You Tend to Grow', *New York Times*, 6 July 2008.

20   G. Crowther, '15 To 18: A Report of The Central Advisory Council for Education (England)', London, Her Majesty's Stationery Office, 1959, p.130. The National Service survey was of 9,000 men recruited to the armed forces between 1956 and 1958.

21   Lord Robbins, 'The Robbins Report: Higher Education', London, Her Majesty's Stationery Office, 1963, p.50, Table 21.

22   Ibid.

23   S. Gurney-Dixon, 'Gurney-Dixon Report: Early Leaving, A Report of the Central Advisory Council for Education (England)', 1954.

24   A. Elliott, *State Schools Since The 1950s: The Good News*, London, Trentham Books Ltd, 2007.

25   Department for Education, 'GCSE and Equivalent Results in England 2010/11, SFR 26/201120', 2011.

26   J. Blanden, P. Gregg, and S. Machin, 'Intergenerational Mobility in Europe and North America', London School of Economics, 2005.

27   J. Blanden and S. Machin, 'Recent Changes in Intergenerational Mobility in Britain', London School of Economics, December 2007.

28   M. Chorley and M. Ledwithy, 'Britain is Run By a Privately-Educated Elite: Ex-Tory PM John Major Condemns "Truly Shocking" Dominance of the Privileged', *Daily Mail*, 11 November 2013.

29   The Crowther Report, Vol II, Table 9, Her Majesty's Stationery Office, 1959, p.130.

30   A. Milburn, 'Unleashing Aspiration: The Final Report of the Panel on Fair Access To The Professions', 2009.

31   The IFS found that 13 per cent of the poorest quartile attended higher education in 2003/4, compared to the 2 per cent of the unskilled that the Robbins Report – quoted in this document – found in 1963. Source: H. Chowdry, C. Crawford, and A. Goodman, 'The Role of Attitudes and Behaviours in Explaining Socio-Economic Differences in Attainment at Age 16', Institute for Fiscal Studies, November 2010.

32   M. Dickson, L. Macmillan, and S. Burgess, 'Hard Evidence: Do Grammar Schools Boost Social Mobility?', *The Conversation*, 18 June 2014.

33   Department for Education, 'School Performance Data: 2012 Download Data', 2012.

34   Only 3 of the grammar schools had levels of disadvantage above 20 per cent. These are Handsworth, King Edward VI Aston, and Stretford.

35   A. Atkinson, P. Gregg, and B. McConnell, 'The Result of 11-Plus Selection: An Investigation into Opportunities and Outcomes for Pupils in Selective LEAs', Working Paper No. 06/150, April 2006.

36   Ibid.

37   A. Skipp, A. Vignoles, D. Jesson, F. Sadro, J. Cribb, and L. Sibieta, *Poor Grammar: Entry into Grammar Schools for Disadvantaged Pupils in England*, London, The Sutton Trust, 2013, p.5.

38   Ibid, p.13.

39   F. Millar, 'State School Pupils Doing Worse in "Tutor-Proof" 11-Plus Tests', *Guardian*, 16 September 2014.

40   Ibid.

41   Ibid.

42   J. Groves, 'Tory Backlash After Ofsted Chief Sneers at Grammars: MPs Challenge Claim That Selective Schools Are Too Middle Class', *Daily Mail*, 15 December 2013.

43   Department for Education, 'School Performance Data: 2014 Download Data', 2014. The ten LEAs with the highest proportion of students starting secondary school defined as 'high prior attainment' were (highest first): Sutton, Trafford, Buckinghamshire, Kingston upon Thames, Slough, Richmond upon Thames, Reading, Southend-on-Sea, Kensington, and Chelsea and Barnet. Of these, only Kensington and Richmond are entirely non-selective.

44   Department for Education, 'School Performance Data: 2012 Download Data', 2012.

45   A. Skipp, A. Vignoles, D. Jesson, F. Sadro, J. Cribb, and L. Sibieta, 'Poor Grammar: Entry Into Grammar Schools for Disadvantaged Pupils in England', The Sutton Trust, 2013, p.5.

46   FOI response from Reading Council, 26/2/2014; 58 per cent is based on removing the effect of the 74 per cent in grammar schools, who are not Reading residents, and adding back the 14.1 per cent of residents who go to schools outside the area – assuming these would achieve GCSEs in the same proportion as those in Reading but not in grammar schools.

47   Just 7.8 per cent of Trafford students were 'low attainment', while 43.9 per cent were 'high attainment'. Department for Education, 'School Performance Data: 2013 Download Data, 2013.' See also J. Bolt, 'Trafford, Its Grammar Schools, What Graham Brady Didn't Say and the Today Programme Didn't Ask', *Socialist Education Association*, 5 December 2014.

48   Department for Education, 'School Performance Data: 2013 Download Data', 2013.

49   Ibid.

50   C. Cook, 'Grammar School Myths', *Financial Times*, 28 January 2013.

51   Ibid.

52   Ibid.

53   T. Young, 'Suzanne Moore's Attack on Michael Gove is a Hysterical, Ill-Informed Rant', *Daily Telegraph*, 31 January 2013.

54   P. Bolton, 'Oxbridge "Elitism"', House of Commons Library, June 2014.

55   P. Bolton, 'Oxbridge "Elitism"', House of Commons Library, February 2013.

56   G. Paton, 'Cambridge University "Admits More State School Students"', *Daily Telegraph*, 27 September 2012.

57   The 85 per cent figure is based on the Sutton Trust reporting 0.8 per cent of comprehensive students and 3.4 per cent of grammar school students get to Oxbridge. This was applied to the latest Year 11 figures of 536,000 students at comprehensives and 23,000 at selective schools. Source: The Sutton Trust, *Degree of Success: University Chances By Individual School*, 2011, p.18.

58   A. Sullivan, 'Grammar Schools Don't Give Pupils a Better Chance of Getting Into Elite Universities', *The Conversation*, 21 November 2014.

59   Department for Education, 'A-level and Other Level 3 Results: Academic Year 2012 To 2013 (Revised)', SFR02/2014, London, Department for Education, Table 1a. It is based on 22,333 students from state schools and colleges achieving 3 A/A* at A-level and 10,336 from independent schools. No Department for Education figures are available for the one A* and two As now generally required by Oxford.

60   The Organisation for Economic Co-Operation and Development (OECD), 'What Students Know and Can Do, PISA', 2012.

61   Ibid.

62   Pearson Foundation, 'Strong Performers and Successful Reformers in Education', 2013.

63   The Organisation for Economic Co-Operation and Development (OECD), 'PISA 2006: Science Competencies for A Modern World, PISA', 11 December 2007.

64   The Organisation for Economic Co-Operation and Development (OECD), 'PISA 2009 Results: What Makes A School Successful', Volume IV, PISA, 2010.

65   E. Hanushek and L. Woessmann, 'Does Educational Tracking Affect Performance and Inequality? Differences-In-Differences Evidence Across Countries', Institute for Economic Research at the University of Munich, 2005.

Free to Pursue an Academic Education

1   W. Mansell, 'The English Bac Causes Fury in Schools', *Guardian*, 11 January 2011.

2   G. Paton, 'Grammar Schools "Fuelling Gap Between Rich and Poor"', *Daily Telegraph*, 29 May 2014.

3   D. Boffey, 'Ofsted Chief Declares War on Grammar Schools', *Guardian*, 14 December 2013.

4   G. Paton, 'GCSE League Tables 2014: Anger as Top Schools Plummet', *Daily Telegraph*, 23 January 2014.

5   C. Iannelli, 'The Role of School Curriculum in Social Mobility', *British Journal of Sociology of Education*, 34(5-6), 2013, pp.907-928.

6   J.S. Mill, *On Liberty*, New York, Cosimo Classics, 2005 (original work published, 1859).

7   Ibid.

Education for New Times

1   C.B. Frey and M.A. Osborne, 'The Future of Employment: How Susceptible Are Jobs to Computerisation?', Oxford Martin School, 17 September 2013.

2   Compass, 'The Bloomsbury Paper', March 2014.

3   J. Cruddas, 'Radical Hope', Speech to the Royal Society of the Arts, 1 July 2014.

4   J. Cridland, 'Education System Must Better Prepare Young People for Life Beyond the School Gates', London, Confederation of British Industry, 7 July 2014.

5   S. Jenkins, 'When Whitehall Meddles in Schools, It's Only Ever Bad News', *Guardian*, 10 June 2014.

How We Got Into This Mess

1   Department of Education and Science, 'Circular 10/65', 12 July 1965.

2   Ibid.

3   W. Churchill, *The Unrelenting Struggle: War Speeches by the Right Hon. Winston S. Churchill*, London, Little, Brown and Company, 1942, pp.19-20.

4   M. Young, *The Rise of the Meritocracy*, London, Thames and Hudson, 1958, p.53.

5   N. Timmins, *The Five Giants: A Biography of the Welfare State*, London, HarperCollins, 2001.

6   R.A. Butler, *The Art of the Possible*, London, Hamish Hamilton, 1971, p.120.

7   M. Young, *The Rise of the Meritocracy*, London, Thames and Hudson, 1958, p.54.

8   Department of Education and Science, 'Circular 10/65', 12 July 1965.

9   C. Woodhead, 'Boys Who Learn to Be Losers', *The Times*, 6 February 1996.

10   R. Pedley, *The Comprehensive School*, London, Penguin, 1963.

11   S. Pollard, *Ten Days That Changed the Nation: The Making of Modern Britain*, London, Simon & Schuster, 2009, p.48.

12   *The Times*, leading article, 13 July 1961.

13   T. Crosland, *The Future of Socialism*, London, Jonathan Cape, 1956.

14   S. Pollard, *Ten Days That Changed the Nation: The Making of Modern Britain*, London, Simon & Schuster, 2009, p.49.

15   Ibid.

16   T. Crosland, *The Future of Socialism*, London, Jonathan Cape, 1956.

17   S. Pollard, *Ten Days That Changed the Nation: The Making of Modern Britain*, London, Simon & Schuster, 2009, p.49.

18   Ibid.

19   D. Marsden, 'Politicians, Equality and Comprehensives', Fabian Society, 1971.

20   S. Pollard, *Ten Days That Changed the Nation: The Making of Modern Britain*, London, Simon & Schuster, 2009, p.51.

21   Ibid, p.52.

22   Ibid.

23   Ibid.

24   Ibid, p.49.

25   A. Wooldridge, 'Meritocracy and the Classless Society', Social Market Foundation, 1995.

26   *Sunday Telegraph*, 7 January 1996.

27   Ibid.

28   S. Pollard, *Ten Days That Changed the Nation: The Making of Modern Britain*, London, Simon & Schuster, 2009, p.56.

29   E. Holmes, *What Is and What Might Be*, London, General Books LLC, 1911.

30   S. Pollard, *Ten Days That Changed the Nation: The Making of Modern Britain*, London, Simon & Schuster, 2009, p.57.

31   M. Phillips, *All Must Have Prizes*, London, Sphere, 1998.

32   Central Advisory Council for Education, 'Plowden Report: Children and Their Primary Schools', 1967.

33   S. Pollard, *Ten Days That Changed the Nation: The Making of Modern Britain*, London, Simon & Schuster, 2009.

34   Ibid.

35   Ibid, p.60.

36   Ibid.

37   Ibid, p.61.

38   Ibid.

39   Ibid, p.64.

40   Ibid.

41   Ibid, pp.62-63.

Will Selection at 11 Ever End?

1   Comprehensive Future, interview, 2002.

2   Ibid, 2006.

3   The Organisation for Economic Co-operation and Development (OECD), 'Viewing the United Kingdom School System Through the Prism of PISA', 2010.

4   Comprehensive Future, 'If These Grammars Didn't Exist Parents Would Be Much Happier', July 2008.

5   Comprehensive Future, 'Chaos in Kent Where Selection Rules', January 2013.

6   Comprehensive Future, 'Eleven-Plus Selection in West Kent Is Actually Social and Economic Selection', January 2013.

7   D. Willetts 'David Willetts Speech on Grammar Schools', *Daily Telegraph*, 16 May 2007.

8   'Tories' Grammar School "Betrayal"', BBC, 2 October 2007.

9   D. Willetts, 'David Willetts Speech on Grammar Schools', *Daily Telegraph*, 16 May 2007.

10   D. Laws, 'David Laws Speech on Grammar Schools', Department for Education, 19 June 2014.

11   Secretary of State for Education and Employment, 'School Standards and Framework Act', 1998; 'The Education (Grammar School Ballots) Regulations 1998', 19 November 1998.

12   Secretary of State for Education and Employment, 'The Education (Grammar School Ballots) Regulations 1998', 19 November 1998.

13   House of Lords, 'Written Answers, Baroness Blackstone HL 1063 and HL 1064', 22 February 2000.

14   Department of Education, 'Education for the 21st Century', Report of Post Primary Review Body Department of Education, Northern Ireland, 2001.

15   'Draft Statutory Instrument: The Education (Northern Ireland) Order 2006', London, The Stationery Office, 19 July 2006.

16   M. Taggart, 'Omagh Catholic Grammar Schools in Bid to End Academic Selection', BBC News, 12 June 2014.

The Case for Grammar Schools

1   D. Laws, Speech on grammar schools to the Grammar School Heads' Association Conference, 19 June 2014.

2   P. Bolton, 'Grammar School Statistics', House of Commons Library, 2013, p.6.

3   Ibid.

4   Department for Education, 'Key Stage 5 Performance Tables', 2013.

5   The Sutton Trust, 'Social Selectivity of State Schools and the Impact of Grammars', 2008, p.4.

6   J. Boulton, 'The Case Against Grammar Schools', parliamentstreet.org blog, 20 November 2013.

7   'Degree of Success: University Chances by Individual School', The Sutton Trust, July 2011, p.2.

8   'Tracking the Decision-Making of High Achieving Higher Education Applicants', The Sutton Trust and Department for Business Innovation and Skills, November 2012, p.6.

9   Ibid.

10   Ofsted, 'The Most Able Students: Are they doing as well as they should in our non-selective secondary schools?', 2013, p.4.

11   Ibid, pp.7-8.

12   K. Jackson, 'Can Higher-Achieving Peers Explain the Benefits to Attending Selective Schools? Evidence from Trinidad and Tobago', *Journal of Public Economics*, Elsevier, vol. 108(C), 2013, pp.63-77.

13   D. Clark, 'Selective Schools and Academic Achievement', Institute for the Study of Labor (IZA), November 2007.

14   D. Deming, J. Hastings, T. Kane, and D. Staiger, 'School Choice, School Quality and Postsecondary Attainment', *American Economic Review*, 104(3), 2014, pp.991-1014.

15   D. Clark and E. Del Bono, 'The Long-Run Effects of Attending an Elite School: Evidence from the UK', Institute for Social and Economic Research, University of Essex, February 2014.

16   S. Burgess, M. Dickinson, and L. Macmillan, 'Do Grammar Schools Increase or Decrease Inequality?', Institute of Education, Department for Quantitative Social Science Working Paper Series, February 2014.

17   The Sutton Trust, 'The Social Selectivity of State Schools and the Impact of Grammars', 2008, p.15.

18   A. Atkinson, P. Gregg, and B. McConnell, 'The Result of 11+ Selection: An Investigation Into Opportunities and Outcomes for Pupils in Selective LEAS', Working Paper No. 06/150, The Centre for Market and Public Organisation, University of Bristol, 2006.

19   Ibid, p.27.

20   Ibid.

21   I. Schagen and S. Schagen, 'The Impact of Selection on Pupil Performance', NFER, Issue 28, Autumn 2002.

22   Ibid, p.4.

23   D.J. Taylor, 'The Problem With Grammar Schools', *Guardian*, 7 March 2014.

24   Grammar School Statistics UK Parliamentary Briefing Paper SN/SG/1398, p.3.

25   Ibid, p.8.

26   The Good Schools Guide, 'Fee-Paying Schools: Bargain Hunting', 2014.

27   Department for Education, 'Statistical First Release National Curriculum Assessments at KS2 in England 2013', 12 December 2013.

28   D. Laws, Speech on grammar schools, Department for Education, 19 June 2014.

29 The Sutton Trust, 'Selective Comprehensives: The Social Composition of Top Comprehensive Schools', 2013, p.4; R. Coe, K. Jones, J. Searle, D. Kokotsaki, A. Mohd Kosnin and P. Skinners, 'Evidence on the Effects of Selective Educational Systems', The Sutton Trust, p.168, 2008.

(Un)natural Selection

1   G. Orwell, *Such, Such Were the Joys*, London, Penguin Great Ideas, 2014, p.9.

2   A. Binet and T. Simon, *The Development of Intelligence in Children*, Baltimore, Williams and Wilkins, 1916, pp.42-43.

3   The principal advocate of Binet's work being adapted for this purpose was Henry Goddard: H. Goddard, *The Kallikak Family: A Study in the Heredity of Feeble-Mindedness*, New York, Macmillan, 1912.

4   Royal College of Paediatrics and Child Health, 'Steep Rise in Children Suffering Depression', News and Campaigns, 30 September 2013.

5   A. Gregory, 'Teen STIs Plague: 15,000 Underage Teenagers Caught Sexually Transmitted Infections in Last Three Years', *Daily Mirror*, 22 March 2013.

6   I. Johnston, 'Number of Children Who Self-Harm Jumps 70 Percent in Just Two Years', *The Independent*, 11 August 2014.

7   C.K. Stead, *Mansfield*, London, Harvill, 2004, p.176.

Why Is Selection by Wealth Better Than Selection by Ability?

1   R. Bloomfield, 'Top London School Catchment Area Premium Hits £54,000', *London Evening Standard*, 29 January 2014.

2   The Grey Coat Hospital Church of England Comprehensive Academy for Girls, 'Admissions Policy 2015-2016', 2015.

3   University of Oxford, *Report of Commission of Inquiry*, Oxford, Clarendon Press, 1966, Volume II, statistical appendix, p.47, table 31.

4   Ibid, p.47, table 31.

5   Ibid, p.47, table 31.

6   Higher Education Statistics Authority website, Column 'V' of Table 1a (T1a) 'Participation of under-represented groups in higher education: UK domiciled full-time first degree entrants 2012/13', linked under heading 'Young full-time undergraduate entrants'.

7   R. Breen and K.B. Karlson, 'Education and Social Mobility: New Analytical Approaches', *European Sociological Review*, 30(1), 2014, pp.107-118; M. Howarth, 'Poor Pupils from Disadvantaged Backgrounds "Benefit Most in a Grammar School System"', *Daily Mail*, 15 March 2014.

8   E. Waugh, *The Diaries of Evelyn Waugh*, M. Davie (ed.), Phoenix, 2010, entry for March 1964.

9   Engineering Council, 'Measuring the Mathematics Problem', 2000.

10 Ibid.

11 P. Tymms and C. Fitz-Gibbon, 'Standards, Achievement and Educational Performance: A Cause For Celebration?', in R. Phillips and J. Furlong (eds.), *Education, Reform and The State: Twenty-five Years of Policy, Politics and Practice*, London, Routledge Falmer, 2002, pp.167-73.

12 J. Russell, 'Drilled, Not Educated', *Guardian*, 20 August 2004.

13 *Daily Telegraph*, 15 October 1975.

14 *Daily Mail*, 25 August 1975.

15 *Daily Telegraph*, 11 November 1974, quoting Sir Rhodes Boyson and Professor Brian Cox, citing surveys by the education authorities of Manchester and Sheffield.

16 Schools Standards and Framework Act 1998, c.31, Part III, Chapter II, Section 99.

17 K. Cochrane, 'TUC Leader Frances O'Grady: "People Want Some Hope for the Future"', *Guardian*, 5 September 2012.

18 F. Elliott, 'Theresa May: "More Than 500 British Muslims Have Gone to Syria – We Face a Real Threat"', *The Times*, 27 September 2014.

19 Theresa May, born 1 October 1956, would have gone to Holton Park Grammar aged 11, in 1967 or possibly 1968. The school became Comprehensive in 1971. J. Chipperfield, 'Girls Were Taught in Idyllic Surroundings at Holton Park', 'Memory Lane', *Oxford Mail*, 8 June 2009.

20 J. Judd and F. Abrams, 'Time to Bring Back Grammar Schools?', *The Independent*, 23 June 1996.

21 Commons Debate between T. Blair and M. Howard, 3 December 2003, col 498.

22 G. Jones, 'I Would Send My Children to State School', *Daily Telegraph*, 10 December 2005.

23 T. Shipman, 'SamCam and PM "Will Send Daughter to a State School"', *Daily Mail*, 10 March 2014.

24 S. Vine, 'Why I've Chosen to Send My Daughter to a State School', *Daily Mail*, 5 March 2014.

25 S. Atkinson, 'Harman Snubs Local Comp for Top Girls School', *Daily Mirror*, 7 April 1998.

26 K.R. Bradford, 'Call This a Comprehensive? Grey Coat Hospital Could Hardly be Called Inclusive – Unlike the Local Secondary Michael Gove Has Passed Up', *The Independent*, 12 March 2014.

27 M. Gove, 'Academic Rigour is Liberating Not Limiting', *The Times*, 15 August 2012.

28 M. Gove, 'The Crude Social Engineering of A-Levels Insults Any Child Who Wants to Succeed on Merit', *Daily Mail*, 28 September 2011.

29 Ibid.

30 K.R. Bradford, 'Call This a Comprehensive? Grey Coat Hospital Could Hardly be Called Inclusive – Unlike the Local Secondary Michael Gove Has Passed Up', *The Independent*, 12 March 2014.

Assessing the Damage:
The Fracturing of Our Comprehensive System

1 The Organisation for Economic Co-operation and Development (OECD), 'PISA 2012 Results in Focus: What 15 Year-Olds Know and What They Can Do With What They Know', The Organisation for Economic Co-operation and Development (OECD), 2014.

2 J. Rose, 'The Independent Review of the Teaching of Early Reading', Department for Education and Skills, March 2006.

3 J. Kirkup, 'Ofsted Will Mark Down Schools that Refuse to Teach all Pupils Five "Core" GCSEs, Pledge Tories', *Daily Telegraph*, 30 August 2014.

4   Department for Education, 'Factsheet: Progress 8 Measure', February 2014.

5   R. Adams, 'Labour Plans to Overhaul Michael Gove's A-Level Reforms', *Guardian*, 11 August 2014.

6   S. Hubble, 'Cuts in Funding for 18 and 19 Year-Olds', London, House of Commons Library, 23 January 2014.

7   Ofsted and Department for Education, 'Ofsted Annual Report 2013-14', 10 December 2014.

8   Education Committee, 'Seventh Report: Careers Guidance for Young People: The Impact of the New Duty on Schools', House of Commons, 23 January 2013; The Humber LEP Skills Commission, 'Lifting the Lid: The Humber Skills Challenge 2013', Humber Local Enterprise Partnership, 2013.

The Dilemma of Selection in Schools

1   A. Smithers and P. Robinson, 'Educating the Highly Able', The Sutton Trust, 2012.

2   PISA, 'What Students Know and Can Do', Volume 1, OECD Publishing, 2010, Table 1.3.1, p.221 and Table S.1.s, p.256.

3   J. Blanden, P. Gregg, and S. Machin, 'Intergenerational Mobility in Europe and North America', The Sutton Trust, 2005.

4   Conservative Party, *General Election Manifesto*, 1997.

5   It is also current UKIP policy and it will be interesting to see how far it takes them in the 2015 election.

6   S. Crosland, *Tony Crosland*, London, Jonathan Cape, 1982, p.148.

7   F. Millar, 'State School Pupils Doing Worse in "Tutor-Proof" 11-Plus Tests', *Guardian*, 16 September, 2014.

8   A. Smithers and P. Robinson, *Beyond Compulsory Schooling*, London, Council for Industry and Higher Education, 1991, p.19.

9   HM Government, 'Higher Standards, Better Schools for All', White Paper, Cm 6677, London, TSO, Chapter 4, 2005.

10   A. Smithers and P. Robinson, *Specialist Science Schools*, Buckingham, The Carmichael Press, 2005.

11   BBC News, 'Specialist Schools' Selection "Illegal"', 11 July 2003.

12   A. Smithers and P. Robinson, 'Educating the Highly Able', The Sutton Trust, 2012.

13   Department for Education and Skills, 'Excellence in Cities: The National Evaluation of a Policy to Raise Standards in Urban Schools 2000-2003', Lesley Kendall *et al*, Research Report RR675A, London, HMSO, 2005, pp.90-94.

14   Department for Education, 'Schools Achieving Success', White Paper, Cm5230, 2001, p.21.

15   D. Eyre, *Room at the Top,* London, Policy Exchange, 2011, p.39.

16   Children Schools and Families Select Committee, House of Commons, April 2010, 'The Gifted and Talented Programme', Oral and Written Evidence, 1 February 2010, HC337-i, London, TSO, 2010.

17   A. Smithers and P. Robinson, 'Educating the Highly Able', The Sutton Trust, 2012.

18   Hansard Written Answers for 31 January 2012.

19 House of Commons Education Committee, 'The English Baccalaureate', Fifth Report of the Session 2010-12, HC851, London, TSO, 2011.

20 A. Wolf, 'Review of Vocational Education', Department for Education, 00031-2011, Recommendations 1 and 3, 2011.

21 Baker, K., *14-18 – A New Vision for Secondary Education*, London, Bloomsbury, 2013, pp.27-41.

22 Department for Education and Education Funding Agency, 'Full-Time Enrolment of 14 to 16-Year-Olds in FE and Sixth-Form Colleges', November 2014.

23 Department for Education, 'Reforming Qualifications and the Curriculum to Better Prepare Pupils for Life After School', 2014.

24 The Sutton Trust, 'Use of an Aptitude Test in University Entrance: A Validity Study', Final Report, 2010.

25 There has been a strand of writing which has downplayed the role of ability and implied that through hard work anyone can do almost anything, for example: M. Syed, *The Bounce*, London, Fourth Estate, 2011; G. Colvin, *Talent is Over-rated*, London, Nicholas Brealey Publishing, 2008; and D. Coyle, *The Talent Code*, London, Arrow, 2010.

26 A. Smithers and P. Robinson, 'Worlds Apart: Social Variation Among Schools', The Sutton Trust, 2010.

27 Ibid.

28 Ibid.

29 M. Benn, *School Wars: The Battle for Britain's Education*, London, Verso, 2011.

30 G. Paton, 'Russell Group Universities to Run Specialist Maths Schools', *Daily Telegraph*, 19 June 2014.

31 The Organisation for Economic Co-operation (OECD) and Development, *Handbook for Internationally Comparative Education Statistics: Concepts, Standards, Definitions and Classifications*, Paris, OECD, 2004. A distinction is drawn between lower and upper secondary education. 'Lower secondary' is the first three years of secondary education and 'upper secondary' the years of schooling that follow. Although these terms with their precise meanings are unfamiliar in England they are widely used elsewhere.

32 A. Smithers and P. Robinson, 'Choice and Selection in School Admissions: The Experience of Other Countries', The Sutton Trust, 2010.

33 F. Musgrove, *Youth and the Social Order*, London, Routledge and Kegan Paul, 1964, p. 74.

34 C. Halsey, N. Postlethwaite, S. Prais, A. Smithers, and H. Steedman, 'Every Child in Britain', Report of the Channel 4 Commission on Education, 1991.

35 A. Smithers, 'Making 14-18 Education a Reality,' in Baker, K. (ed.), *14-18 A New Vision for Secondary Education*, London, Bloomsbury, 2013, pp.57-69.

36 A. Hodgson and K. Spours, *Education and Training 14-19: Curriculum, Qualifications and Organization*, London, Sage, 2008.

37 A. Wolf, 'Review of Vocational Education', Department for Education, 00031-2011, 2011.

38 A. Smithers, 'Making 14-18 Education a Reality,' in K. Baker (ed.), *14-18 A New Vision for Secondary Education*, London, Bloomsbury, 2013, pp.57-69.

39 For a highly critical account see A. Smithers and P. Robinson, *The Diploma: A Disaster Waiting to Happen?*, Buckingham, Carmichael Press, 2008.

Selection by Stealth

1   P. Bolton, 'Grammar School Statistics', House of Commons Library, 2013, p.8.

2   G. Paton, 'Michael Gove: "Progressive" Teaching Undermines Social Mobility', *Daily Telegraph*, 24 May 2012.

3   Department for Education, 'School Admissions Code: Statutory Guidance for School Leaders, Governing Bodies and Local Authorities', 2012.

4   M. Peters, H. Carpenter, and G. Edwards, 'Cost of Schooling 2007', DCSF-RR060, 2007.

5   Hansard, House of Commons Debate, 19 July 2010, vol 514, columns 24-129.

6   Hansard, House of Commons Debate, 26 July 2010, vol 514, columns 808-809.

7   Hansard, House of Commons Debate, 26 July 2010, vol 514, column 820.

8   The National Archives, Education Act 2011, November 2011.

9   Department for Education, 'New Admissions Code: A Fairer and Simpler System', 27 May 2011.

10   The Academies Commission, *Unleashing Greatness – Getting the Best from an Academised System*, London, Pearson/RSA, 2013.

11   Office of the Children's Commissioner, 'It Might Be Best If You Looked Elsewhere: An Investigation Into the School Admissions Process', April 2014.

12   The National Archives, Education Act 2011, November 2011.

13   NASUWT, 'The Cost of Education Survey 2013/14', 2013.

14   Ibid.

15   Ibid.

16   NASUWT, 'The Cost of Education Survey 2012/13', 2012.

17   NASUWT, 'The Cost of Education Survey 2013/14', 2013.

18   Ibid.

19   Child Poverty Action Group, 'Child Poverty Facts and Figures', 2014.

20   NASUWT, 'The Impact of Financial Pressures on Children and Young People', 2014.

Church of England Schools for the Common Good

1   St Luke's Church of England School, Kingston upon Thames, Letter from the Head Teacher, January 2015.

2   Bury Church of England High School, Interview with the Head Teacher, January 2015.

Divisive Faith Schools Urgently Need Reform

1   Home Office, 'The Cantle Report – Community Cohesion: A Report of the Independent Review Team', January 2001.

2   H. Ouseley, 'Community Pride Not Prejudice – Making Diversity Work in Bradford', The Bradford District Race Review Panel, January 2001.

3   S. Jeffery, 'Violence at Holy Cross School', *Guardian*, 4 September 2001.

4   S. Tough and R. Brookes, 'School Admissions Report: Fair Choice for Parents and Pupils', Institute for Public Policy Research, 2007, p.7.

5   R. Berkeley, 'Right to Divide? Faith Schools and Community Cohesion', Runnymede Trust, 2008, p.68.

6   A. West, E. Barham, and A. Hind, 'Secondary School Admissions in England: Policy and Practice', London School of Economics, 2009.

7   R. Berkeley, 'Right to Divide? Faith Schools and Community Cohesion', Runnymede Trust, 2008, p.18.

8   T. Cantle, 'The Cantle Report into Community Cohesion in Blackburn with Darwen (Interim Findings)', 2009.

9   Fair Admissions Campaign, 'Map of English Secondary Schools by Religious and Socioeconomic Selection', 2013.

10 House of Commons Library, 'Faith Schools: Admissions and Performance', 10 March 2009, p.5.

11 Fair Admissions Campaign, 'Schools Adjudicator: London Oratory School Must Overhaul Admissions Criteria', 29 August 2013.

12 Fair Admissions Campaign, 'Church Baptisms Move Away from Birth and Towards School Admissions Deadlines', 6 January 2014.

13 Accord, 'Widespread Socioeconomic Segregation Caused by Religiously Selective Admission Arrangements Revealed', 22 September 2014.

14 A. Donald, 'Religion or Belief, Equality and Human Rights in England and Wales', Equality and Human Rights Commission Research Report 84, Human Rights and Social Justice Institute, London Metropolitan University, 2012.

15 D. Marley, 'CoE Opens School Gates to Non-Believers', *Times Educational Supplement*, 28 April 2011.

16 R. Gledhill, 'Church in "Move Away" from School Selection', *The Times*, 14 November 2013.

17 Accord, 'Religious Leaders Launch First Manifesto for Faith Schools', 2 September 2014.

18 Ibid.

In Defence of Faith Schools and Religious Selection

1   Department for Education, 'Schools, Pupils and Their Character', 12 June 2014.

2   Department for Children, Schools and Families, 'Faith in the System', 2007, p.2.

3   R. Barker and J. Anderson, 'Segregation or Cohesion: Church of England Schools in Bradford', in R. Gardner, *et al.*, *Faith Schools: Consensus or Conflict*, London, Routledge, 2005, p.122.

4   Department for Education, 'Schools, Pupils and Their Character', 2014.

5   Fair Admissions Campaign, 'Ten Reasons Why We Should Object to Religious Selection by Schools', 2013.

6   Ibid.

7   British Humanist Association, 'Faith Schools', 2015.

8   Fair Admissions Campaign, 'Ten Reasons Why We Should Object to Religious Selection by Schools', 2013.

9   'State schools: The Top 50 "Most Socially-Exclusive"', *Daily Telegraph*, 21 September 2013.

10 Fair Admissions Campaign, 'Ten Reasons Why We Should Object to Religious Selection by Schools', 2013.

11   J. Shepherd and S. Rogers, 'Church Schools Shun Poorest Pupils', *Guardian*, 5 March 2013.

12   S. Tough and R. Brooks, 'School Admissions: Fair Choice for Parents and Pupils', IPPR, 2007, p.16.

13   J. Shepherd and S. Rogers, 'Church Schools Shun Poorest Pupils', *Guardian*, 5 March 2013.

14   Department for Education, 'School Admissions Code', 19 December 2014.

15   YouGov for Westminster Faith Debates, 'New Poll Shows the Debate on Faith Schools Isn't Really About Faith', 19 September 2013.

16   E. Oldfield, L. Hartnett, and E. Bailey, *More Than an Educated Guess*, London, Theos, 2013, pp.33-34.

17   Fair Admissions Campaign, 'Ten Reasons Why We Should Object to Religious Selection by Schools', 2013.

18   Office of the Schools Adjudicator, 'The London Oratory School', 15 July 2014.

19   D. Hinds, 'Select Committee Questions Media Reporting of Church Schools' Admissions Criteria', House of Commons, 4 February 2011.

20   T. Cantle, 'Community Cohesion', Home Office, 2001, p.9.

21   D. Conway, 'Faith Schools: Enrichment or Division', Civitas, 7 April 2012, p.7.

22   Department for Education, 'Guidance on Promoting British Values in Schools Published', 27 November 2014.

23   M. Holness, 'Ofsted Questioned as Two Schools Face Closure', *Church Times*, 30 January 2015.

24   Ibid.

25   R. Berkeley, *Right to Divide?*, London, Runnymede, 2008, p.41.

26   Ibid.

27   Ibid.

28   D. Jesson, 'A Study of Recent Ofsted Data Assessing Schools' Progress on the Duty to Promote Community Cohesion and Tackle Inequality', in *Strong Schools for Strong Communities: Reviewing the Impact of Church of England Schools in Promoting Community Cohesion*, Church of England Archbishops' Council Education Division, 2009, p.7.

29   E. Oldfield, L. Hartnett and E. Bailey, *More Than an Educated Guess*, London, Theos, 2013, p.25.

30   A. Lipsett, 'Children Bullied Because of Faith', *Guardian*, 17 November 2008.

31   YouGov for Westminster Faith Debates, 'New Poll Shows the Debate on Faith Schools Isn't Really About Faith', 19 September 2013.

32   W. Temple, Speech to the National Society, 1942, quoted in F. A. Iremonger, *William Temple: Archbishop of Canterbury. His Life and Letters*, London, New York and Toronto, Oxford University Press, 1948, p.571.

Banding: Selecting for a Comprehensive Intake

1   Banding could also be used explicitly to admit intakes with greater proportions of higher-attainers. Only one school in 2008 did so and admission authorities are prohibited from adopting any new arrangements that select by ability including selective banding.

2   J. Coldron, E. Tanner, and S. Finch *et al*, 'Secondary School Admissions', Department for Children, Schools and Families RR020, 2008; P. Noden, A. West, and A. Hind, 'Banding and Ballots: Secondary School Admissions in England: Admissions in 2012/13 and the Impact of Growth of Academies', The Sutton Trust, 2014.

3   I have partly adopted Noden *et al*'s useful terminology here to distinguish the different types.

4   J. Coldron, E. Tanner, and S. Finch *et al*, 'Secondary School Admissions', Department for Children, Schools and Families RR020, 2008.

5   P. Noden and A. West, 'Secondary School Admissions in England: Admission Forums, Local Authorities and Schools', Research and Information on State Education Trust, 2009.

6   P. Noden, A. West, and A. Hind, 'Banding and Ballots: Secondary School Admissions In England: Admissions in 2012/13 and the Impact of Growth of Academies', The Sutton Trust, 2014.

7   Ibid.

8   J.D. Willms, 'School Composition and Contextual Effects On Student Outcomes', *Teachers College Record*, 112, 1008–1037, 2010; L.B. Perry and A. McConney, 'Does the SES of The School Matter? An Examination of Socioeconomic Status and Student Achievement Using PISA 2003', *Teacher College Record*, 112, 1137–1162, 2010; G. Palardy, 'High School Socioeconomic Segregation and Student Attainment', *American Education Research Journal*, 50(4), 2013, pp.714–754.

9   S. Bonhomme and U. Sauder, 'Recovering Distributions in Difference-in-Differences Models: A Comparison of Selective and Comprehensive Schooling', *The Review of Economics and Statistics*, May 2011, 93(2), pp.479-494.

10 I. Schagen and S. Schagen, 'Analysis of National Value-Added Datasets to Assess the Impact of Selection on Pupil Performance', *British Educational Research Journal*, 29(4), 2003.

11 S. Burgess, E. Greaves, A. Vignoles, and D. Wilson, 'What Parents Want: School Preferences and School Choice', CMPO Working Paper No. 09/222, University of Bristol, 2009; S. Burgess, E. Greaves, A. Vignoles, and D. Wilson, 'Parental Choice of Primary School In England: What Types of School Do Different Types of Family Really Have Available to Them?' *Policy Studies*, 32(5), 2011, pp.531-547.

12 The Sutton Trust, 'Selective Comprehensives: The Social Composition of Top Comprehensive Schools', June 2013.

13 H. Pennell, A. West, and A. Hind, 'Religious Composition and Admission Processes of Faith Secondary Schools in London', Comprehensive Future, 2007; R. Allen and A. West, 'Why Do Faith Secondary Schools Have Advantaged Intakes? The Relative Importance of Neighbourhood Characteristics, Social Background and Religious Identification Amongst Parents', *British Educational Research Journal*, 37(4), 2011, pp.691-712; The Sutton Trust, 'Selective Comprehensives: The Social Composition of Top Comprehensive Schools', June 2013.

14 A. Atkinson and P. Gregg, 'Selective Education: Who Benefits from Grammar Schools?' *Market and Public Organisation*, Issue 11, Autumn 2004.

15 J. Cribb, D. Jesson, L. Sibieta, A. Skipp, and A.Vignoles, 'Poor Grammar: Entry into Grammar Schools for Disadvantaged Pupils in England', The Sutton Trust, 2013.

16 S. Burgess, E. Greaves, A. Vignoles, and D. Wilson, 'What Parents Want: School Preferences and School Choice', *The Economic Journal*, 21 August 2014; S. Burgess, E. Greaves, A. Vignoles, and D. Wilson, 'Parental Choice of Primary School in England: What Types of School Do Different Types of Family Really Have Available to Them?' *Policy Studies*, 32(5), 2011, pp.531-547.

17 S. Gorard, R. Hordosy, and B.H. See, 'Narrowing Down the Determinants of Between-School Segregation: An Analysis of the Intake to All Schools in England', 1989–2011, *Journal of School Choice: International Research and Reform*, 7(2), 2013, pp.182-195.

18 R. Allen and A. Vignoles, 'What Should an Index of School Segregation Measure?' *Oxford Review of Education*, 33(5), 2007, pp.643–68; R. Harris, and R. Johnston, 'Primary Schools, Markets and Choice: Studying Polarization and the Core Catchment Areas of Schools', *Applied Spatial Analysis and Policy*, 1(1), 2008, pp.59-84.

19 S. Gorard, R. Hordosy, and B.H. See, 'Narrowing Down the Determinants of Between-School Segregation: An Analysis of the Intake to All Schools in England', 1989–2011, *Journal of School Choice: International Research and Reform*, 7(2), 2013, pp.182-195.

20 J. Coldron, L. Cripps, and L. Shipton, 'Why Are English Secondary Schools Socially Segregated?' *Journal of Education Policy*, 25(1), 2010.

21 P. Noden, A. West, and A. Hind, 'Banding and Ballots: Secondary School Admissions in England: Admissions in 2012/13 and the Impact of Growth of Academies', The Sutton Trust, 2014.

22 S. Burgess, E. Greaves, A. Vignoles, and D. Wilson, 'Parental Choice of Primary School in England: What Types of School Do Different Types of Family Really Have Available to Them?' *Policy Studies*, 32(5), 2011, pp.531-547; R. Allen, S. Burgess, and T. Key, 'Choosing Secondary School by Moving House: School Quality and the Formation of Neighbourhoods', CMPO Working Paper, No. 10/238, 2010.

23 J. Coldron, E. Tanner, and S. Finch *et al*, 'Secondary School Admissions', Department for Children, Schools and Families RR020, 2008.

24 J. Coldron, E. Tanner, and S. Finch *et al*, 'Secondary School Admissions', Department for Children, Schools and Families RR020, 2008; S. Burgess, E. Greaves, A. Vignoles, and D. Wilson, 'Parental Choice of Primary School in England: What Types of School Do Different Types of Family Really Have Available to Them?' *Policy Studies*, 32(5), 2011, pp.531-547.

25 P. Noden, A. West, and A. Hind, 'Banding and Ballots: Secondary School Admissions in England: Admissions in 2012/13 and the Impact of Growth of Academies', The Sutton Trust, 2014, p.35.

26 Ibid.

27 The 2014 Code states in paragraph 1.34: Local authorities **must not** use random allocation as the principal oversubscription criterion for allocating places at all the schools in the area for which they are the admission authority.

28 P. Noden, A. West, and A. Hind, 'Banding and Ballots: Secondary School Admissions in England: Admissions in 2012/13 and the Impact of Growth of Academies', The Sutton Trust, 2014.

29 R. Allen, S. Burgess, and L. McKenna, 'The Early Impact of Brighton and Hove's School Admission Reforms', CMPO Working Paper No. 10/244, 2010.

30 P. Noden, A. West, and A. Hind, 'Banding and Ballots: Secondary School Admissions in England: Admissions in 2012/13 and the Impact of Growth of Academies', The Sutton Trust, 2014.

Selection and the Independent Sector

1 M. Toseland, *The Ants Are My Friends*, London, Portico, 2007, p.111.

2 The Independent Schools Council, 'ISC Census 2014', 2014, p.21.

3 Advertising Standards Authority ruling, 16 October 2013.

4 Office of Fair Access, 'Access Agreements for 2015-16: Key Statistics and Analysis', 2014, p.7.

5 T. Lello, Interview with author, 2014.

6 J. Wilding, Interview with author, 2014.

7 Ibid.

8 V. Smit, Interview with author, 2014.

9 Ibid.

10 S. Welch, Interview with author, 2014.

11 Ibid.

12 M. Adshead, Interview with author, 2014.

13 F. Galindo-Rueda and A. Vignoles, 'The Heterogeneous Effect of Selection in Secondary Schools: Understanding the Changing Role of Ability', IZA Discussion Paper No. 1245, 2004.

14 D. Jesson, 'The Comparative Evaluation of GCSE Value-Added Performance by Type of School and LEA', University of York, 2000, p.2.

15 C. Crawford, 'The Link Between Secondary School Characteristics and University Participation and Outcomes', CAYT Research Report, London, Department for Education, 2014.

16 S. Welch, Interview with author, 2014.

17 Populus poll for the Independent Schools Council, 'Attitudes Towards Independent Schools', Independent Schools Council, 16 November 2011.

18 G. Paton, 'Rising Private School Fees Pricing Out the Middle-Classes', *Daily Telegraph*, 30 September 2013.

19 Independent Schools Council, 'ISC Census 2014', London, Independent Schools Council, 2014, p.20.

20 N. Fraser, *The Importance of Being Eton: Inside the World's Most Powerful School*, London, Short Books, 2006.

21 V. Shaw, 'Top Catchment House Price Premiums Revealed', *The Independent*, 26 March 2012.

22 P. Lampl in A. Smithers, and P. Robinson, 'Worlds Apart: Social Variation Among Schools', The Sutton Trust, 2010.

23 F. Green, S. Machin, R. Murphy, and Y. Zhu, 'The Changing Economic Advantage From Private School', Centre for the Economics of Education, London School of Economics, 2010.

Using the Comprehensive Ideal to Drive Education Standards and Equality

1 The pupil premium gives schools extra funding to raise the attainment of disadvantaged pupils.

2   G. Greene (ed), *The Old School,* London, Jonathan Cape, 1934.

3   Ibid, p.17.

4   Ibid.

5   Ibid.

6   Speech to the Social Market Foundation, 5 February 2013.

7   P. Walker, 'Michael Gove Reveals the Surprising Inspirations Behind His Reforms', *Guardian*, 5 February 2013.

8   M. Gove, Speech to the Social Market Foundation, 5 February 2013.

9   Ibid.

10   D. Wiliam, 'Optimizing Talent: Closing Educational and Social Mobility Gaps Worldwide', Dylan Wiliam Center, 2014.

11   D. C. Berliner and G. V. Glass, *50 Myths and Lies That Threaten America's Public Schools: The Real Crisis in Education*, New York, Teachers College Press, 2014, p.7.

School Selection by Gender: Why It Works

1   RSAcademics, study of aggregated annual *SchoolPulse* parental satisfaction surveys conducted by individual schools between 2011 and 2013.

2   Department for Education, 'Statistics, 16-19 Attainment', 17 October 2013; A-level results ranked by average points scored per student (schools where the full-time equivalent of fewer than 30 pupils took the qualifications were not included).

3   Department for Education, 'Destinations of Key Stage 4 and Key Stage 5 Pupils: 2011 to 2012', 26 June 2014.

4   Ibid.

5   N. Morrison, 'Single-Sex Education Belongs in the 21st Century', *Forbes*, 30 April 2014.

6   Ibid.

7   Ibid.

8   Independent Schools Council, *ISC Annual Census 2014* (based on a survey carried out in January 2014).

9   H. Hollingsworth and J. Bonner, 'More Public Schools Splitting up Girls, Boys', *Associated Press*, 8 July 2012.

10   YouGov, End Violence Against Women Survey, November 2010.

11   OECD, 'PISA: Are Boys and Girls Equally Prepared for Life?', 2014.

12   S. Coughlan, 'Maths Confidence Gap Leaves UK Girls Trailing, OECD Says', BBC News, 23 January 2014; OECD, 'PISA: Are Boys and Girls Equally Prepared for Life?', 2014.

13   Ibid.

14   Institute of Physics, 'Closing Doors: Exploring Gender and Subject Choice in Schools', December 2013.

15   Ibid.

16   Ibid.

17   Institute of Physics, 'It's Different for Girls: The Influence of Schools', October 2012.

18   Ibid, Foreword.

19   Ibid, p.15.

20 Ibid.

21 Ibid.

22 Independent Schools Council, 'How Good Are Girls', 20 November 2013.

23 Ibid.

24 C. H. Riordan, *Girls and Boys in School: Together or Separate?*, New York, Teachers College Press, 1990.

25 L. J. Sax, 'Women Graduates of Single-Sex and Coeducational High Schools: Differences in their Characteristics and the Transition to College', The Sudikoff Family Institute for Education & New Media, UCLA Graduate School of Education & Information Studies, March 2009.

26 Ibid.

27 L. J. Sax, 'Women Graduates of Single-Sex and Coeducational High Schools: Differences in their Characteristics and the Transition to College', The Sudikoff Family Institute for Education & New Media, UCLA Graduate School of Education & Information Studies, March 2009, p.9.

28 A.L. Booth and P. Nolan, 'Gender Differences in Risk Behaviour: Does Nurture Matter?', IZA Discussion Paper 4026, Institute for the Study of Labor, 1990.

29 Ibid, p.4.

30 Ibid, p17.

31 H. Park, J.R. Behrman, and J. Choi, 'Causal Effects of Single-Sex Schools on College Entrance Exams and College Attendance: Random Assignment in Seoul High Schools', University of Pennsylvania, *Demography*, Volume 50, Issue 2, pp.447-469.

32 Ibid, Abstract, p.447.

33 Ofsted, 'Girls' Career Aspirations', April 2011.

34 Ibid, p.9.

35 Ibid.

What Does the Research Tell Us About Single-Sex Education?

1 R. Dale, *Mixed or Single-Sex Schooling? Vol.1: A Research Study in Pupil-Teacher Relationships*, London, Routledge and Kegan Paul, 1969; R. Dale, *Mixed or Single-Sex Schooling? Vol.2: Some Social Aspects*, London, Routledge and Kegan Paul, 1971; R. Dale, *Mixed or Single-Sex Schooling? Vol.3: Attainment, Attitudes and Overview*, London, Routledge and Kegan Paul, 1974.

2 M.B. Ormerod, 'Subject Preference and Choice in Coeducational and Single-Sex Secondary Schools', *British Journal of Educational Psychology*, 45, 1975, pp.257-267; D. Spender and E. Sarah, *Learning to Lose: Sexism and Education*, London, The Women's Press, 1980; R. Deem, *Coeducation Reconsidered*, London, Open University Press, 1984.

3 J. Steedman, 'Examination Results in Mixed and Single-Sex Schools', Equal Opportunities Commission, 1983, p.98; J. Steedman, 'Examination Results in Selective and Non-Selective Schools', National Children's Bureau, 1983.

4 H. Goldstein, J. Rashbash, M. Yang, G. Woodhouse, H. Pan, D. Nuttall, and S. Thomas, 'A Multilevel Analysis of School Examination Results', *Oxford Review of Education*, 19(4), 1993, pp.425-433; S. Thomas, P. Sammons, P. Mortimore, and R. Smees, 'Differential Secondary School Effectiveness: Comparing the Performance of Different Pupil Groups', *British Educational Research Journal*, 23(4), 1997, pp.451-469.

5   T. Spielhofer, T. Benton, and S. Schagen, 'A Study of the Effects of School Size and Single-Sex Education in English Schools', *Research Papers in Education*, 19(2), 2004, pp.133-159.

6   A. Sullivan, H. Joshi, and D. Leonard, 'Single-Sex Schooling and Academic Attainment at School and Through the Lifecourse', *American Educational Research Journal*, 47(1), 2010, pp.8-38.

7   E. Malacova, 'Effect of Single-Sex Education on Progress in GCSE', *Oxford Review of Education*, 33(2), 2007, pp.233-259.

8   A. Bryk, V. Lee, and P. Holland, *Catholic Schools and the Common Good*, Cambridge, Mass., Harvard University Press, 1993; V.E. Lee, and A.S. Bryk, 'Effects of Single Sex Secondary Schools on Student Achievement and Attitudes', *Journal of Educational Psychology*, 78(5), 1986, pp.381-395.

9   H. Marsh, 'Public, Catholic Single-Sex and Catholic Coeducational High Schools: Their Effects on Achievement, Affect and Behaviours', *American Journal of Education*, 99, 1991, pp.320-356; J.E. Gilson, 'Single-Gender Education Versus Coeducation for Girls', ERIC, 2002.

10 C.H. Riordan, *Girls and Boys in School: Together or Separate?*, New York, Teachers College Press, 1990; C. Riordan, 'What Do We Know About the Effects of Single-Sex Schools in the Private Sector? Implications for Public Schools', in A. Datnow and L. Hubbard (eds.), *Gender in Policy and Practice: Perspectives on Single-Sex and Coeducational Schooling*, New York, RoutledgeFalmer, 2002.

11 D.F. Hannan, E. Smyth, J. McCullagh, R. O'Leary, and D. McMahon, *Coeducation and Gender Equality*, Dublin, Oak Tree Press/ESRI, 1996.

12 P. Carpenter, 'Single-Sex Schooling and Girls' Academic Achievements', *The Australian and New Zealand Journal of Sociology*, 21(3), 1985, pp.456-472; R. Harker, 'Achievement, Gender and the Single-Sex/Coed Debate', *British Journal of Sociology of Education*, 21(2), 2000, pp.203-218.

13 E. Pahlke, J.S. Hyde, and C.M. Allison, 'The Effects of Single-Sex Compared with Coeducational Schooling on Students' Performance and Attitudes: A Meta-Analysis', *Psychological Bulletin*, 140(4), 2014, pp.1042-1072.

14 T. Spielhofer, T. Benton, and S. Schagen, 'A Study of the Effects of School Size and Single-Sex Education in English Schools', *Research Papers in Education*, 19(2), 2004, pp.133-159.

15 V.E. Lee and A.S. Bryk, 'Effects of Single-Sex Secondary Schools on Student Achievement and Attitudes', *Journal of Educational Psychology*, 78(5), 1986, pp.381-395.

16 J. Ainley and P. Daly, 'Participation in Science Courses in the Final Year of High School in Australia' in A. Datnow and L. Hubbard (eds.), *Gender in Policy and Practice: Perspectives on Single-Sex and Coeducational Schooling*, New York, RoutledgeFalmer, 2002, pp.243-262.

17 E. Smyth and C. Hannan, 'School Effects and Subject Choice: The Uptake of Scientific Subjects in Ireland', *School Effectiveness and School Improvement*, 17 (3), 2006, pp.303-327.

18 R. Dale, *Mixed or Single-Sex Schooling? Vol.1: A Research Study in Pupil-Teacher Relationships*, London, Routledge and Kegan Paul, 1969; R. Dale, *Mixed or Single-Sex Schooling? Vol.2: Some Social Aspects*, London, Routledge and Kegan Paul, 1971; R. Dale, *Mixed or Single-Sex Schooling? Vol.3: Attainment, Attitudes and Overview*, London, Routledge and Kegan Paul, 1974.

19   F. Mael, A. Alonso, D. Gibson, K. Rogers, and M. Smith, 'Single-Sex Versus Coeducational Schooling: A Systematic Review', US Department of Education, 2005.

20   A. Bryk, V. Lee, and P. Holland, *Catholic Schools and the Common Good*, Cambridge, Mass., Harvard University Press, 1993.

21   A. Sullivan, 'Academic Self-Concept, Gender and Single-Sex Schooling', *British Educational Research Journal*, 35(2), 2009, pp.259-288.

22   F. Schneider, L.M. Coutts, and M.W. Starr, 'In Favour of Coeducation: the Educational Attitudes from Coeducational and Single-Sex High Schools', *Canadian Journal of Education*, 13(4), 1988, pp.479-496.

23   A. Sullivan, H. Joshi, and D. Leonard, 'Single-Sex Schooling and Academic Attainment at School and through the Lifecourse', *American Educational Research Journal*, 47(1), 2010, pp.6-36.

24   S.M. Billger, 'On Reconstructing School Segregation: the Efficacy and Equity of Single-Sex Schooling', *Economics of Education Review*, 28, 2009, pp.393-402.

25   A. Datnow and L.Hubbard, *Gender in Policy and Practice: Perspectives on Single-Sex and Coeducational Schooling*, New York, RoutledgeFalmer, 2002; M. Younger, M. Warrington, with J. Gray, J. Rudduck, R. McLellan, E. Bearne, R. Kershner, and P. Bricheno, 'Raising Boys' Achievement', Department for Education and Skills, 2005.

26   M. Younger and M. Warrington, 'Would Harry and Hermione Have Done Better in Single-Sex Classes? A Review of Single-Sex Teaching in Coeducational Secondary Schools in the United Kingdom', *American Educational Research Journal*, 43(4), 2006, pp.678-820.

Selection by Choice

1   While some argue in favour of a philosophical right to choose taxpayer-funded goods and services, just like people have a right to choose goods and services in the private marketplace, this argument is unlikely to persuade those who do not value freedom of choice to the same extent as its proponents. The chapter therefore takes a purely instrumental approach: choice is desirable as a method to allocate pupils to schools because it is more efficient and more equitable than other methods.

2   A. Adnett and P. Davies, *Markets for Schooling: An Economic Analysis*, London, Routledge, 2002.

3   J. E Chubb and T. M. Moe, 'Politics, Markets, and the Organization of Schools', *American Political Science Review*, vol. 82, no. 4, 1988, pp.1065-1087.

4   C. M. Hoxby, 'School Choice and Productivity: Could School Choice Be a Tide That Lifts All Boats?, in C. M. Hoxby (ed.), *The Economics of School Choice*, Chicago, University of Chicago Press, 2003, pp.287-341.

5   W. B. MacLeod and M. Urquiola, 'Competition and Educational Productivity: Incentives Writ Large', Discussion Paper no. 7063, Institute for the Study of Labor, Bonn, 2012, p.17.

6   C. M. Hoxby, 'School Choice: The Three Essential Elements and Several Policy Options', Keynote speech delivered on 30 June 2005 to the New Zealand Association of Economists, Christchurch, New Zealand, 2005.

7   W. W. McMahon, 'The External Benefits of Education', in D. Brewer and P. J. McEwan (eds), *The Economics of Education*, Oxford, Elsevier, 2010, pp.68-79.

8   D. J. Deming, 'Using School Choice Lotteries to Test Measures of School Effectiveness', *American Economic Review: Papers & Proceedings*, vol. 104, no. 5, 2014, pp.406-401.

9   For more information regarding the construction of such measures, see G. *Heller Sahlgren, Incentivising Excellence: School Choice and Education Quality*, London, CMRE and IEA, 2013.

10   See, for example, E. A. Hanushek, J. F. Kain, S. G. Rivkin, and G. F. Branch, 'Charter School Quality and Parental Decision Making with School Choice', *Journal of Public Economics*, vol. 91, 2007, pp. 823-848; S. Gibbons, S. Machin, and O. Silva, 'Valuing School Quality Using Boundary Discontinuities', *Journal of Urban Economics*, vol. 75, 2013, pp.15-28.

11   J. S. Hastings and J. M Weinstein, 'Information, School Choice, and Academic Achievement: Evidence from Two Experiments', *Quarterly Journal of Economics*, vol. 123, no. 4, 2008, pp.1373-1414.

12   J. Buckley and M. Schneider, 'Shopping for Schools: How Do Marginal Consumers Gather Information About Schools?', *Policy Studies Journal*, vol. 31, no. 2, 2003, pp.121-145.

13   D. Neal, 'Aiming for Efficiency Rather than Proficiency', *Journal of Economic Perspectives*, vol. 24, no. 3, 2010, pp.119-132.

14   This is the information problem applied to education. See F. A. Hayek, 'The Use of Knowledge in Society', *American Economic Review*, vol. 35, no. 4, 1945, pp.519-530.

15   B. A. Jacob and L. Lefgren, 'What Do Parents Value in Education? An Empirical Investigation of Parents' Revealed Preferences for Teachers', *Quarterly Journal of Economics*, vol. 122, no. 4, 2007, pp.1603-1637.

16   For a review, see G. Heller Sahlgren, *Incentivising Excellence: School Choice and Education Quality*, London, CMRE and IEA, 2013.

17   Ibid; A. Böhlmark and M. Lindahl, 'Independent Schools and Long-Run Educational Outcomes: Evidence from Sweden's Large-Scale Voucher Reform', *Economica*, forthcoming.

18   See, for example, R. Chakrabarti, 'Can Increasing Private School Participation and Monetary Loss in a Voucher Program Affect Public School Performance? Evidence from Milwaukee', *Journal of Public Economics*, vol. 92, no. 5-6, 2008, pp.1371-1393; V. Lavy, 'Effects of Free Choice Among Public Schools', *Review of Economic Studies*, vol. 77, 2010, pp.1164-1191.

19   H. F. Ladd, 'School Vouchers: A Critical View', *Journal of Economic Perspectives*, vol. 16, no. 4, 2002, pp.3-24.

20   D. Epple and R. Romano, 'Economic Modeling and Analysis of Educational Vouchers', *Annual Review of Economics*, vol. 4, 2012, pp.159-183.

21   G. Caetano and H. Macartney, 'Quasi-Experimental Evidence of School Choice Through Residential Sorting', Unpublished Manuscript, Princeton University, 2014.

22   For a review of the literature on the impact of school performance on house prices, see S. E. Black and S. Machin, 'Housing Valuations of School Performance', *Handbook of the Economics of Education*, vol. 3, 2011, pp.485-519.

23   E. A. Hanushek, S. Sarpca and K. Yilmaz, 'Private Schools and Residential Choices: Accessibility, Mobility, and Welfare', *B.E. Journal of Economic Analysis & Policy*, vol. 11, no. 1, 2011, article 44; D. Neal, 'How Vouchers Could Change the Market for Education', *Journal of Economic Perspectives*, vol. 16, no. 4, 2002, pp.24-44.

24 G. Heller Sahlgren, 'Lika barn leka bäst? Kamrateffekter och utbildningspolitiska slutsatser', IFN Policy Paper, Stockholm, forthcoming.

25 For a review, see G. Heller Sahlgren, 'Dis-Location: School Choice, Residential Segregation, and Educational Equality', CMRE Research Report no. 4, London, 2013.

26 E. J. Brunner, S-W. Cho, and R. Reback, 'Mobility, Housing Markets, and Schools: Estimating the Effects of Inter-District Choice Programs', *Journal of Public Economics*, vol. 96, no. 7-8, 2012, pp.604-614; S. Machin and K. G. Salvanes, 'Valuing School Quality Via a School Choice Reform', Discussion Paper no. 4719, Institute for the Study of Labor, Bonn, 2010; A. E. Schwartz, I. Voicu, and K. M. Horns, 'Do Choice Schools Break the Link Between Public Schools and Property Values? Evidence from House Prices in New York City', Working Paper 2014-03, Department of Economics, University of Massachusetts, Boston.

27 G. Heller Sahlgren, 'Dis-Location: School Choice, Residential Segregation, and Educational Equality', CMRE Research Report no. 4, London, 2013.

28 P. L. Baude, M. Casey, E. A. Hanushek and S. G. Rivkin, 'The Evolution of Charter School Quality', NBER Working Paper no. 20645, National Bureau of Economic Research, Cambridge, MA, 2014.

29 G. Heller Sahlgren and J. Le Grand, 'How to Get School Competition Right', *Standpoint*, June, 2014, pp.36-37.

30 S. Burgess, E. Greaves, A. Vignoles, and D. Wilson, 'What Parents Want: School Preferences and School Choice', *Economic Journal*, forthcoming.

31 G. Heller Sahlgren and J. Le Grand, 'How to Get School Competition Right', *Standpoint*, June, 2014, pp.36-37.

32 W. B. MacLeod and M. Urquiola, 'Anti-Lemons, School Reputation, Relative Diversity, and Educational Quality', IZA Discussion Paper no. 6805, Institute for the Study of Labor, Bonn, 2012.

33 A. Böhlmark and M. Lindahl, 'Independent Schools and Long-Run Educational Outcomes: Evidence from Sweden's Large Scale Voucher Reform', Working Paper 6/2013, Swedish Institute for Social Research (SOFI), Stockholm University, 2013; C-T Hsieh and M. Urquiola, 'The Effects of Generalized School Choice on Achievement and Stratification: Evidence from Chile's Voucher Program', *Journal of Public Economics*, vol. 90, 2006, pp.1477-1503.

34 J. A. Correa, F. Parro, and L. Reyes, 'The Effects of Vouchers on School Results: Evidence from Chile's Targeted Voucher Program', *Journal of Human Capital*, vol. 8, no. 4, 2014, pp.351-398.

35 G. Elacqua, M. Martínez, H. Santos, and D. Urbina, 'School Closures in Chile: Access to Quality Alternatives in a School Choice System', *Estudios de Economía*, vol. 39, no. 2, 2012, pp.179-202.

36 G. Elacqua and F. Alves, 'Rising Expectations in Brazil and Chile', *Education Next*, vol. 14, no. 1, 2014, pp.54-61.

37 For a review, see G. Heller Sahlgren, *Incentivising Excellence: School Choice and Education Quality*, London, CMRE and IEA, 2013.

38 R. Chakrabarti, 'Do Vouchers Lead to Sorting Under Random Private School Selection? Evidence from the Milwaukee Voucher Program', *Economics of Education Review*, vol. 34, 2013, pp.191-218.

39 E. Duflo, P. Dupas, and M. Kremer, 'Peer Effects, Teacher Incentives, and the Impact of Tracking: Evidence from a Randomized Evaluation in Kenya', *American Economic Review*, vol. 101, no. 5, 2011, pp.1739-1774.

40   K. Yang Hansen, J-E. Gustafsson, and M. Rosén, 'School Performance Differences and Policy Variations in Finland, Norway, and Sweden', in *Northern Lights on TIMSS and PIRLS 2011*, Copenhagen, Nordic Council of Ministers, 2011.

41   Author interview with Dr Sirkku Kupiainen at the University of Helsinki, September 2014.

42   Author interviews with Dr Sirkku Kupiainen of the University of Helsinki and Professor Jouni Vilijärvi of the University of Jyväskylä, September 2014.

43   For evidence on positive incentive effects prior to the point of selection, K. Koerselman, 'Incentives from Curriculum Tracking', *Economics Education Review*, vol. 32, 2013, pp.140-150.

Unlimited Potential

1   J. Rawls, *A Theory of Justice*, Executive Summary, Cambridge, Massachusetts, Harvard University Press, 1971.

2   M. Orton and K. Rowlingson, 'Public Attitudes to Economic Inequality', Executive Summary, Joseph Rowntree Foundation, July 2007.

3   R. Wilkinson and K. Pickett, *The Spirit Level*, London, Penguin, 2010, p.195.

4   R. Cairns, 'A-Level Results: Proof That Not All Teenagers Think the World Owes Them a Living', *Daily Telegraph*, 19 August 2011.

5   R. Pring *et al.*, *Education for All: The Future of Education and Training for 14-19 Year-Olds*, London, Routledge, 2009.

6   A. Seldon, Sir John Cass's Foundation Lecture, 'Why Schools? Why Universities?', 8 December 2010.

7   Ibid.

8   Ibid.

9   Ibid.

10   Ibid.

11   Ibid.

12   BBC Radio 4, *Today* programme, 1 February 2010.

13   R. Mason, 'Nigel Farage Lays Out UKIP Plans for Schools and Taxes', *Guardian*, 1 June 2014.

14   C. Cook, 'Grammar School Myths', *Financial Times* Blogs, 28 January 2013.

15   The Sutton Trust, 'Degree of Success: University Chances by Individual School', July 2011, p.18.

16   The Organisation for Economic Co-operation and Development (OECD), 'PISA: Snapshot of Performance in Mathematics, Reading and Science', *PISA 2012 Results in Focus*, 3 December 2013.

17   S. Burgess, M. Dickson, and L. Macmillan, 'Selective Schooling Systems Increase Inequality', Institute of Education Working Paper, May 2014.

18   B. Bernstein, 'Education Cannot Compensate for Society', *New Society* 15(387), 1970, pp.344-347.

19   A. Seldon, Sir John Cass's Foundation Lecture, 'Why Schools? Why Universities?', 8 December 2010.